Coronado's Children

Barker Texas History Center Series, No. 3

J. FRANK DOBIE

Coronado's Children

Tales of Lost Mines and Buried
Treasures of the Southwest

Foreword by Frank H. Wardlaw
Illustrations by Charles Shaw

University of Texas Press, Austin & London

International Standard Book Number 0-292-71050-X (cloth);
0-292-71052-6 (paper); 0-292-71053-4 (special)
Library of Congress Catalog Card Number 78-58925
Copyright 1930 by the Southwest Press;
copyright © 1958 by J. Frank Dobie;
copyright © 1978 by the University of Texas Press
All rights reserved
Set in Sabon by G&S Typesetters and
printed in the United States of America
by Edwards Brothers
First University of Texas Press Edition

To my mother
ELLA BYLER DOBIE
who has so often delighted me with
conversational sketches of such
characters as enter this book
and to the memory of my father
R. J. DOBIE
a clean cowman of the Texas soil

Contents

"The Precious Ability to Wonder"

"Great literature transcends its native land, but none that I know of ignores its soil," wrote J. Frank Dobie in 1936.

When his colleagues in the English department at the University of Texas objected to his proposal that he teach a course on "life and literature in the Southwest" on the grounds that the region had produced little literature worthy of note, Dobie responded: "It has plenty of life; I'll teach that."

Life and literature, while not always synonymous, were closely linked in the thinking of this remarkable man. Few American writers have contributed so much to the preservation of the history and legends of a region or done so much to enrich its literature and its life. It is a fortunate thing indeed that the Southwest's foremost apostle of regionalism should have also been an implacable foe of provincialism. "Unless the region has elements of the universal, it is country-minded and is, therefore, damned," he wrote.

There was always much of the universal in Dobie's own writings, even though they sprang straight from the rocky Texas soil. Not only the Southwest but American literature in general would be vastly poorer without *A Vaquero of the Brush Country*, *Coronado's Children*, *Apache Gold and Yaqui Silver*, *The Voice of the Coyote*, and his remarkable companion volumes *The Longhorns* and *The Mustangs* which reveal him as a solid historian as well as a fine teller of tales.

Nothing could be more fitting than for *Coronado's Children*, Dobie's second major work and one of his finest, to be republished by the University of Texas Press. Although he was no longer a member of the University of Texas faculty when the Press was established in 1950 he contributed enormously to the development of its program. With the single exception of Walter Prescott Webb, he did more than anyone to establish the character and tone of its regional list. Nearly every Texas book which we published was subjected to his scrutiny. The slightest hint of provincialism drew his instant wrath. He couldn't resist writing on the margins of manuscripts he read for us. Of one book he wrote, "The author is a damned egotistic Philistine." Of another, "His world is no bigger than the Texas Panhandle." Of yet another, "There are three lies in the first paragraph." Once we had to erase the word "bullshit" twenty times from the margins of a manuscript before returning it to its author.

Frequently Frank Dobie would telephone me at the office and say, "Come by to see me, but make it the right time of day." I would find him, with our mutual friend Jack Daniel, under a big Spanish oak in the backyard of his home on Waller Creek, his boots off and his hat pushed back on his tousled white head. There we would sit until the evening star grew dim talking about all sorts of things but mostly about books.

Once we were joined by an ancient and bedraggled treasure hunter —one of Coronado's children—who had read Frank's tales of lost mines and buried treasures and who wanted more specific advice about how to find them. Dobie greeted him warmly and engaged him in extended but indeterminate conversation before sending him on his way to El Dorado. On another occasion, Frank told me, a treasure hunter turned up with a map of an area discussed in *Coronado's Children* and demanded that Dobie pinpoint the location of a lost mine. Dobie told him sadly that he didn't really know where it was, but the prospector persisted. Finally Frank closed his eyes and marked a spot on the map with his pen; the old man left happy.

In Herbert Faulkner West's copy of *Apache Gold and Yaqui Silver*, Dobie wrote in 1951: "These people had nothing but hope. They were rich in it. As I grow older I wonder if any other form of wealth is more enriching to lives ..."

In the pages of *Coronado's Children* you will meet many of these men of hope, following the same gleam which lured Coronado across half a continent and sent the gold-rushers over the mountains and deserts to California. In essence, but not in detail, these tales of treasure hunters are preserved just as Frank Dobie heard them. He never claimed to be a folklorist in the professional sense. He admitted that he had "a constructive memory" and that "after I have heard a tale I do all I can to improve it." He had no patience with folklorists who were slaves to tape recorders.

The readers of this new book will find as much delight in it as did the readers of the first edition in 1930. "Coronado's Children," wrote Dobie, "still have the precious ability to wonder."

During his last illness Frank Dobie told his doctor: "I don't want any more of your damned pills. I just want my vitality." His vitality persists, as strong as ever, in the hearts of his friends and in the pages of his books, one of the finest of which you now hold in your hands.

College Station,   Frank H. Wardlaw
Texas   Director, University of Texas Press, 1950–1974
April, 1978   Director, Texas A&M University Press, 1974–1978

In the Beginning

These tales are not creations of mine. They belong to the soil and to the people of the soil. Like all things that *belong*, they have their roots deep in the place of their being, deep too in the past. They are an outgrowth; they embody the geniuses of divergent races and peoples who even while fiercely opposing each other blended their traditions. However all this may be, the tales are just tales. As tales I have listened to them in camps under stars and on ranch galleries out in the brush. As tales, without any ethnological palaver, I have tried to set them down. So it is with something of an apology that I make even a brief explanation before plunging into a veritable Iliad of adventures.

In March, 1536, four hundred years ago tomorrow, a party of Spaniards scouting in the wild lands against the Gulf of California came suddenly upon a spectacle more strange and unexpected than the footprints which greeted Robinson Crusoe's eyes on the desert island. The spectacle was a white man all but naked, his nakedness partly concealed by an uncouth tangle of long hair and beard, his nationality revealed only by wild and whirling words. He was accompanied by a Moor called Estevanico, or Stephen, and eleven Indians. He gave his name as Cabeza de Vaca. He told how he had been shipwrecked on the coast of Florida a continent away and how, passing from tribe to tribe, his life often threatened by starvation, thirst, and savage enemies, he had for eight long years been beating west. He had seen much and heard more. Somewhere to the north, he said, was a galaxy of cities the inhabitants of which wore civilized raiment, lived in palaces ornamented with sapphires and turquoises, and possessed gold without end—the Seven Cities of Cíbola.

As the great scholar Adolph F. Bandelier has pointed out in *The Gilded Man*, the story of seven rich cities in an unknown land was old before Columbus discovered America. Despite that, Cabeza de Vaca's story was new—new in a new land where men with fresh hearts were looking for the fabled Fountain of Youth, the giant Amazons, the anthropophagi with heads growing out of their breasts, and many another marvel.

Search for the wondrous Cities was inevitable. The expedition led by Francisco Vásquez Coronado was the first made by white men into what is now known as the Southwest and it was surely the most amazing of all expeditions ever made on the North American continent. Fitted out at an immense cost, it included 300 Spaniards, 1000 Indians, 1000 extra horses, herds of swine and sheep, six swivel guns, and a temperament as superbly sanguine as young men are capable of enjoying.

Ahead of him Coronado sent a Franciscan monk known as Fray Marcos de Nizza, and ahead of Fray Marcos scouted Black Stephen, the Moor who had been with Cabeza de Vaca. If the gorgeous reports about the riches of Cíbola turned out to be only partly true, Black Stephen was to send back a small cross "two handfuls long"; if the reports had not been exaggerated, and the Seven Cities really contained more wealth than the palaces of the Montezumas, he should send back "a larger cross." Four days after he had ridden out, the Moor sent back a cross "as high as a man," and the priest relayed the message to Coronado.

Black Stephen was killed; the name of Nizza became a term for contempt; instead of cities with gates of gold and houses with sapphire-studded doors that flashed in the sun, Coronado found among the Zuñis of what is now Arizona walls of mud and naked burrows in barren cliffs. The Seven Cities of Cíbola were a dream, but *más allá*— on beyond—so an Indian known as the Turk said, was the Gran Quivira. It was a place "where ordinary dishes were made of wrought plate and the jugs and bowls were of gold." Coronado rode on—*más allá*. He rode a thousand miles across unknown mountains and parched plains—and he found the Gran Quivira to be a handful of naked savages squatting under wind-whisked thatches or skulking at the heels of drifting buffaloes.

At the very time Cíbola and Quivira seized the Spaniards of North America, expeditions fitted out by Spanish princes, Dutch bankers, and English sea-dogs were beginning to scour South America in search of El Dorado. El Dorado, the Gilded King, so the story went, had attendants to anoint his body with oil every morning and then to blow gold dust upon him until he was decently clad. At evening he washed himself clean in a lake—a lake somewhere in the uncharted outyonder. Presumably he slept in undress, but always at sunrise he was freshly robed in golden plating. Thus for uncounted generations kings by the lake had dressed and undressed. It might well be supposed that the lake was paved with golden sands. It might well be supposed that the people who gave their king a fresh suit of gold every day possessed immense stores of it. For more than a hundred years *conquistadores* marched and counter-marched from one extremity of South America to the other, spending the lives of thousands upon thousands of men and the wealth of prodigal treasuries, enduring starvation, fever, cold, thirst, the pests of swamps, and the pitiless heat of deserts—in search of El Dorado. El Dorado was a man, a lake, a city, a country, a people, a name, a dream—a dream at once absurd and sublime—an allegory of every phantom that the high heart of man has ever pursued.

El Dorado and the Seven Cities of Cíbola but represented a multitude of tales pointing the buoyant way to untold wealth. La Ciudad Encantada de los Cesares; the fabled palace of Cubanacan in Cuba; the golden mirage of Manoa, in quest of which Raleigh at the age of sixty-three came out of prison to fare forth a second time up the Orinoco; the nebulous treasures of a Casa del Sol, of the Gran Moxo, and of the Golden Temple of Dabaiba, all in South America; a gilded rainbow somewhere in the northern Pacific called the Straits of Annian; the Laguna de Oro in New Mexico hard by the Peak of Gold in the same region; the Seven Hills of the Aijados in Texas, where gold was so plentiful that the natives, "not knowing any of the other metals," tipped arrows and lances with it—all these were but duplications of one theme. Far up the bleak New England coast French voyagers sought "the northern El Dorado" under the name of Norembega—

> And Norembega proved again
> A shadow and a dream.

But despite the madness and fantasticality of such rumors, the Spaniards had a basis for hope and belief. How much the wealth of Montezuma amounted to has never been known, but Cortés plundered enough of it to inflame the imagination of the Old World. In Peru the Inca called Atahualpa heaped up for Pizarro, as the price of ransom, golden vessels almost sufficient to fill a room twenty-two by seventeen feet square to a height of nine feet. In a courtyard of Bogotá, Quesada piled up golden booty so high "that a rider on horseback might hide behind it."

When, in 1542, Coronado returned and told the truth about his barren search, men refused to believe him. One who did believe him, Castañeda, chronicler of the expedition, set down an exquisite point of view in these words: "Granted that they did not find the riches of which they had been told, they found a place in which to search for them." The opportunity that Coronado thus opened has never since his time been neglected; the dream he dreamed has never died. For thousands of happy folk the mirage that lured him on has never faded, and today all over the wide, wide lands where *conquistadores* trailed and *padres* built their simple missions—and in yet more places never glimpsed by Spanish eyes—tradition has marked rock and river and ruin with illimitable treasure. The human imagination abhors failure. Hope and credulity are universal among the sons of earth, and so when English-speaking men took over the *sitios* and *porciones* of Spanish lands in the Southwest, they acquired not only the land that Spanish pioneers had surveyed but the traditions they had somehow made an ingredient of the soil itself.

The fact of California gold, which stampeded a nation, and the fact of Nevada silver, which stampeded California, added immensely to the tradition of Spanish wealth and gave it a flavor and coloring characteristic of the American frontier. As a result, the legends of lost mines and buried treasures that pass current today all over the Southwest and West are a blend. An amazing thing about them is that they seem to be increasing rather than diminishing in number; they are incredibly, astoundingly numerous—as are the people who tell them and halfway, at least, believe them.

These people, no matter what language they speak, are truly Coronado's inheritors. I have called them Coronado's children. They follow Spanish trails, buffalo trails, cow trails; they dig where there are no trails; but oftener than they dig or prospect they just sit and tell stories of lost mines, of buried bullion by the jack load, of ghostly *patrones* that guard treasure, and of a thousand other impediments, generally not ghostly at all, that have kept them away from the wealth they are so sure of.

Coronado's children still have the precious ability to wonder. And you who are so sophisticated, unless you can feel at home in the camps of Coronado's children, never imagine that you understand bold Drake or eager Raleigh or stout Cortés or any of the other flaming figures of the spacious, zestful, and wondering times of great Elizabeth and splendid Philip. They are of imagination all compact.

As readers of *The Alhambra* know, generations of Spaniards preceding those who came to America to hunt gold had been bred on tales of wealth hidden by the Moors. Yet the legends of the Old World that have persisted with most vitality and have called most powerfully to the imaginations of men are legends of women: Venus, too supernally beautiful for earth, too lush of flesh for heaven; Helen with a face that burnt the topless towers of Ilium and a kiss that was fair exchange for a man's soul; sacrificial Iphigenia and love-lorn Philomela; Semiramis and fair Rosamond; Egyptian Cleopatra, with Roman Antony against her fragrant bosom, and majestical Lucretia, who made Roman womanhood a synonym for virtue; tragic Dido of Carthage and burning Thisbe of Babylon; wronged Brunhilde and Queen Guinevere, more potent than the whole Round Table of knights; the Maid of Orleans leading armies by the sound of voices and confounding judges by the simplicity of truth; waiting Hero beyond the Hellespont and unfading Deirdre of the Sorrows. To be sure, the Old World has begot and transmitted many fine legends other than those about women; the Old World is very, very old and it has experienced everything. It has imagined legends of strong men like Hercules, Samson, and the Norse giants; of adventurers like Ulysses; of outlaws like Robin Hood and Rob Roy; of treasures like the Golden Fleece and of lost mines like those of King Solomon. But these legends are minor compared with those in which woman has prefigured for all races and times man's conception of loveliness, and even into these minor legends woman is always entering. A woman shears Samson's locks; among women Ulysses makes his most adventurous wanderings. Jason finds Medea more precious than the Golden Fleece; the golden apples are but an incident in the race for marble-limbed Atalanta.

The New World has been a world of men neither lured nor restrained by women. It has been a world of men exploring unknown continents, subduing wildernesses and savage tribes, felling forests, butchering buffaloes, trailing millions of longhorned cattle wilder than buffaloes, digging gold out of mountains, and pumping oil out of hot earth beneath the plains. It has been a world in which men expected, fought for, and took riches beyond computation—a world, indeed, if not of men without women, then of men into whose imaginings woman has hardly entered. The brawny subduers of this New World have conceived legends about a Gargantuan laborer and constructor, Paul Bunyan; about a supreme range rider, Pecos Bill; about matchless mustangs, lost canyons, and mocking mirages of the desert. But above all, their idealizations—their legends—have been about great wealth to be found, the wealth of secret mines and hidden treasures, a wealth that is substantive and has nothing to do with loveliness and beauty. The representative legends of America are the legends of Coronado's children.

In the tales that follow and in the notes herded into the back of the book, I have acknowledged my indebtedness to many helpers. As will be seen, I have drawn freely from *Legends of Texas*, now out of print, which I compiled and edited for the Texas Folk-Lore Society in 1924. Especially would I here thank Mrs. Mattie Austin Hatcher, archivist, and Miss Winnie Allen, assistant archivist, of the University of Texas, for directing me to many a curious item of Southwestern lore. Who preside over the genial branches of the Grasshoppers' Library in the sunshine of the Pecos, beside the elms and oaks on Waller Creek, down the mesquite flats of the Nueces River, up the canyons of the Rio Grande, under the blue haze of the Guadalupes, deep in the soft Wichitas, over the hills of the San Saba, and in many another happily remembered place where I have pursued "scholarly enquiries," I cannot name. I wish I could, for in the wide-spreading Grasshoppers' Library I have learned the most valuable things I know.

Some of Coronado's children and their tales have appeared in *The Country Gentleman, American Mercury, Yale Review, Southwest Review, Holland's Magazine, Texaco Star,* and *The Alcalde.*

One person has helped me so much and so continuously that in all justice her name should appear on the title page—Bertha McKee Dobie.

University of Texas   *J. Frank Dobie*
Austin, Texas
June 19, 1930

Coronado's Children

CHAPTER I

The Lost San Saba Mine

O brave new world
That has such people in't!
The Tempest.

What the Golden Fleece was to the Greeks or what El Dorado—the Gilded Man—has been to South America, the lost mines on the San Saba and Llano rivers in Texas have been to all that part of the United States once owned by Spain. The story of these mines is a cycle made up of a thousand cantos. Housed mechanics, preachers, teachers, doctors, lawyers, earth-treading farmers, and home-staying women, as well as roaming cowboys, rangers, outlaws, and miners, have told the strange story—and believed it. It is a story of yesterday, as obsolete as the claiming of continents by priority in flag-hoisting; it is a story of today, as realistic as the salt of the earth; it is also a story of tomorrow, as fantastic and romantic as the hopes of man. Through it history walks unabashed and in it fancy sets no limit to extravagance.

Sometimes the name of the fabled source of wealth is Los Almagres; sometimes, Las Amarillas; again, La Mina de las Iguanas, or Lizard Mine, from the fact that the ore is said to have been found in chunks called *iguanas* (lizards); oftener the name is simply the Lost San Saba Mine or the Lost Bowie Mine. In seeking it, generations of men have disemboweled mountains, drained lakes, and turned rivers out of their courses. It has been found—and lost—in many places under many conditions. It is here; it is there; it is nowhere. Generally it is silver; sometimes it is gold. Sometimes it is in a cave; sometimes in water; again on top of a mountain. Now it is not a mine at all but an immense storage of bullion. It changes its place like will-o'-the-wisp and it has more shapes than Jupiter assumed in playing lover.

Only the land that hides it does not change. Except that it is brushier, groomed down in a few places by little fields, and cut across by fences, it is today essentially as the Spaniards found it. A soil that cannot be plowed under keeps its traditions—and its secrets. Wherever the mine may be, however it may appear, it has lured, it lures, and it will lure men on. It is bright Glamour and it is dark and thwarting Fate. It is the Wealth of the Indies; it is the Wealth into which Colonel Mulberry Sellers so gloriously transmuted water and turnips.

The preface to this cycle of a thousand cantos goes back to a day of the seventeenth century when a Spanish *conquistador* set out from Nueva Viscaya "to discover a rumored Silver Hill (Cerro de la Plata) somewhere to the north."[1] At a later date La Salle's Frenchmen wandering forth from Saint Louis Bay on the Texas coast listened to Indians tell of "rivers where silver mines are found." Like most great legends, the legend of the San Saba Mine is a magnification of historical fact. The chief fact was Miranda.

MIRANDA'S REPORT

In February, 1756, Don Bernardo de Miranda, lieutenant-general of the province of Texas, with sixteen soldiers, five citizens, an Indian interpreter, and several peons, rode out from the village of San Fernando (San Antonio) with orders from the governor to investigate thoroughly the mineral riches so long rumored.[2] After traveling eight days towards the northwest, he pitched camp on the Arroyo San Miguel (now called Honey Creek), a southern tributary of the Río de las Chanas (Llano River). Only one-fourth of a league beyond he reached the Cerro del Almagre (Almagre Hill), so called on account of its color, *almagre* meaning *red hematite*, or *red ochre*. Opening into the hill Miranda found a cave, which he commanded to be called the Cave of Saint Joseph of Alcasar. He prospected both cave and mountain—with results that brought forth the most sanguine and fulsome predictions.

"The mines which are in the Cerro del Almagre," he reported, "are so numerous that I guarantee to give to every settler of the province of Texas a full claim. . . . The principal vein is more than two varas in width and in its westward lead appears to be of immeasurable thickness." Pasturage for stock, wood and water for mining operations, irrigable soil—all the natural requirements for a settlement of workers—were, Miranda added, at hand. The five citizens with him denounced ten mining claims.

On the way back to San Antonio Miranda met a well-known and trusted Apache Indian, who informed him that "many more and better mines" were at "Los Dos Almagres near the source of the Colorado

River." Here the Apache people were accustomed to get silver for their own use—not ore, but solid silver, "soft like the buckles of shoes." Miranda offered the bearer of these tidings a red blanket and a butcher knife to lead him to Los Dos Almagres, but the Apache said that the Comanches out there were too numerous and hostile. However, he promised to guide the Spaniards thither later on—*mañana*.

After having been away only three weeks, Miranda reentered San Fernando. He at once dispatched to the viceroy in Mexico City a statement of his findings, together with recommendations. He declared that no mining could be carried on at El Almagre unless a presidio of "at least thirty men" were established near by as a protection against hostile Indians. And since "an abundance of silver and gold was the principal foundation upon which the kingdoms of Spain rested," Miranda urged the establishment of a presidio and the commencement of mining operations.

As evidence of his rich findings, Miranda turned over three pounds of ore to be assayed. This ran at the rate of about ten ounces of silver to the hundredweight—a good showing. But, as Manuel de Aldaco, a rich mine owner of Mexico, pointed out to the viceroy, three pounds of handpicked ore could not be relied upon to represent any extensive location. Moreover, some silver had been present in the reagent used for assaying the three pounds. Aldaco recommended that before Miranda's glowing report was acted upon "at least thirty mule loads of the ore" be carried for reduction to Camp Mazapil, seven or eight hundred miles away from the veins collectively called Los Almagres. Ten of the thirty loads were to be from the surface, ten from a depth of one fathom, and ten from a depth of at least two fathoms. "It is not prudent," concluded Aldaco, "to be exposed to the danger of deception in a matter so grave and important." Finally, to Aldaco it seemed but fair that Miranda and the citizens who had denounced mining claims should pay the cost of transporting the thirty *cargas*.

Miranda had followed his report to Mexico City, where he engaged an attorney to push his enterprise. He strongly objected that the citizens associated with him could not bear the expense of transporting so much ore, for at twenty pesos per *carga* the total cost would amount to more money than all five of the citizens together possessed. However, Miranda at length agreed to pay the cost himself on condition that he be placed in command of a presidio at Los Almagres; such an office would bring valuable perquisites. He professed to have no doubt that, once the ore was assayed, extensive mining would result and a

5

presidio would be required to protect the miners. The haggling went on. At last, on November 23, 1757—more than twenty months after Miranda had made his "discovery"—the viceroy acceded to his proposition.

Meantime Captain Miranda had been dispatched on a mission to the eastern part of Texas. And at this point, so far as the mines are concerned, approved history stops short, drops the subject without one word of explanation. Did Miranda or anyone else ever so much as load the thirty *cargas* of ore on mules to be carried nearly a thousand miles away for assaying? Did Spanish miners then swarm out to the Almagres veins and extract fortunes from the earth?[3] If authenticated documents cannot finish out the half-told story, other kinds of documents,[4] as we shall see, can—and plenty of things have happened in Texas that the records say nothing about.

In the absence of positive testimony we may be sure that no presidio was established on the Llano for the protection of Almagres silver, but even while Miranda was proposing one, the Spanish government had actually planted a fort called San Luis de las Amarillas on the north bank of the San Saba River sixty miles to the northwest. At the same time a mission, for the conversion of Apaches, had been set up three miles below the fort on the south side of the river. This military establishment on the San Saba, though history may regard it as a buffer against Comanches, was according to tradition designed to protect vast mining operations. Thus hunters for the lost Spanish mine—the lost Almagres Mine, the Lost San Saba Mine, or whatever they happen to call it—look for it oftener on the San Saba than on the Llano. The mountain—of silver—went to Mahomet.

It is necessary to trace out the fate of the San Saba enterprise. Captain Diego Ortiz de Parrilla was placed in command, and on June 30, 1757—even before the stockade about his quarters was completed—he asked the viceroy to permit him to move his garrison of one hundred men to the Llano River. The Almagres minerals there should, he said, be protected, for, "*if* worked," they would be "a great credit to the viceroy and of much benefit to the royal treasury." The viceroy evidently thought otherwise, for the move was not allowed. In March, 1758, the mission, three miles away from military assistance, was besieged by two thousand Comanche warriors, who so thoroughly burned and killed that it was never reestablished.

Following this disaster, it was again officially proposed that the presidio be moved south to Los Almagres, "for protection and defense of the work on some rich veins of silver, which, it is claimed, have been discovered by intelligent men who know such things." Nothing came of the proposal. The presidio, always poorly manned and almost constantly terrorized, held out for twelve years and was then (1769) abandoned forever.[5]

The ruins of San Luis de las Amarillas and of a rock wall enclosing three or four acres of ground are still visible about a mile above the present town of Menard. Various old citizens of the region assert that in early days they saw signs of a smelter just outside the stockade, though these signs have been obliterated. Marvin Hunter remembers that his father, a pioneer editor of West Texas, picked up at the smelter a piece of slag weighing about fifteen pounds and containing silver. For years it was used as a door prop in the office of the Menard *Record*. The Hunters had eleven silver bullets, too, found in and around the old presidio—but many years ago Marvin shot them at a wild goose on the Llano River. From the smelter, so the oldest old-timers assert, a clear trail led to what is yet called Silver Mine on Silver Creek to the northwest. Of this creek more later.

In 1847 Doctor Ferdinand Roemer, a German geologist, traveled over Texas gathering material for a book that was printed in Germany two years later. In this book he describes the San Saba ruins and says that, although he looked for a smelter and for slag, he found no sign of either. It is possible that Roemer overlooked the smelter as he most certainly overlooked the old irrigation ditch, remains of which can still be seen. It is also possible that he was too sophisticated to take burnt rocks about an Indian kitchen midden for a smelter—a mistake often made by ranchmen, farmers, and treasure seekers.

Two or three aged men living in Menard recall that when they were boys swimming in the water hole below the old fort they used to stand on a submerged cannon barrel and stick their toes in the muzzle. In 1927 the town authorities diverted the river through an irrigation ditch and drained the water hole in an attempt to find the cannon. No cannon was revealed. Years before this municipal investigation, W. T. Burnum spent fifteen hundred dollars pumping out a cave on the divide north of the old presidio. Failing to find the mine there, he moved his machinery to a small lake just above Menard and pumped it dry. The Spaniards had, before evacuating the region, created the lake and diverted the river into it, thus most effectually concealing their rich workings.

Another persistent rumor has it that a great bell to be hung in the mission was cast within sight of it, gold and silver from near-by mines having been molten into the metal to give it tone. On account of the massacre, however, the bell was never hung, and so to this day certain people versed in recondite history disturb the soil about the mission site looking for it.

THE FILIBUSTERS

The first Americans who came to Texas came for adventure: Philip Nolan to catch mustangs, Doctor Long to set up a republic, and at least one man in Magee's extraordinary expedition to dig a fortune out of the ground. In 1865, more than fifty years after the remnant of Magee's followers were dispersed, this man, whom history forgets to mention, appeared in the Llano country. He gave his name as Harp Perry, and he told a circumstantial story to explain his presence.

Following the last battle in which the Magee forces took part, he said, he and a fellow adventurer, together with thirty-five Mexicans, engaged in mining on the Little Llano River. Here they had a rich vein of both gold and silver, a vein that bore evidence of Spanish exploitation. It was their custom to take out enough ore at one time to keep their smelter, or "furnace," as he called it, busy for a month. It was some distance from the mine, and ore was carried to it in rawhide kiaks loaded on burros. Always, Perry said, after taking out a supply of ore he and his associates concealed the entrance to the mine. At the smelter they had no regular moulds for running the refined metal into but poured it into hollow canes; the bars, or rods, thus moulded were buried.

The miners had to be constantly on guard against Indians. In the year 1834 a numerous band of Comanches swooped down upon their camp at the smelter, killing everybody but the two Americans and a Mexican girl. The three survivors made their way to Mexico City, where Perry's partner married the girl. Many things postponed their return to Texas—and to wealth. In 1865, however, Perry, an old man now, was back on the Little Llano. He was not looking for the mine. He was looking for twelve hundred pounds of gold and silver that he had helped mould in hollow canes and bury on a high hill a half mile due north of the smelter.

He was utterly unable to orient himself. Brush had encroached on the prairies; gullies had cut up the hillsides. A few frontiersmen were out on the Llano daring the Comanches, who still terrorized the country. Perry offered a reward of $500 to any one of them who would lead him to the old furnace, the key landmark. He said that it was near a spring and that seventy-five steps from it, in a direct line towards the storage of gold and silver, a pin oak should be found with a rock driven into a knot-hole on the east side. But no furnace or stone-marked pin oak could be found. Perry then announced that he was going to Saint Louis and attempt to find his old partner, whom he believed to be living there. He left the Llano. It was afterwards learned that he threw in with a trail outfit going north from Williamson County and that while he was mounting his horse one morning his six-shooter went off accidentally, killing him instantly.

No further attempt was made to locate the furnace until 1878, when a man by the name of Medlin, his ambition having been aroused by Harp Perry's story, engaged to herd sheep for a ranchman on the Llano. Every day while herding he prosecuted his search, and within the year he found the ruins of the old furnace, the tree with a stone fixed in the knot-hole, and the high hill half a mile due north. Medlin's excavations were as wide as the Poor Parson's parish, but the high hill, where Harp Perry had said over and over the sticks of silver and gold were buried, presented such an indefinite kind of mark that the sheep herder did most of his work about the old furnace. Beneath the ruins themselves he unearthed the skeleton of a man, by its side a "miner's spoon," which was made of burnt soapstone and which showed plainly that it had been used for stirring quicksilver into other metals. Shortly after this find, without waiting to dig up anything else, Medlin left his sheep and the Llano hills for South America.

In Galveston, where he had to wait a few days to take ship, a newspaper writer chanced to find him and took down verbatim his story of Harp Perry's unsuccessful and his own successful search for the furnace. In evidence of his veracity he showed the "miner's spoon" he had dug up. Thus, with little chance for error or exaggeration, has been preserved a record of probably the first American—Harp Perry of Magee's expedition—to be lured to Los Almagres.[6]

BOWIE'S SECRET

Flaming above all the other searchers is the figure of James Bowie. It is a great pity that we have no biography of him such as we have of

Davy Crockett. This biography would tell—often with only legend for authority—how he rode alligators in Louisiana; how, like Plains Indians chasing the buffalo, he speared wild cattle; how, with the deadly bowie knife, he fought fearful duels in dark rooms; how he trafficked for black ivory with the pirate Laffite on Galveston Island; and then how he came to San Antonio and married the lovely Ursula de Veramendi, daughter of the vice-governor of Texas.

Bowie was a master of men and a slave to fortune. He was willing to pawn his life for a chance at a chimerical mine, and he asked no odds. Out on the Nueces and Frio rivers, far beyond the last outpost of settlement, he prospected for gold and silver. In his burning quest for the fabled Spanish mines on the San Saba he engaged in one of the most sanguinary and brilliant fights of frontier history. Four years later, at San Antonio, he mistook some bundles of hay loaded on Mexican mules for bags of silver, and led in the so-called Grass Fight.[7] Then on March 6, 1836, leaving not one "messenger of defeat," he and one hundred eighty-odd other Texans died in the Alamo. Thousands of men have believed and yet believe that he died knowing the location of untold riches. At any rate, dying there in the Alamo he carried with him a secret as potent to keep his memory fresh in the minds of the common people as his brave part in achieving the independence of Texas. Thenceforth the mine he sought and that many believe he found took his name.

In the accounts dealing with Bowie's search history and legend freely mingle. I tell the story as frontiersmen and hunters for the Bowie Mine have handed it down.

When Bowie came to western Texas, about 1830, a band of Lipan Indians, a branch of the Apaches, were roaming the Llano region. Their chief was named Xolic, and for a long time Xolic had been in the habit of leading his people down to San Antonio once or twice a year to barter. They always brought with them some silver bullion. They did not bring much at a time, however, for their wants were simple. The Spaniards and Mexicans thought that the Lipan ore had been chipped off some rich vein; there was a touch of gold in it. Of course they tried to learn the secret of such wealth, but the Indians had a tribal understanding that if any man of their number revealed the source of the mineral he should be tortured to death. At length the people of San Antonio grew accustomed to the silver-bearing Lipans and ceased to pry into their secret. Then came the curious Americans.

Bowie laid his plans carefully. He at once began to cultivate the friendship of the Lipans. He sent back east for a fine rifle plated with silver. When it came, he presented it to Chief Xolic. A powwow was held and at San Pedro Springs Bowie was adopted into the tribe. Now followed months of life with the savages. Bowie was expert at shooting the buffalo; he was foremost in fighting against enemies of the Lipans. He became such a good Indian and was so useful a warrior that his adopted brothers finally showed him what he had joined them to see.

He had expected much, but he hardly expected to be dazzled by such millions as greeted his eyes. Whether it was natural veins of ore that he beheld or a great storage of smelted bullion, legend has not determined. Anyway, it was "Spanish stuff." The sight seemed to overthrow all caution and judgment. Almost immediately after learning their secret, Bowie deserted the Lipans and sped to San Antonio to raise a force for seizing the wealth.

He was between two fires. He did not want too large a body of men to share with; at the same time he must have a considerable number in order to overcome the guarding Indians. It took some time to arrange the campaign. Meanwhile old Chief Xolic died, and a young warrior named Tres Manos (Three Hands) succeeded to his position. Soon after coming to power, Tres Manos visited San Antonio. There he saw Bowie, accused him of treachery, and came near being killed for his effrontery.

The story of Bowie's adventures with the Indians thus far has no support from history. What follows is of record. On November 2, 1831, Bowie set out to find the Spanish mine. His brother, Rezin P. Bowie, was in the company and was perhaps the leading spirit. It has been claimed that he had made a previous trip of exploration into the San Saba country. Both of the brothers were remarkable men and both of them left accounts of the expedition.[8] With them were nine other men, the name of one of whom, Cephas (or Caiaphas) K. Ham, will weave into odd patterns through the long Bowie Mine story.

If James Bowie knew exactly where he was going, he coursed in a strange manner. In fact, he took so much time in "examining the nature of the country," to use his own words, that three weeks after setting out from San Antonio he had not yet arrived at the abandoned presidio on the San Saba only a hundred and fifty miles away. Yet the San Saba fort was a chief, if not the chief, objective of the expedition, for the Bowies were certain that it had protected the Spaniards "while working the silver mines, which are a mile distant." Why then did the Bowies not go directly to the fort and the mine? Did Jim Bowie know —from a Lipan's confidence—of some other place? Where had he spent the three weeks in scouting before he was stopped? *¿Quién sabe?*

On the nineteenth of November a friendly Comanche warned him that hostile Indians were out. Whether Tres Manos was among them is not recorded; they were mostly Caddos, Wacos, and Tehuacanas. About daylight on the twenty-first one hundred and sixty-four hostiles —fifteen against one—swooped down upon the Bowie camp. The Texans were not unready. They had the advantage of a thicket and of being near water in a creek. The fight lasted all day. One man was killed; three others were wounded. The Indians had fifty dead and thirty-five wounded. With a comrade named Buchanan shot so in the leg that he could not ride and with most of their horses killed or crippled, the mine hunters remained in camp for eight days. They were not provided with surgical instruments or with medicines of any kind, "not even a dose of salts." They "boiled some live oak bark very strong, and thickened it with pounded charcoal and Indian meal, made a poultice of it, and tied it around Buchanan's leg." Then they sewed a piece of buffalo skin around the bandage. The wound healed rapidly.

While waiting for the disabled to recover sufficiently to travel, some of the Bowie party found a cave near camp. This is a point to remember. Ten days were required for the hobbling journey back to San Antonio.

It is generally said that the fight was on what is now known as Calf Creek in McCulloch County, twenty-five miles or so east of the San Saba fort. At any rate, the remains of a barricade called Bowie's Fort are yet visible on Calf Creek, though "the hand of the impious treasure seeker" long since scattered the stones. Rezin P. Bowie said that the fight took place six miles east of the San Saba fort, and there is good reason for accepting his word. Some six or seven miles east of the old presidio a strip of brush growing on what is known to moderns as Jackson's Creek, a tributary of the San Saba, hides a collection of rocks that looked to many frontiersmen like a hastily arranged fortification. Not a great distance from this place is a cave. Jackson's Creek is dry now, but before the country was grazed off it usually furnished water during several months of the year. Thus it affords a site corresponding to Rezin P. Bowie's description. Exact location of the battle ground

12

would be interesting to some seekers of mine and treasure, for they say that the cave near the Bowie camp held "something."

When Doctor Roemer visited the San Saba ruins in 1847, he observed among other carvings on the stone gateposts near the northwest corner of the stockade the name of Bowie and the date 1829. Those gateposts have been shamefully mutilated, but on one of them this legend, neatly carved, is yet visible:

BOWIE
MINE
1832

Whether James Bowie carved his name with either of those discrepant dates can never be determined.

Without exception, one might say, the men of that highly individualized class who called themselves Texians knew about the Bowie Mine. Most of them who left any kind of chronicle make mention of it. The unpublished *Memoirs*[9] of Colonel "Rip" (John S.) Ford, border ranger, journalist, and a Texian among Texians—aye, a *Texican*—contains a sequel to the Bowie expedition. This sequel came to "Old Rip" from Cephas K. Ham, who survived "the Calf Creek Fight" for many, many years and became a veritable high priest to the Bowie Mine tradition.

According to Ham's story, he (and not Bowie) was adopted by the Indians and was—*almost*—shown the mine. His warrior brothers were a band of Comanches under the leadership of Chief Incorroy. In 1831 he was wandering around with these Comanches, trading for horses and catching mustangs in order to make up a bunch to drive to Louisiana. One pint of powder, eight balls of lead, one plug of tobacco, one butcher knife, and two brass rings made the price of a good horse. "A certain fat warrior," Ham narrates, "was frequently my hunting companion. One day he pointed to a hill and said: 'There is plenty of silver on the other side. We will go out by ourselves, and I will show it to you. If the other Indians find I have done so, they will kill both of us.'" But camp was hurriedly moved next day and the fat warrior never fulfilled his promise.

Not long afterwards Bowie sent a message to Ham advising him that, as the Mexicans were about to make war on the Comanches, he had better cut loose from them. He came into San Antonio, only to find that Bowie's real motive in sending a warning was to get him to join an expedition in search of the San Saba Mine.

Rezin P. Bowie, Ham's story goes on, had already visited the mine. "It was not far from the fort. The shaft was about eight feet deep." Rezin P. Bowie went down to the bottom of it "by means of steps cut in a live oak log" and hacked off some ore "with his tomahawk." He carried the ore to New Orleans and had it assayed. "It panned out rich." He came back to San Antonio. The results of his next move have already been recounted.

Here Rezin P. Bowie drops out of the story, but Jim Bowie did not give up the quest. Ham and other like authorities agree that he raised a second expedition of thirty men. This time, according to Ham, Bowie reached the San Saba but could not find the shaft, as it had been filled up either by rains or by Indians. Others say that about the time Bowie got ready to exploit the mineral riches he had located, the Texan war for independence broke out. Among many Texans the legend is persistent that Bowie's chief motive in searching for the San Saba treasure was to secure means for financing the Texas army[10]—a view hardly tenable by anyone who knows anything about the real Bowie.

Thus Bowie's name lives on. Wes Burton, a lost mine hunter who has been very successful in telling of his hunts, says that the Lipan Indians never showed Bowie a mine but merely five hundred jack loads of pure silver stored in a cave. The Spaniards mined the silver and moulded it into bars faster than they could transport it. Consequently, when the Indians forced them to abandon their workings they left behind an immense store of bullion. Burton also knew a man who paid $500 to a Mexican in San Antonio for a document purporting to have been taken off Bowie's dead body in the Alamo by one of Santa Anna's officers. The Mexican who sold it claimed to be a descendant of the officer. It gave full and explicit directions to the Bowie Mine; yet somehow the purchaser could never follow them.

Well, James Bowie set out for the San Saba Mine. Therefore he must have known where it was. Miranda found the Almagre vein south of the Llano and powers who did not listen to him established the presidio of San Luis de las Amarillas on the north bank of the San Saba twenty leagues away. Rezin P. Bowie asserted that *the Spanish mine* was only a mile from the presidio. But the Lost San Saba, or Bowie, Mine envelops both these locations as well as many others.

Sometimes it is as far east as the Colorado and sometimes it is as far west as the Nueces.

The early settlers of the San Saba and Llano country found an old road leading south from the presidio of San Luis de las Amarillas. As it was their belief that the Spaniards had hauled bullion over it to San Antonio and Mexico, they called it Silver Trail and they traveled it themselves until the country was fenced. Like other roads laid out by men who must beware of ambuscade, it kept as much as possible to high and open ground. The land it traversed on the North Fork of the Llano came to be known as Lechuza Ranch.

In 1881 the Lechuza came into the possession of a young Scotchman, Captain George Keith Gordon, who, after having hunted slavers on the East Coast of Africa and mapped many of its harbors, had lately retired from the British Navy. Nearly fifty years have passed now since Captain Gordon became interested in the San Saba Mine; he is still interested and has a trail to hunt out. This is his story.

Twenty-five miles or so northwest of the Lechuza Ranch was Fort McKavett, occupied during the seventies for the purpose of frontier defense. After it was abandoned, the camp sutler remained in the country. He was not an uncommunicative sort of being, and he was not tardy in letting the newly arrived owner of the Lechuza know that the hillsides and valleys of his estate contained something more valuable than the eye-delighting mesquite grass.

One day while scouting out in the vicinity of a large cedar brake on the Lechuza range, the sutler, so he said, saw three Indians. He himself was hidden on a hill above them, and he watched. Presently they disappeared in a very queer manner—vanished as if into the earth—then reappeared and left. Curious to see what they had been up to, the sutler rode down to the spot. He found a hole in the ground about thirty inches in diameter. Looking down into it, he could distinguish nothing clearly and so became more curious. He dragged up a small log, tied his lariat to it, and lowered himself. Something over twenty feet down he struck bottom.

He was in a concave about fifteen feet across. Against the wall on one side, the disheveled skeleton of a man sprawled over a heap of silver bars. The bars were so heavy that the sutler could not take even one with him, for it would be all he could do to pull his own weight out of the hole. He would return to the fort, he told himself, and make immediate preparations for securing the silver bars and hauling them away. After clambering to the surface, he marked the spot carefully and left. But a man attached to the army even in the loosest way is very often not his own master. For reasons not necessary to delineate here, it was a full two years before the sutler got back to haul out the silver.

When he did get back, he found that a fire had swept the cedar brake, obliterating all surface markings. The hole thirty inches in diameter was lost.

This account reminded Captain Gordon of a cavity he himself had observed in a cedar brake in his pasture but had not investigated. He was thinking of investigating it when one morning a stranger drove up to the Lechuza headquarters and, after the usual beating about the bush, asked permission to hunt silver on the ranch. He was willing to give the owner half of whatever he should find. Telling him nothing, Captain Gordon hitched up his buggy and drove the prospector to a spot on the old Silver Trail where some irons from a burnt wagon had given rise to a tale about Spanish treasure.

"It was a hot July day," Captain Gordon narrates. "I was not feeling very well; so I sat in the shade and let the stranger have his way. He produced a divining rod and followed its pull into a dense cedar brake—directly away from the wagon irons but towards the cave I knew about. After an hour's struggle with the heat and cedar limbs, he returned, claiming that the farther he went the harder the rod pulled. 'There must be a wagon load of the stuff at least,' he said. I now told him the sutler's story.

"The next morning he, two young Englishmen who were staying with me, and I, all well provided with ropes, picks, crowbars, and shovels, got into a wagon and headed for the cave. On our arrival the rod in the stranger's hand at once told us that the silver was still in the hole. We let him down and I entered also. The rod pulled towards one side. The cave was not so deep as the sutler had described his as being and it appeared to have been filled with loose rocks. My theory was that the cedar fire had ignited bat guano in the cave and that the heat had caused rocks to crack and fall. The young Englishmen flew in to moving the debris and within three hours were down to solid rock bottom—but not to silver. The mineral rod still pointed to the spot, but we were disgusted and quit."

So much for the silver cache. The mine out of which the Spaniards took silver affords the problem that Captain Gordon has really been interested in. Some time after the experience in the cave, he was over on the Nueces River and there met General John R. Baylor, whose exploits as a mineralogist will be told of in the next chapter of this book. Baylor showed Captain Gordon an outcropping of curious sandstone from which he had assayed a showing of silver. The Captain began tracing that formation. He found that, cropping out in various places, it led in a north-northeast direction, across his own ranch, and on straight towards the old presidio at Menard. He and his brother assayed some of the rock found on the Lechuza and got a good percentage of silver.

The way to find the San Saba Mine is to trace this sandstone to the vicinity of the old Spanish fort. Captain Gordon never tracked the outcroppings to the inevitable shaft on the San Saba. Few people realize how tied down the average ranchman is, how little time he has for taking up asides. But the old captain, living now in San Antonio— his house a veritable museum of objects of art and aboriginal artifacts collected from many lands—is at last free of ranch bondage. At the very moment of this writing he is preparing to follow the sandstone trail to its end—the long-hidden Spanish silver mine on the San Saba.

YELLOW WOLF: ''THREE SUNS WEST''

Even if there were no "Spanish charts" to the mineral wealth on the Llano and the San Saba, no Silver Trail, no rocks pointing always *más allá*, there would yet remain as a guide to Coronado's trustful children the tales of the aboriginal red men. In the beginning it was Indians who inspired the search for the Hill of Silver. An Apache told Miranda of the Dos Almagres, where solid silver, "soft like the buckles of shoes," could be found. A Comanche pointed out, somewhere over the hill, a mine to Cephas K. Ham. A legendary Lipan gave the secret to Bowie himself. Years after Bowie's death another Lipan led, for the modest reward of $300, some Austin citizens to "the old Spanish mine" near the San Saba mission. It was out in a "bald-open prairie." According to the latest available report, in the *Telegraph and Texas*

Register, Houston, June 22, 1842, the ore from this Lipan's mine "has not yet been accurately analysed."

Oftener than either Spaniards or Bowie, the Comanches appear as witnesses in tales of the great lode. A century and a quarter ago these fierce and extraordinary people boasted their nation to be the peer of the United States, whose citizens they at that time respected and treated as friends. Towards Spanish power, however, never did they express any other feelings than contempt and hatred. They learned to outride the race of horsemen who had introduced the horse to America; they ran Spaniards and Mexicans down, roped them, and dragged them to death. They were particularly jealous of the Llano–San Saba territory, from which they evicted the Apaches; they prevented the Spaniards from getting a firm foothold in the region; they fought against Anglo-American settlement of it until the very end.

Living at Liberty Hill is an old mustanger and trail driver named Andy Mather. The mountains of the West and canyons of the Plains are mapped in his grizzled features. I see him now, a great hat on his head, wearing a vest but no coat, "all booted and spurred and ready to ride," but sitting with monarchial repose in an ample rawhide-bottomed chair on his shady gallery. He was born in 1852 on the North Fork of the San Gabriel River in Williamson County, where his father owned a wheat mill and blacksmith shop. Two miles above the Mather place a band of Comanches under Chief Yellow Wolf made their headquarters. They were peaceable at the time and were friendly with the few settlers.

"In 1851," says Andy Mather, "Yellow Wolf brought some silver ore to my father to be hammered into ornaments. Of course I was not yet born, but one of my earliest and clearest recollections is of my father's telling me about the silver. He knew a good deal about metals and said that the ore was almost pure silver. Yellow Wolf told him that he got it from a place 'three suns to the west.' He described the deposit as being under a bluff near the junction of two streams. He offered to show it, but my father would not at that time think of leaving his family in order to go prospecting into the wild country beyond.

"How far 'three suns west' would be I do not know. A Comanche warrior could go a far piece in a day's time. From our place west to the old San Saba fort it was close to a hundred miles—just about three days' travel as we used to ride. Some people have figured that Yellow Wolf must have got his silver in the vicinity of the fort. I have known plenty of men to lose what little money they had in looking for silver in the hills west of here. I never hunted for the mines myself. All I know is what my father told me. I know that he was a calm man and that he told nothing but the truth. He knew Yellow Wolf well. He hammered Yellow Wolf's ore on his own anvil."

CAPTIVE WITNESSES

As if to corroborate the Indians, Indian captives have added their tales to the ever-increasing cycle. Captain Jess Billingsley, who won his fame in the Texas Revolution, was the "old rock" itself. Such was his prowess that his followers as long as they lived called themselves and were proud to be called "the Billingsley men." In the speech to his men that preceded the charge at San Jacinto Billingsley used a phrase that became a nation's battle cry and that seems destined to live as long as the name of Texas lives: "Remember the Alamo! Remember Goliad!"[11]

Along in the forties, while San Jacinto and the Alamo were yet freshly remembered, Captain Billingsley heard a Baptist preacher tell how for years he had been held captive by the Comanches and how through them he had obtained knowledge of the Bowie Mine. As proof of his knowledge of the mine he offered to lead the way to it. Billingsley organized a small expedition and with the preacher as guide set out for the San Saba. Up in the hills somewhere the Comanches attacked the party and killed their escaped captive. The survivors of the fight nearly starved to death before they got back to a country in which they were not afraid to shoot a deer—and that was the last of that search.

One time in the early fifties a *comanchero* (a Mexican trader with the Comanches) while out in the hills north of San Antonio bought a Mexican woman from a band of Comanches, with whom she had been for several years. He took her to San Antonio and released her. Naturally many people questioned her as to her experiences with *los indios broncos*. Among other things she told of how she had helped them gather silver ore up on the San Saba and beat it into ornaments.

Now, about this time a bachelor named Grumble was ranching on the San Saba below the mouth of Brady Creek—a good seventy-five miles east of the old fort. He had fought Comanches a plenty; he had seen silver on their buckskin trappings; he had even picked up spent silver bullets from their guns. When echoes of the Mexican woman's story reached his ears, he determined to visit her in San Antonio and find out more concerning the source of Comanche silver. This was a year or two after the captive's liberation, she having married in the meantime. She talked to Grumble without reservation.

"The Comanches often camped," she said, "at the old presidio, and right there they made bracelets and conchas and other ornaments out of silver. I have helped to bring the ore into camp, but I will not deceive you by telling you that I saw where it was taken out of the ground. I was a slave and had to obey others. I tell you only what I myself have seen.

"The Indians would leave their camp at the fort and cross the San Saba River. Then they would go on south for about two miles, following up Los Moros Creek. Then the men would leave the squaws and captives at a regular stopping place. Sometimes they would be gone a long time; sometimes not over an hour. I do not think the mine was over half a mile away. When the men got back to where we were waiting, they always gave us their ore to carry on in. It was well understood that the mine was kept hidden so that no stranger could find it."

After hearing this account, Grumble asked the woman if she would go with him to the San Saba and guide him as far as she could towards the Comanche mine.

"All I could do," she answered, "would be to lead you to our waiting ground on Los Moros Creek. At this place I could only point out the brush into which I saw the warriors enter empty-handed and from which I saw them return carrying silver."

All that Grumble asked was to be "put on the right track." The woman and her husband were willing to undertake the trip under his protection. Arrangements were made for immediate departure.

Grumble was a race horse man and gambler. He had formerly lived in New Braunfels, and he chose now to pass through that place and several other towns that offered chances for profitable games and races. Riding at his own convenience, he was sometimes ahead of the Mexicans and sometimes behind them. The arrangement with them was kept secret. Late one evening all three arrived in the village of San Saba, where Grumble went to the hotel while the Mexicans made camp.

As soon as he arose the next morning, the American entered a saloon to get a drink. At the bar he saw another gambler and racer named Sinnet Musset with whom he had recently had a "difficulty."

Each man "reached." Musset drew a fraction the quicker, and Grumble was a dead man. This was in 1857.

The Mexicans were naturally frightened. The woman had no desire to fall again into the hands of the Comanches. They went back to Lampasas, through which they had passed on their way up, got work there, and for five years did not tell a soul of their secret engagement with Grumble. When, finally, they did tell, no man was enterprising enough to take up the trail that Grumble had so precipitately quitted.[12]

Perhaps there is some connection between the silver up Los Moros Creek and Mullins' chart. Mullins is a bachelor. He lives at Menard in a feed store and makes money trading real estate. He uses some of his money to keep two or three men digging for San Saba treasure. He is not particular where they dig, provided they dig the holes deep enough. Sometimes they dig above the old presidio, sometimes below it; sometimes on one side of the river, sometimes on the other. The laborers get their wages every Saturday night and are satisfied; so is Mullins.

His prize chart is drawn in blue ink on the scraped hide of a javelina. He bought it from a young man who confessed to have stolen it from an old trapper in East Texas. I doubt if Mullins would sell it for a thousand dollars. It shows the San Saba River and Los Moros Creek. A cross represents the presidio. Near it an Indian with a long scalp-lock is drawing a bow. An owl looks down from a tree. A half dozen irregular stars sprinkled conspicuously over the map indicate where silver is to be found. The largest of the stars is up Los Moros Creek. A line projected southward from the old presidio up Los Moros Creek would very nearly coincide with the line of silver-bearing sandstone that Captain George Keith Gordon traced to the Lechuza Ranch.

The silver ledge on the Frio River must be too many suns west for the location that Yellow Wolf alluded to, and it could not be the location on Los Moros Creek that the Mexican woman told Grumble of. Yet it belongs to the tradition of captives who ranged with their captors over the San Saba territory. A "little rancher" named Whitley out in McMullen County told me about it. Could I reproduce the starlight on his beard, as we sat in front of his house, and the far-away barking of coyotes that mingled with his tones, the story would be a thousand times more real.

"When I was a young man in Refugio County," Whitley said, "I got to knowing an old, old Mexican named Benito who had been raised by the Comanches. They had captured him down on the Rio Grande as a boy and they kept him until he was grown. Whenever the Indians came to San Antonio to trade, he said, they always put him and other captives under the supervision of squaws, who stayed hid out.

"The main thing these Indians had to trade was ore. They made bullets out of it too. It was mostly silver. For a long time Benito didn't know where they got it, but finally they trusted him far enough to let him see. There was a big ledge of it up towards the head of the Frio.

"Well, Benito finally slipped away from the Indians and took in a couple of Mexican pardners to go with him for a lot of the ore. The Indians got on their trail and killed both his *compañeros*, and he barely escaped. After that he never tried to go back to the Frio.

"When I knew him he was over a hundred years old, and he would often tell me about the rich silver vein. I wanted to go in search of it, and he thought he could make the trip in spite of his feebleness if we fixed it so he could ride in a hack. He knew he could find the ledge if he ever got up the Frio Canyon, but he would not go unless a good-sized party went. He said that he would pick six Mexicans to go and I could pick six white men.

"Well, we got everything about ready, wagon, provisions, and so forth, when the man in our party who was bearing most of the fitting-out expense up and took down sick. So we naturally had to put the trip off. The man got well and a while after that we got ready to go again. But luck seemed to be against us. This time the old Mexican guide was taken down. It was out of the question for him to go. He was dying. He gave us the clearest directions he could and thought we could follow them. From what he said, the vein of silver could not be got to on horseback. It is in the south bank of one of three arroyos that run into the Frio close together. At it the arroyo makes a sharp turn, and a man would have to get down and go afoot along the bank. No doubt it was concealed, for the Indians always covered it up well after they had hacked off what they wanted. Benito said that if he could get just one sight of the lay of the land, he could tell which one of the three arroyos the vein was in. But he never got that sight; so he gave the best way-bill he could and died.

"The treasure hunting party broke up and things rocked along for years without me doing anything. Meanwhile a brother-in-law of mine had moved into the upper Frio country. I decided to pay him and my sister a visit and to find the ore at the same time. I took my dogs along, and the first thing we struck the very first morning we rode out to find those three arroyos was a bear. Well, sir, I got to hunting bear, and we never looked for that silver at all. But I know good and well if I had left my dogs at home, I'd 'a' had it.

"I say I know, because my brother-in-law found it after I left. I gave him the directions and he agreed to notify me if he made the find. Well, he made it and was leaving his place to come down the country to tell me, when he was murdered in cold blood. But that is another matter. He had confided in his wife, and of course she told me; but as he hadn't explained to her where he located the vein, that didn't do much good.

"You see, I have known two living witnesses to that silver. It wasn't hearsay with them. If I just had time, I believe I could go up there yet and find it myself."

Living in Fort Worth is an old-time Texas frontiersman named W. A. McDaniel. He appears to have swung a wide loop and to have heard the owl hoot in all sorts of places. The following is one of many tales that he tells.[13]

"Soon after the Civil War, while I was just a kid, my father went out to Coleman County to work for the Stiles and Coggin outfit. The Indians were so bad that at times only about half the cowboys worked on the range, the others keeping guard over the horses and the ranch quarters. My mother cooked on the fireplace for a couple dozen men, but the work and anxiety were so hard on her that father said he wouldn't let her stay in such a country any longer. So one day he put her and us children in a wagon and drove us to Burnet County to stay with an uncle and aunt. The Comanches were raiding there too, but not so bad, and there were more settlers to afford protection.

"Not long after we got there, two or three neighbor families came to see us. Of course, we boys must go swimming and fishing in the creek. The grown folks were afraid for us to go alone—afraid of Indians; so a kind of picnic party was made up. After we got to the creek another boy and I slipped across and ran to a hole that was hid by a bend.

"We were pulling fish out and bragging about our luck when twelve Comanche warriors rode down upon us out of the bushes. Two of them dragged the other boy and myself up on their horses behind them. As soon as they got off a little distance they stopped and blindfolded us. They did not torture us.

"It was about eleven o'clock when they captured us, and all that afternoon and into the night we rode like the devil beating tan bark.

We could not see a wink, but we knew by the coolness of the air and the sounds of insects and coyotes when night came. We also knew that we were traveling over a hilly country. At last the Indians stopped, pulled us off, undid our bandages, and told us to lie down and go to sleep. We slept.

"When we awoke next morning, we found ourselves in a shallow cave. I noticed some of the Comanches picking up what looked to be gravel. They had a fire, a little iron pot, and a bullet mould. They were melting these pebbles and running them into bullets. I picked up four or five of the pebbles and put them in my pocket. We stayed in the cave all that day, all the next night, and until late the third night. Of course both of us boys were looking for a chance to escape, but we were afraid to make any move. We were not tied but we were guarded.

"On the second afternoon of our captivity, the Comanches brought

in a jug of fire water—regular old tarantula juice—from somewhere and they all got as drunk as a covey of biled owls. By good dark the warrior guarding us was as drunk as the other Indians. He let the fire go out and keeled over dead to the world. We were in a kind of pen made by the cave wall on one side and the sleeping Comanches on the other. Now was our time.

"We slipped out and found a horse tied in the hollow. We both got on him and headed him southeast. He kept a general course except when we misguided him, which we frequently did; it later turned out that he had been stolen from a settler on the Lampasas. After riding the night out and then, with a few stops, until nearly sundown next day, we struck the settlement from which we had been stolen. While we were telling the story, I pulled the pebbles from my pocket. They proved, upon examination by a man who knew, to contain gold and silver as well as lead.

"I have tried many a time to ride back to the cave. It's been like looking for the white cow with a black face. I went to that cave in darkness; I left it in darkness; it is still in darkness. It can hardly be more than fifty miles from Burnet. When the Comanches saw that the white men were going to take the country for good, they doubtless filled up the entrance to the cave. Some day—perhaps it may be a hundred years from now—the cave and the mine will be found."

Whether this cave paved with pebbles of silver is the same as the one hung with icicles of silver, I cannot say. Living in Sweetwater, Texas, until recently was a blind man named Johnson, very old. Back in the fifties he was a ranger and Indian fighter. One time the band of rangers to which he belonged struck a party of Indians west of the Colorado River and, after killing two or three of them, scattered in pursuit. It was seldom that rangers bothered with Indian prisoners, but the captain of this company took his man alive. The prisoner turned out to be a Mexican.

The Indians, he said, had stolen him as a child, reared him, and shared with him a great secret. If his life were now spared, he would show his captor *mucha plata*. The ranger agreed, and the Mexican led him back into the hills for a few miles until they arrived at a very thick motte of hog, or Mexican, persimmons. Crawling into this, they came upon a broad rock slab. They lifted it back. Underneath was a slanting hole. Peering in, the ranger saw what appeared to be a myriad "icicles of silver." They hung glistening from the roof of the cavity like stalactites.

The captain now regarded himself a wealthy man, but what with chasing Comanche raiders, fighting Mexican bandits, and quelling domestic outlaws, he had no time to realize immediately on his wealth. In fact, he saw the icicles of silver but the one time. He confided the secret to Johnson, and was shortly afterwards killed. The years passed, and by the time Johnson got ready to search for the wonderful hole amid the hog persimmons he was blind. He knew the hill country, every canyon of it; he knew where he and his fellow rangers had met the Indians and in what direction his captain had followed the warrior captive who surrendered and paid such a wonderful ransom for his life; he had the captain's directions in minute detail. But a blind man cannot make his way through dense thickets and into box canyons; a blind man cannot lead the blind.

BEASLEY'S CAVERN

Beasley has been dead more than ten years now, and he was perhaps eighty-five years old when he died.[14] As a youth he came to live in the ettlement about Lampasas. Following one of the Comanche raids he vent with a little band of settlers in pursuit. The trail was plain, and hey rode fast towards the west. They crossed the Colorado and veered 10rthward in the direction of the San Saba. The moonlight was too dim to reveal tracks and so at dark the trailers camped to await dawn.

When Beasley went out early next morning to get his horse, he found that a coyote had chewed the picket rope, a rawhide reata greased with fresh tallow, in two, and that his horse had "made tracks." It was well after sunup before he found the animal, on the side of a rocky draw. He caught him and was making a *bozal*—a nose-hitch, used in place of a bridle—preparatory to mounting bareback, when his eye caught the mouth of a cave near at hand.

There is something about a cave that draws all natural men. A cave may conceal anything. This cave faced east, and the rising sun was shining directly into it. Beasley led his horse over and peered within. For fifteen or twenty feet the hole sloped down at a steep angle and then seemed to become a horizontal tunnel. The walls of the opening were reflecting and refracting the sun's rays like a chamber of mirrors. Beasley forgot at once both murderous Indians and his impatient comrades. He made a pair of hobbles out of a bandana, thus securing his mount, and then with the free rope lowered himself into the cave.

Now that he could examine the walls near at hand, he saw that they were lined, plated, cased with ore almost pure—ore that was undoubtedly silver.

However, he did not tarry. As quickly as possible he climbed out of the cavern, unhobbled his horse, mounted, and galloped to camp, where he found all hands awaiting him. He privately told the leader of the party what he had found. The leader chided him for having delayed the pursuit of the Indians and at once took up the trail. It was a long trail, a twisting trail, and at the end of it there was blood. When the frontiersmen turned back towards the Lampasas country, they left their leader behind them.

Beasley had communicated his secret to no one else. He alone now possessed it. There was only one other person in the world with whom he would share it. Almost immediately he went east to marry the girl who had been waiting for him to make a stake. He told his bride that their fortune was found, though not yet gathered. Daring the privations and hazards of the then utmost frontier, the couple settled a few miles below the mouth of the San Saba River. Beasley picked the site as being near his silver cavern. He remembered exactly, he thought, where his party had camped that night, where he had found his horse, and where he had seen the metal plating flash against the early sun. He was a good man in the ways of camp, trail, and unfenced range.

Yet after he had established a home—a base of operations—and set out to work his mine, he could not find it. He was so disturbed that for a long time he would not tell his wife of his failure. When he told her, she encouraged him by going out with him. The country settled up, and he went on looking for his cavern. In time he told neighbors of his quest—of his rich find and of his loss. The years by fives and tens shuttled by; he farmed and ran a few cattle; he worked hard; he raised a family; but he never entirely gave up the search. When death came he was still hopeful of some day recovering the fortune that one bright morning in his youth, when the land was youthful like himself, had gleamed before his eyes. To this good day, however, Beasley's cavern, like the tomb of Moses, remains an unseen monument.

> *Perchance the bald, old eagle*
> *On gray Packsaddle's height*
> *Out of his rocky eyrie*
> *Looks on the wondrous sight;*
> *Perchance the panther stalking*

Still knows *that* hunted *spot;*
For beast and bird have seen and heard
That which man knoweth not.

PEBBLES OF GOLD

Some—many—there are who hold that Beasley's cavern, the cave in which drunken Comanches held McDaniel prisoner, and likewise the cave with icicles of silver are all identical with the Bowie Mine, hasty revelations of it under extraordinary circumstances. However that may be, while the hunters are looking for cavern walls of shining metal, roof of argent stalactites, and floor strewn with pebbles of rich alloy, they had as well look also for pebbles of gold in a brook that flows somewhere in the same country.[15]

About the time that Captain Ben McCulloch of the Texas rangers was helping introduce the six-shooter to the horseback world, he detailed two of his men to scout for Indian signs west of the upper Colorado River. One morning they arose from their pallets out in that lonely and unsettled region to find their horses gone. A dense fog enveloped the hills and valleys so that they could see nothing. Nevertheless, they struck out to find the horses. The fog held on for hours. The best of woodsmen can become lost in such a fog. When this one lifted, the rangers discovered that they were lost. They had not found the horses and now they could not find the way back to their saddles and canteens. They wandered all day. It was hot summer, in a time of drouth, and they were in a region utterly devoid of water. By the time night came they were so thirsty they could not sleep. The lead, taken from cartridges, that they chewed afforded no relief. Their whole object now was to find water; as soon as they could see to travel, they pushed on.

At length, from the summit of a low range of hills, they saw below them far to the west a winding line of green. What stream it marked they knew not, for they had never seen it before. Its waters were life, and they were so clear that the sun danced on the pebbles at the bottom.

As one of the rangers, after the burnings of thirst were quenched, lay looking into the sun-lit pool from which he had drunk, he was startled to discover that the bottom of it was strewn with minute particles shining like gold. Calling to his companion, he said: "We have lost our horses, our saddles, and our guns, but we have found something better than all of them. Here is gold, gold, world without end!"

The shining particles, some of them as large as coarsely ground corn grits, were so thick among the sand and gravel that they had the appearance of having been sown by the handful. The rangers waded into the water and gathered them until each had a pocketful. Then one of them crept up on a turkey gobbler that was watering and shot it with a six-shooter. That night they feasted.

On their way out they stopped to rest high up on the shoulder of a long, rough hill. They were sprawled out on the ground, neither talking, when suddenly their attention was arrested by that peculiar cry of a hawk so resembling the call of a young wild turkey. Looking towards the hawk, which was alit in a stunted, half-dead post oak, they noticed something sticking out from a crotch of the tree.

It proved to be an ancient rust-eaten pick, its handle gone and one point encased so deeply that it could not be removed. The other point stuck out toward the head of the little stream they had just left. Then the rangers realized that they were not the first to have discovered gold in the region. They went on, leaving the unknown prospector's signboard still pointing. Late in the afternoon they saw Packsaddle Mountain looming in the distance. From this well-known landmark they got their bearings.

A few weeks later they exhibited their gathering of nuggets to an expert on minerals. He pronounced the stuff to be what miners call "drift gold," gold that has washed downstream from a mother lode. The mother lode, he added, might be miles away, but wherever it was it must be exceedingly rich. On many a long ride in after years the rangers sought the golden pool, but though they were Ben McCulloch's own men—plainsmen and woodsmen right—they never found it again. It may be that the mute finger of the old pick on the shoulder of a long, rough mountain still points to the source of the drift gold. The granite hills of the Llano guard well their secrets.

THE MAGIC CIRCLE ON PACKSADDLE

Had McCulloch's rangers on their way to camp climbed Packsaddle Mountain instead of using it merely as a landmark, they might have had an additional story to tell. Every fifteen or twenty years some "prospector" comes along, finds an old shaft on the mountain, imagines that he has discovered the original Spanish mine, and cleans it out, digging it a little deeper down. After he has spent his last two-bits, he goes away, and within a few years the abandoned shaft has the appearance of being as old as the hills—just the appearance to delight searchers for Spanish mines. But never doubt that there is a real mine on or in or under or somewhere around Packsaddle; the shafts have just not been sunk at the right places.

A Spaniard by the name of Blanco, they say, found the right place;

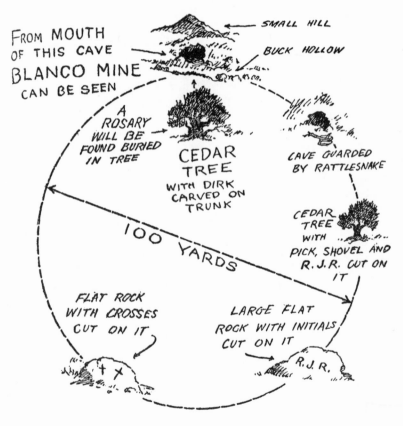

The magic circle. Landmarks within its circumference are supposed to afford a key to the Lost Blanco Mine. (Courtesy Miss Julia Estill.)

hence the object of search is often called the Blanco Mine. Whether it is the same as the Bowie Mine, I shall not undertake to determine. Men have all but shot each other in arguments over this very question. Certainly a plat to it in the form of a "magic circle" is sometimes applied to the Bowie Mine as well.

Among the earliest settlers in Llano County was a man by the name of Larimore. One day while he was hunting javelinas (peccaries) on Packsaddle Mountain his dogs ran three of them into a den. During the tedious process of smoking them out, Larimore discovered that the den was an old mine—maybe Blanco's—maybe Bowie's. Back in it a profusion of mineral was still exposed. The mineral proved to be lead with a strong percentage of silver. It made excellent bullets; and bullets, with powder, were the most urgent need that Larimore had.

Along in the fall of 1860 Jim Rowland went with Larimore into the mine and helped bring out about a hundred pounds of the ore. This they spent several days moulding into bullets. Larimore was preparing to leave the country. "I don't mind fighting for life," he said to Jim Rowland, "but I am tired of living just to fight. When I leave I'm going to leave that mine so well hidden that no other man can find it." In carrying out his word, Larimore is said to have turned a mountain gully so that it filled the valuable javelina den with silt and then to have covered the entrance with a large flat stone, over which he strewed soil. Grass and weeds soon sealed the last trace of the secret.

Such is the account given in two letters written towards the beginning of the present century by Jim Rowland himself and now in my possession. He knew a good deal more about the Blanco mine than he ever set down on paper.[16] He had even cut his initials, R. J. R., on the flat rock with which Larimore sealed up the entrance. One time a fellow named Chaney who was in the country looking for the mine offered Rowland a thousand dollars to show him the famous rock. Rowland agreed to the offer and took Chaney to Packsaddle Mountain, where he proceeded to lead him about in a manner rather devious for one who knew exactly where to go. Finally Chaney, becoming impatient, told his guide he was tired of "fooling."

"I'm tired too," Rowland replied. "Show me that thousand dollars and I'll show you the mine."

Chaney, however, refused to pay in advance, whereupon Rowland turned on his heel and strode indignantly down the hill. In telling, some time afterwards, what "a damned fool" Chaney had showed himself to be, Rowland concluded: "And just to think, at the very

31

minute I told Chaney to hand over them thousand dollars I was a-standing right on top of that mine."

It is a long way from Packsaddle Mountain to Calf Creek, and the faith that J. T. Merchant places in that location is based on no ambiguous magic circle. Mr. Merchant lives at Breckenridge, Texas. He used to be a schoolteacher; he is night watchman for an oil company now. He reads *Current History, Scientific American, The National Geographic Magazine,* and anything he can find bearing on geology and mineralogy. His interest in anthropology and paleontology has led him on long excursions following the tracks of prehistoric animals in rocks and getting evidence on "the Long-Headed Tribe." He has a strange story about a chart to the San Saba Mine.

"While I was a boy attending high school," he says, "I lived at New Boston, near Texarkana, with my sister and her husband, R. H. Jones, who was judge of Bowie County. In April, 1896, legal business took him to San Antonio. There he met a young Mexican, Aurelio Góndora by name, who was looking for a job tutoring Spanish. The young man was a graduate of the University of Mexico and had studied English in New York. As Judge Jones had four children of his own as well as myself to educate and as his experience with Spanish laws and land grants operating in Texas had caused him to value highly a knowledge of the Spanish language, he engaged the tutor and brought him home."

Aurelio's history was a sad one. At the death of his father, who had been quite wealthy, his mother married her dead husband's brother, a drunkard and a gambler. He had quickly run through with most of the estate and had made the life of Aurelio—like Hamlet, "a little more than kin and less than kind"—so wretched that he left home determined never to return. Shy, sensitive, lonely, the young tutor soon became passionately devoted to the member of the Jones household who was nearest his own age and most sympathetic towards him. This was Tom Merchant. The youths roomed together for two years, "often talking for hours on Spanish history."

Towards the end of the second year of this friendship, Tom fell in love. Aurelio as a result showed himself miserable and jealous. Every time the lovers stepped out, they found Aurelio dogging them. He generally took a position about fifteen or twenty steps to the rear. The town talked and joked. The lonely Mexican lad shrank more into himself and craved more the possession of his friend. The girl protested. Tom protested also—and Aurelio took a position a little more to the rear of the lovers. The girl now said that Merchant must either give up her company or force Aurelio to quit following them. Merchant, his patience exhausted, stormed at his friend, nagged him, tried to anger him. The break which finally came brought about a most singular revelation.

"I have always been sorry for my words," says Mr. Merchant. "At the same time it seems to me that an inscrutable fate made me say what I did. Aurelio and I were together in our room. I had been nagging him about the way he followed me around. He was so innocent and kind that it was hard to abuse him. I was looking for something that I could accuse him of in such a way as to shake him. Presently my eye fell on my trunk. It was open, the tray out on the floor, several rumpled garments exposed to view. The idea at once occurred to me that Aurelio was never so untidy. Then another idea came.

" 'Aurelio,' I said, 'there is my trunk open so that you can see everything in it. If you wanted to take anything you could. My trunk is always unlocked. But look at that damned trunk of yours. I have never seen it when it wasn't locked. I have never seen you open it. You follow me around like a sick kitten and yet you do not even trust me with your trunk.'

"I shall never forget the expression that this speech produced on Aurelio's face. For three days we slept together and ate together without exchanging a word. I managed to keep away from him most of the waking hours. On the fourth day one of those dreary, almost interminable drizzles that East Texas is noted for kept us inside. I went into our room, where I found Aurelio. I had broken him from following me; now I wanted to regain his friendship. I tried to start a conversation, but we could not talk.

"Presently Aurelio got up from his chair and closed the wooden shutters to each of the three windows in the room. Then he pulled down the windows and the shades over them. He even adjusted the lace curtains. Next he shut and locked the two doors opening into the room. A kerosene lamp gave us light.

" 'Now, Tom,' he said, 'your words about my trunk have hurt me so much that I can hardly sleep. I am going to show you why I keep it locked.'

"I remonstrated, telling him I had no desire to see what was in the trunk. 'Let us forget our differences and be the friends that we have been,' I said.

" 'No,' he replied, 'I must put before your eyes what has made me keep the trunk shut. First, though, I must explain some things to you.'

"Then he drew a passionate picture of his idealized father, a Castilian gentleman, highly intelligent, well educated, wealthy. 'When I was a mere child,' Aurelio went on, 'my father took me into his confidence and told me that he possessed the key to a fortune that would be mine even if everything else he had were lost. He repeated over and over the history of this key, specifying how I should use it. He put the details into writing. When he died, this instrument, along with other papers, came into the hands of my mother. After she married my wasteful and debauched uncle and I found I could endure home no longer, I told her that in leaving I wanted but one thing from the estate, that I would never claim anything else—the document my father had made for me. She protested that her husband knew about this document and that he would be terribly angry when he missed it. I took it anyhow. I came to the United States, for here I am to recover the fortune which it describes.'

"Aurelio declared that his uncle would, if he had the chance, murder him in order to possess the document. 'You will see now,' he concluded, 'why I keep my trunk locked.'

"With these words he took the document from his trunk. He showed me a series of plats relating to mines and treasures in Texas, Oklahoma, and New Mexico. There was a good deal of writing, and to this Aurelio added many details that he had heard from his father. I did not, as I shall presently explain, see all the plats. I shall tell of two. While the account of the first has nothing to do with the San Saba Mine, it will establish the validity of Aurelio's information on that subject.

"After finishing school, I parted from my friend and went to live in what is now Haskell County, Oklahoma. One day a man invited me to go fishing at Standing Rock on the Canadian River.

"Standing Rock on the Canadian! That was the key to one of Aurelio's plats. I asked the man if a hatchet was cut into the rock fifty feet up on the east side. He looked at me queerly and said that he had seen that very hatchet. Then I told him that there were nineteen mule loads buried near the rock.

"We went to Standing Rock on the Canadian. Yes, there fifty feet up, on the east side of the rock, just as Aurelio and the plat had described it, was the figure of a hatchet. Six hundred varas away at an angle of seventy degrees east of north should be a cedar tree with a turtle cut on it. We found it. The shaft we sank in the river and all that makes another story."

The plat to the San Saba Mine was so precious to Aurelio that he would not allow a close examination of it. He merely remarked that the Spaniards a short while before leaving the San Saba lost their entire stock of horses to the Comanches and as a result had to abandon all but one mine. It, "the main mine," he added, "was near the junction of a creek with the San Saba River to the east of the presidio. Here the Spaniards had a kind of sub-fort."

This creek Mr. Merchant has, by means of certain rock ruins, identified as Calf Creek, in McCulloch County. "Nevertheless," he concludes, "doubt seems to be the most destroying element to any argument. The contents of Aurelio's trunk would, I am confident, remove all errors and doubts. But many years ago Aurelio was stabbed to death—by an unknown man—in the Indian Territory and at the same time his trunk mysteriously disappeared."

THE RELIC

It is a persistent belief among treasure seekers, despite the fact that they do not live up to it, that treasure appears only when unsought and always in the most unexpected form. Late one evening some twenty years ago a man in a rickety wagon, hitched to a pair of "crow-bait" horses, drove up to a farmhouse in the hill country. He called, "Hello," got out, and stepped into the yard. A widow and her grown son lived on the place, and both of them were at home.

"I'm out buying relics," the stranger said. "Have you got anything to sell?"

"No, I guess not," laughed the widow, "leastwise nothing that you'd carry off."

"Well, just any kind of relic," went on the stranger. "Maybe an old picture, an old gun of some kind, locked deerhorns, queer rocks, Indian spear points. I buy anything."

"But we don't have a thing," repeated the widow. "You can see for yourself that this ain't much like a museum, even if the plows is all wore out and the stove so caved in that I have to bake bread in the yard."

"What's this?" interrupted the stranger, as he walked over and kicked a leaden ball that he had been eyeing most of the time.

"Oh, that's just an old lead ball that one of the boys plowed up in the field years ago," mildly explained the woman. "You can see how the plow grazed it. The boys used to roll it about as a plaything. It's a wonder it wasn't lost long ago."

"Now, that's what I call a relic," exclaimed the stranger. "What'll you take for it?"

"It's not worth anything, I know," slowly answered the woman, "but I'd rather not part with it. It was such a plaything for the boys."

"I'll give you twenty-five dollars," popped out the stranger.

Such a price almost overwhelmed the widow, and she accepted it immediately. The stranger paid down the twenty-five dollars, and then walked towards the wood pile.

"Loan me your axe," he said.

The young man got the axe. Selecting a clean, hard spot of ground, the stranger put the ball between two logs so that it could not roll. "I've been looking for this particular relic a good while," he explained.

Then he cut the ball in two. It was full of gold nuggets. If the plow had gone a little deeper, it would have cut into them.

The stranger was not stingy or mean. Gathering up the spilled nuggets before the speechless widow and son, he mounded them into two equal piles.

"By rights," he said, "at least half is yours. Take it." And a few days later that half was disposed of for exactly $7000.

"This is just one of four lead balls," went on the stranger. "I've been looking for them for fifteen years. According to my directions, the stuff in them come from one of the San Saba mines and the Spaniards planted them. The four balls formed the corners of an exact square four hundred yards to the side. Just by accident the other day while I was up in the Santa Anna Mountains I heard of this old relic in your yard, and I come a hundred miles as fast as my old plugs could travel."

A prolonged attempt was made to find the other three balls. But the exact spot in which the one ball was plowed up had long since been forgotten. So not one of the four corners could be established. The only definite clue was that the ball had been turned up along one of several washes that seamed the field. If any of the other balls is ever exposed, it will probably be by some plowhand as ignorant of its history as were the widow and her sons.

THE PICTURED COPPER PLATES

There were two Kirkpatrick brothers, Moses and James. They lived in the sober and sequestered village of Mullin, where Moses combined banking with his mercantile business and was the stout pillar, both moral and financial, that the Presbyterian church rested upon. He seldom glimpsed the wild flowers growing along the path of dalliance which his brother James so softly trod. James had been educated to medicine in Kentucky, their native state, and riding with his "pill bags" over the far-stretched hills of the Colorado River satisfied his ambition. The people in the country called him "Doctor Jim." He knew a little about rocks and he often brought them home in his saddle pockets or tied to his saddle horn. Home was with his good Scotch parents. Sometimes he fancied a rock too big to carry on horseback; he did not mind spending a day going after it in a buggy. He had a fondness for art. He was a loiterer with the tastes of an adventurer. When he was close to fifty he married a woman twenty-five years his junior. He was a great hand at story-telling, and however idle the heroes of his narratives may have appeared to Brother Moses, they were life and life's romance to nephews and nieces. He never had any children of his own. Thus lived

Twa Duries in Durrisdeer,
Ane to tie and ane to ride.

In 1900 "a foreigner" came to Mullin. He was either a Frenchman or a Spaniard—it could not be, or was not, determined which. He was very non-communicative, but as he was in quest of information he had to make human contacts. It was natural that he should "take" to Doctor Kirkpatrick, the easiest-going and the most tolerant man in the country.

He was looking, so he told the doctor, for a wrought-iron spike in an oak tree that should be somewhere north and a little east of the junction of the San Saba River with the Colorado. If he could find the spike, then he could find "the treasure of the banking mission"—the San Saba. The San Saba, according to the foreigner, handled the funds for all the Spanish missions to the northwest and was also a concentration point for bullion from mines in New Mexico and Colorado. It was a kind of clearing house for everything costly freighted between Santa Fe and New Orleans and naturally it had a storage vault for so much wealth. Rather unnaturally, however, this vault was far distant from the mission itself. In view of the danger of Indian attacks, a diagram to it was sent to "headquarters."

Where headquarters were, the foreigner did not say. Perhaps they were in New Orleans, perhaps in Mexico, perhaps in Spain. At any rate, after the San Saba massacre, headquarters alone knew where the wealth was stored; and for a century and a half headquarters took more pains to conceal than to utilize the information. Then, somehow, the foreigner came into possession of it. He went so far as to let Doctor Kirkpatrick get a hurried glimpse at his chart—but not to copy it. After having spent several weeks in a vain search for the wrought-iron spike, he left. No one in Mullin ever heard of him again.

Doctor Jim soon spread the foreigner's story. Consequently, when one morning during the following winter a resident of the village found a wrought-iron spike in the ashes he was cleaning out of his fireplace, he naturally mentioned the matter to the doctor.

Doctor Jim at once traced down the man who had hauled in his neighbor's wood. Then he got the woodhauler to show him where he had cut up a dead live oak tree. It is worth mentioning that a good deal of random digging had been going on in that very vicinity. Doctor Jim now entered into a loose oral understanding with the owner of the land and began operations. He interested Bob Urbach to the extent that Bob nearly broke his back and his credit digging and furnishing grub for a camp of hearty eaters. At last Doctor Jim had an occupation that was a passion.

A great deal of the exploration was through matted shinnery and cedar that a man could hardly penetrate without an axe. The first thing found was a flat limestone rock, perhaps four feet long, near the stump of the tree from which the spike had been taken. One side of it was covered with a picture, partly etched and partly painted, of an extraordinary pageant. The paint seemed to be red and yellow ochre, such as Indians commonly used. What the numbers and certain geometrical signs on this rock were has been forgotten; but many people are alive to testify to the train of ten pack burros that trailed across the stone as if to enter the mouth of a cave. On each of three packs and over the mouth of the cave was pictured a small yellow half-moon —the sign of treasure.

Doctor Kirkpatrick was as fond of deciphering codes as was Edgar Allan Poe of inventing them; he dawdled with mathematics. The figures on the stone fitted into memories of the foreigner's chart. Following Doctor Jim's directions, the laborers dug into what seemed to be the masonry of an ancient altar.

Here, between rocks that had protected them from becoming in the least tarnished, were found two "raw-beaten" copper plates, roughly circular in shape, each about twelve inches in diameter and about a quarter of an inch thick. The plates were covered with crude but clearly marked engravings. The first plate showed a trail winding down a hill, crossing a ravine, and then twisting up a hill to the east. Near the crossing, over what appeared to be a mining shaft, was the half-moon —a sign as magnetic to treasure seekers as the bright star was to the Magi. The second plate showed a setting sun near the mouth of a cave. A man standing by this cave looked across a valley towards another man who approached leading a pack burro. Between the two men three trees formed a triangle. The waiting man was dressed in a long coat of antiquated cut that reached below his knees—a coat too long to be a Prince Albert and too short to be a cassock. He wore on his head something between a derby and a helmet. He had a French appearance. Some of the details were remarkably well finished. A series of bars along one side of the plate meant something to Doctor Kirkpatrick. Taken together, the two plates seemed to suggest the dual character of the San Saba wealth: mines and stored treasure.

Doctor Kirkpatrick now located a triangle of trees a half mile east of the place where the plates were found. At the root of one of these trees, hardly two feet down, Bob Urbach and his fellow laborers dug up a hand-hammered copper box, not more than ten or twelve inches long. The lid of it was etched with the same string of pack burros, headed for the mouth of a cave, that had been found painted on the flat rock. In addition appeared the name Padre López over the date 1762. Within the box were a crucifix set with pearls and two rosaries, one of ivory and the other of exquisitely carved rosewood.

The intermittent hunting that resulted in the finding of these various objects extended over a period of two or three years. As they were unearthed, the public was allowed to look at them, but only Doctor Kirkpatrick understood the ciphers. He translated them into orders.

At last, when he was ready to open the treasure vault, a work that would require a vast amount of excavation, he considered it wise to draw up a written agreement with the landowner. The landowner, who had in the beginning been contemptuous of the whole business, now demanded a lion's share of the treasure; he would not sign a con-

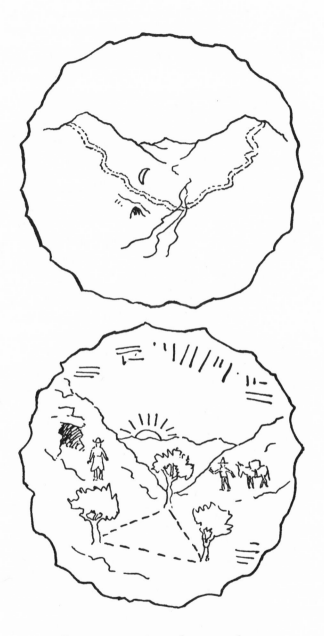

Doctor Jim's pictured copper plates.

tract for less. His Scotch stubbornness aroused and his sense of justice outraged, the doctor refused to agree to any such division. He would wait.

His health had been bad for a long time. He and his thrifty brother were not always in accordance, but at this juncture he went to Moses Kirkpatrick and detailed to him the whole story of the search.

"I now have all the information I need," he concluded. "I know where to find the treasure. But I am not going to dig it out until this hog who owns the land becomes more reasonable. I'll wait if I have to wait until I die—and that may be at any time. You are my brother, and I want to tell you where the treasure is so that if anything happens to me the secret will not be lost."

"No," retorted the austere Presbyterian elder and banker, "you will not tell me. I have already listened to too much idle talk. You neglect your practice, you neglect your wife. I have no patience with all this Spanish treasure foolishness."

Shortly after this conversation the doctor became critically ill. For two days he suffered and then he died. This was in 1904.

Following the death of the doctor two things important to the sequel happened: the Moses Kirkpatrick home in Mullin burned down; at the annual fair in Dallas Moses Kirkpatrick for the first time in his life entered the booth of a palmist.

The palmist pored over the deep wrinkles in his hand. "Your house has recently burned down." She described the house. He believed in her clairvoyance.

"You are on the brink of great wealth," she continued.

"How am I going to get the wealth?" the Scotchman asked.

"That is not clear. Your riches are in the ground. You or someone near you has been very close to them already."

Years after this incident Moses Kirkpatrick used to lament in his scriptural manner, "My heart was turned away so that I would not hear. My ears were dull of hearing and my eyes they were closed." He had stood on the brink of wealth—and scorned the hand that beckoned him to knock and enter. That hand now, alas, was invisible beyond the chasm of death.

Not long after Doctor Jim's death, his brother surrendered the copper plates, the stone, and the copper box with its contents to the doctor's young widow.[17] She sold the crucifix, the exquisite rosaries, and the curious box to a dealer in Dallas. She gave the stone to some stranger. The copper plates she took with her to California, where she married again and died. By expending time and money a good detective might trace down those extraordinary objects, but they seem to be lost forever. Even if they were recovered, however, it is very doubtful if any person could be found with Doctor Jim's skill and knowledge to decipher them. The doctor had made copies of the stone and plates on some wooden lids of old-fashioned candy buckets, but when the Kirkpatrick home burned they burned also.

The natives are still digging sporadically and blindly out in the hills where Doctor Jim dug up some very interesting copper objects—quite untarnished.

AN INNOCENT OLD LIAR

Of all the men who have searched for the Lost Bowie Mine I have heard of only one who in the end admitted that the mine might not exist or that his account of it was not gospel truth.[18]

In the fall of 1876, Mr. J. T. Estill, a pioneer lawyer of "the hill country," and a fellow barrister, D. Y. Portis, were driving in a two-horse buggy from Mason to attend court in Menard. Portis was at that time perhaps seventy years old, a typical plantation gentleman as well as lawyer of the old school. Rich in anecdote and repartee, he made a fine traveling companion for the equally genial Mr. Estill.

Some fifteen miles west of Mason the soil suddenly changes from a light color to a deep red, and as the travelers approached this divide, Mr. Estill remarked: "Well, we are getting into the Almagres—the Red Hills of the San Saba. We must be in the neighborhood of the great Bowie Mine."

"The Bowie Mine," retorted Portis with unusual animation, "is a myth. In my time I have been personally acquainted with a man who accompanied Bowie into the San Saba hills. One night down in Brazoria County a crowd of us young fellows were smoking pipes and telling yarns around a camp fire at which this old Bowie adventurer was present. He told us all about his marvelous experiences with Bowie, and he ended by swearing that he himself had hacked off pure silver from the Bowie vein with a hatchet. Well, sir, such a tale set us wild, and we all agreed right there to fit out an expedition to find the lost mine. We got together teams, wagons, and enough supplies to last us several weeks; we even hired some men to go along to help fight the Indians.

"Our party came through San Antonio and on up into this very country. It hasn't changed much. Bowie's old right bower would tell us where to camp but he stayed with us very little. He was out scouting for the lost mine. Sometimes he would be gone all day, returning only to tell us to move camp.

"By the time the old man had acted in this manner for four or five days, we came to the conclusion that he either knew nothing about the Bowie Mine or was holding back on us, refusing to live up to his contract. The leaders took him aside and in plain terms told him of our suspicions. If he had really hacked ore off a silver vein, they announced, he must tell of its location then and there or else be hanged.

"At this the old guide broke down and actually cried. 'There is no Bowie Mine,' he said. 'It is true that I was with Bowie, but the only thing we found was Indians. They turned us back, for we were only a handful. In after years, with Bowie and the other members of the hunting party dead, I began telling about the mine. I told the story so often and so long that I came to believe it. I am a liar, but I have told you the truth for once. Gentlemen, hang me if you will.'

"The innocent old liar was not hanged, and if the facts were known," concluded Portis, "a half dozen fellows who threatened to hang him have since appropriated his yarns and told them as personal experiences. When I have the right kind of audience, I myself never admit having failed to glimpse the silver of the San Saba."

THE BROKEN METATE

It would be erroneous to conclude that most of the hunters for the Lost Bowie Mine who tell their stories, however they may excel in oral narration, are merely artistic liars. The majority of these men have bought their experiences—the subject of their tales—at the price of years of grinding labor and that habitual abstemiousness which devotion to any single purpose exacts. Many of them have suffered jibes and ridicule only, like other martyrs, to have their patience and confidence strengthened.

We were in a Mexican restaurant in San Antonio. Dishes shoved to one side of him, Longworth[19] was indenting lines in the tablecloth with the point of his knife, occasionally dipping it into *enchilada* sauce for a drop of red to indicate where a hill stood or where a copper peg had been dug up. He was a tall, spare man, perhaps nearer fifty than sixty, not a white streak in his mop of coarse black hair.

"But where did you get this map?" I asked him. "It must have a history."

"Yes," he replied, "it has a history, and God knows in trying to follow it I have had a history too."

The story was told with many backings and windings, and I did not get the whole of it until nearly a year after our first talk, when I found Longworth one day in a little room out in the yard behind the boarding house his wife keeps. He was working on an electrical device for locating minerals that he calls the "radio sleuth." After explaining its mechanism, he brought out a thick pile of documents. From them and from his own testimony I have put Longworth's story together. Like all good stories, it begins far away and long ago.

About 1830, while Texas was still a part of Mexico, a man by the name of Dixon settled on the San Marcos River near the present town of San Marcos. He was a poor man, but not too poor to keep an Indian in his hire. This Indian seems to have been a kind of outcast from his tribe. One day an aged Mexican appeared at Dixon's cabin inquiring for rocks marked in a certain way. Dixon knew of some rocks on his own land that bore the signs described. He, his Indian, and the old Mexican went to them, and in a short time the Mexican dug up a small *olla* of silver coins, which he divided with the landowner.

Not long after this episode the Indian asked Dixon if it was his desire to possess a great deal of silver. Dixon admitted that it was.

"Then," replied the Indian, "I will lead you to it. Yonder to the west in Summer Valley is a cave full of it. The mouth of the cave is stopped up with rocks, but I have been inside. I can go inside again."

It turned out that by Summer Valley the Indian meant the valley of the San Saba River. Thither he and Dixon set forth. When they got into the hills, they saw Indian sign everywhere; the Comanches and the Apaches were at war. Dixon's guide was afraid of both war parties, but from a concealed position he pointed out the vicinity of the cave. Dixon took a good look at the features of the country so that he could recognize the place when he should return at a safer time. Then the two men went back to the San Marcos. The next year the Indian died. This was not long after the close of the Mexican War.

Dixon now took into his confidence three neighboring settlers: Sam Fleming, G. B. Ezell, and Wiley Stroud. The four partners felt that they needed something more definite and reliable than the Indian's tale to guide them. The truth is that the Indian had not on other occasions distinguished himself for veracity. Therefore, they decided to send Dixon at common expense to Monclova, Mexico, once the capital of the united provinces of Texas and Coahuila, to find out what he could from the archives there.

Upon arrival in Monclova, Dixon found that the archives were in the custody of the Catholic Church and that outside examination of them was, for the time being, prohibited. He was on the verge of returning home when he met a Spaniard whom he had known in Texas. He frankly told him his difficulty.

Now it happened that the Spaniard had a daughter, named Carlota, who was engaged in some minor capacity by the priests in charge of the archives. Her father thought she might help in getting the desired information. She readily assented to the plan. She declared that some of the reports in the archives bore on the San Saba mines, though she had no idea of their contents. They were kept secret. She could copy them, she added, only at risk to her life. She would probably have to wait a long time for a chance to get full information. With the understanding that he would hear when it was obtained, Dixon came home.

Months went by without a word, then years—so many years that Dixon and his partners had almost given up hope of ever learning anything from the Monclova documents. Then one day in 1858, the north-bound stage through San Marcos brought a letter. It was from Carlota. She was in San Antonio and she had, she said, information too valuable to trust to the mail. She wanted Dixon to come to her immediately. He went.

In the interview that followed, Carlota was at once open and secretive, definite and indefinite. She was willing to tell only part of what she knew, though that part she disclosed without reservation. She had dug out, she said, documentary evidence concerning fourteen mines located around the old San Saba fort, some of them more than six leagues distant from it, the richest being Las Iguanas. In the bottom of the shaft leading to the Iguanas Mine reposed two thousand bars of silver weighing fifty pounds to the bar. To this vast storage she agreed to furnish a detailed *derrotero* (chart), with the understanding that a fifth of the silver should go to her. Once the silver was secured, it could be utilized in reopening and working the great mines from which it had been extracted before hostile Indians ran the Spanish miners out of the country.

"Dig up this silver," she said, "and then you shall have all the other charts."

Dixon could not read Spanish, but he brought home the *derrotero* to the two thousand bars of silver, and Wiley Stroud, the only "Spanish scholar" in the company, read it. It stated that the shaft was filled up with rocks. The partners agreed that it and the old Indian's "cave" were one. They were on fire with enthusiasm and confidence.

But it always takes lost mine hunters a good while to organize their expeditions. The greater the wealth at stake and the poorer the searchers, the longer the time required. The San Saba wealth was immense; Dixon and his company were as poor as Job's turkey. It took

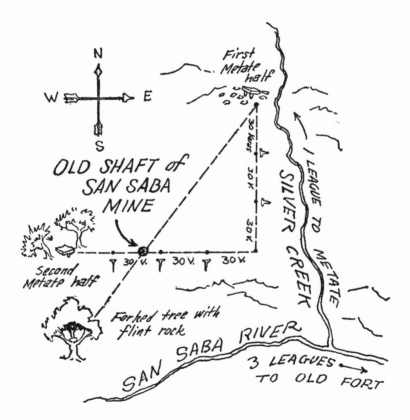

The chart that Carlota brought from the archives of Monclova, Mexico.

them over two years to get ready to go to the San Saba. Just as they were at last about to set forth, the Civil War began. All four entered the Confederate Army; when the war was over, all four were still alive. Meanwhile Carlota had gone back across the Rio Grande. The Texans lost all trace of her.

In 1868, exactly ten years after Carlota's appearance in San Antonio, and twenty years after the Indian's guidance towards a cave in "Summer Valley," the San Marcos adventurers, with several grown sons accompanying them, reached the San Saba. They carried along a few spades, axes, and grubbing hoes—and a keg of homemade corn whiskey.

The *derrotero*, as Wiley Stroud spelled it out, directed that they go three leagues towards the west up the San Saba River from the old fort and then turn north and follow up Silver Creek one league. The searchers had no trouble in finding the ruins near Menard. Approximately three leagues (about eight miles) to the west they came to the mouth of a creek called Silver and proceeded another league northward.

The *derrotero* now called for a mound of stones on a hillside. They found a mound of stones. Under the stones, buried shallow, should be the half of a Mexican *metate* (a stone used to grind corn on). They found half of a *metate*. Now they were to measure off thirty varas due south and dig; there they should find a copper peg. They found it. Another thirty varas to the south should be another copper peg. It was there. Still another thirty varas to the south they should go and then turn west. At intervals of thirty varas each they should on this east-to-west line find three more copper pegs. They found them all. Next, going on west for an unnoted distance, they should come to two mesquite trees growing close together; in the ground between these twin trees they should dig up another half of a *metate*.

As the men ran their lines and dug up copper peg after copper peg, their excitement, as may be imagined, was intense. They worked in a trot. Finding the two mesquites with the piece of *metate* at their roots proved a tedious business. Finally, however, the stump of one tree was located, and, surely enough, excavation around it brought to light the half of a *metate*. This half fitted exactly with the other. Across the gray surface of the rejoined halves the letters of one word showed plainly. The word was EXCAVAD. Dig where?

The chart directed that a tree with three prongs would be found to the south of the last half of the *metate*, and that fixed between these three prongs should be a flint rock "about the size of a turkey egg." It was only after three or four trees had been chopped down and the branches cut out that the flint was found, deeply embedded.

The next step was to sight from the flint in a northeast direction to the initial mound of rocks. The intersection of this line with the east-and-west line was the place to dig into the old shaft. The point of intersection proved to be almost in the bed of Silver Creek, which is generally dry. According to directions, the shaft must be opened for sixty feet straight down; then a complicated tunnel that twisted in various directions on several levels must be cleaned out before the "store room" of two thousand silver bars could be broken into. Dixon and his men began tearing into the earth. As they worked, it became evident to them that they were clearing out a big hole that had been dug through solid rock and later filled. It did not take them long to realize that they could never remove all the rocks without hoisting machinery and the expenditure of an immense amount of labor. Some of the men became discouraged and skeptical. "If it is necessary to tunnel this whole damned hill out to get the silver," said one, "I don't want none of it." Another man swore that "the whole business was a cheat" and that "not even a Spaniard would go to so much work to hide his stuff."

During the discussion several of the malcontents had frequent recourse to the whiskey keg. Finally G. B. Ezell's son grabbed the *derrotero* out of the hands of Wiley Stroud, who was for the fortieth time interpreting some item, and threw it into the fire. It was immediately consumed. Fortunately, Stroud had spelled out the way-bill aloud so many times that its contents were indelibly impressed upon his own mind and the minds of his partners.

Discouraged and quarreling, the San Marcos men gave up the search, never to renew it. The first rise in Silver Creek after their departure filled up with rocks and gravel the shallow excavation they had made to mark the site of the original Iguanas shaft. The six copper pegs were scattered, and now, so far as is known, not one remains. The pieces of *metate* were carried home by Sam Fleming, who cemented them together. Later he moved to Benton, in Atascosa County, where he ran a blacksmith shop, and it is remembered that his wife used the repaired *metate* as a clabber trough for her chickens. After her death he went to San Antonio, where for fifteen years he lived with his niece and her husband, a man by the name of W. J. Parker.

Now Parker, likewise a Confederate veteran, was for years keeper of the West End Pavilion. Here in 1902, W. M. Longworth met him and was taught the history of the San Saba Mine as it has thus far been recorded.

"Night after night," Parker assured Longworth, "I have heard old man Fleming tell how Dixon was guided by the Indian, how he represented his partners in Monclova, how the Spanish lady, Carlota, brought the *derrotero* to San Antonio, and then how the hunt for the two thousand bars of silver came to a disastrous end. Fleming never varied in a single detail. His story had to be true."

It took Longworth a long time to act. Before he ventured greatly he wanted to make sure of the alleged chain of fourteen mines from which the great storage of silver bars had been extracted. He wanted to see those documents that Carlota claimed to have found in the archives of Monclova but would not show to Dixon.

So, about ten years after becoming interested, he raised five hundred dollars and turned it over to a trusted Mexican, instructing him to go to Monclova and "use the money right." The Mexican seems to have "used the money right." He came back with a copy of a very long document purporting to have been written by one Pablo Bernalles. This document recites how two thousand miners under the direction of a certain José de la Amelgamese worked "fourteen rich mines" on the San Saba in the eighteenth century.

"The San Saba hills are bald hills of limestone," so the document quotes José de la Amelgamese. "They are without surface indications of minerals. But we prospected and found a lead to much silver."

True, the directions to the "fourteen mines" seem a little vague. Yet Longworth felt recompensed for the five hundred dollars he had spent to get them. He went up Silver Creek to a place that he verified as being where Dixon and company had made their location. There he set to work. When he had cleaned out the shaft for sixty feet straight down, he struck a wall that appeared to have been cemented. He broke through it into "a kind of natural cave"—the Spanish tunnel. But the tunnel was also filled with rocks and dirt, "*mostly surface material.*" For months he and his helpers carted rocks in wheelbarrows and hoisted them up the shaft. Then he struck a powerful vein of water.

His funds were exhausted, but he managed to buy a good pump. It proved to be inadequate. About this time the United States entered the World War. Longworth made good money working on the cantonments around San Antonio. He bought another pump. It would not do the work. Thus alternating between cantonment jobs and pumps, he spent two years.

Meanwhile he became acquainted with a major in the United States Army who owns an island off the coast of Florida on which pirate loot is buried. As soon as the war was over, this major sent from his home in Kansas City a new kind of "radio machine" guaranteed to indicate any mineral in its vicinity. When the machine got near the San Saba diggings, it "squalled," "bellered," "roared," simply "cut up" beyond all precedent. Longworth felt more certain than ever that he was over a room full of silver bars.

But there was the water. He could find no pump to control it. He was at his row's end, it seemed. Then he heard that a San Antonio lawyer owned some powerful pumps that had proved very successful in a Mexican mine. He went to see the lawyer.

"When I told him what I wanted with pumps and where I was working," says Longworth, "he jumped straight up out of his chair. 'Man,' he exclaimed, 'I've been looking for that location myself. Undoubtedly you are at the right place.' "

In short, for a half interest in the project, the lawyer agreed to finance the search. He secured long leases on the land around the workings. He installed adequate pumps. He put a crew of Mexicans to tunneling. For weeks they carried out from twelve to twenty tons of rock a day.

To describe the labyrinth of holes that Longworth and his moneyed partner now made would be tedious. The farther they dug, the more ambiguous became some of the directions inherited from the San Marcos adventurers. One night, however, Longworth had a dream that set them straight again. Then a series of floods in Silver Creek refilled the tunnel with silt. It had to be reopened.

The lawyer is still spending money. "It may be tomorrow," he says; "it may be a week from now; it may be a year. But some day we are going to break into what is perhaps the greatest treasure chamber known to history. It will create a sensation equalled only by the tomb of King Tut."

This is the dream that never dies.

Always on beyond and beyond! Oh, Spanish *conquistadores* who rode your last ride three centuries back to find the Cerro de la Plata, what think you now of the beyond? Oh, Captain Bernardo de Miranda with your report of silver varas—and nothing else—to keep your memory green while you have been to most unsilvern dust this long while, could you have loaded thirty mules with *cargas* as rich as the viceroy was promised? And you, brave, bloody, rough, romantic, real enigmatical Jim Bowie, who fought for nebulous treasure as hardily as for a nation's liberty, what besides hostiles did you find in the wild San Saba hills? And you, Captain Jess Billingsley, your cry "Remember the Alamo! Remember Goliad!" with its antiphony, "Me no Alamo! Me no Goliad!" echoing down the vaults of time, what is your judgment at last on the captive preacher's tale? Say, Pioneer Dixon, have Carlota and the secretive priests yet revealed what for so many years you waited for and dreamed of beside the clear San Marcos? Doctor Jim Kirkpatrick, brother to the sober elder of Scotch Presbyterianism, could you really have finished the tale you left half told of pictured copper plates and rosewood rosary in plain Mills County? Shades of old Ben McCulloch's rangers, could you find your way back now to that brook paved with golden pebbles and marked by a dead man's pick? Shade of patient Beasley, leading at last, one may hope, your faithful wife in a land that has fulfilled its promises, have you seen there any light to reillumine the walls of the silver cavern that dazzled your youth? Shades of dead dreamers all, is there somewhere on the Llanos a Hill of Silver, somewhere three suns west of the San Gabriel a ledge of Comanche ore, somewhere about the shattered and silent ruins of the Mission San Saba a shaft down to thousands of bars of Almagres bullion once marked by fragments of a peon's *metate*—is there somewhere a Lost Bowie Mine?

CHAPTER II

Down the Nueces

Those old credulities, to Nature dear,
Shall they no longer bloom upon the stock
Of history?
WORDSWORTH

In 1762 a detachment of the San Saba presidio, together with some priests, moved over to the Nueces and at a site marked by the present village of Camp Wood established a fort and mission called San Lorenzo de la Santa Cruz. The Spaniards often referred to this establishment simply as El Cañon. Like that on the San Saba, it was almost constantly harassed by the Comanches, who on one raid alone drove a thousand horses away from it. It was never well garrisoned and was abandoned only seven years after its founding. Contemporaneous with it, another mission of little significance known as Nuestra Señora de la Candelaria was set up some five leagues downstream, at what is now Montell; it was abandoned in 1766.[1]

No doubt the Spaniards prospected the broken lands up the Nueces. What they found is unknown. Maps of the thirties and forties showing a "Silver Mine" on the San Saba indicate another on the high divide between the Nueces and Frio canyons. The adventurous Bowie prospected in the Frio-Nueces country even before he led the famous expedition to the San Saba.[2] Wherever the Spaniards went they left their sign; the clank of their spurs and the thump of their picks still echo down El Cañon.

Human tracks and human blood will not wash out of a soil, although cement may hide them. The region between the Nueces and the Rio Grande is not cemented over; comparatively little of it will ever be cemented over; it will always be a land with a past. While the Apaches and Lipans were making here their most desperate stand against the encroaching Comanches, a few Spanish rancheros built fortified homes and began stocking the country with horses and cattle, which before long ran as wild and unclaimed as the deer. The bands of maverick horses sometimes numbered thousands, and "Mustangs" was the word that on early maps described the wide blank. Nevertheless, a few roads across it were traversed by all traffic from Mexico to the interior of Texas and by the occasional trains of carts or pack animals to New Orleans and Saint Louis. Counterclaims by the Republic of Texas and Mexico made the strip a kind of no man's land. Long after the claim of Texas was established, the Nueces was called "the dead line for sheriffs." Below it bandits of two languages raided and rendezvoused, and the sparse ranchers who survived to possess the land, where it was possessed at all, were as hardy a breed as ever justified the law of the fittest. Their descendants who hold now the vast thickets of thorned brush, prickly pear, and dagger preserve the frontier temper. They cling to the traditions of their soil. For them the tracks made in that soil by Spanish fortune seekers of the eighteenth century have no more been washed away than the outlaw steer's tracks of yesterday.

GENERAL BAYLOR'S ASSAY

Along about the time of the Civil War, so the story runs, General John R. Baylor was talking with a shaggy trapper who had just come out of the Nueces Canyon.

"Is there any gold up there?" Baylor asked.

"Gold!" exclaimed the trapper. "You can pick up gold nuggets along the gravel bar as big as a cow's liver!"

"Well, why didn't you get some of it?" asked the blunt frontiersman.

"Huh," the trapper explained, "a man has to run too fast in that country to pick up anything. Indians won't let him stop."

Now John R. Baylor was a frontiersman if ever Texas produced one. He was high-handed, high-headed, and high-spirited. He had been sub-agent on the Comanche Reservation on the Clear Fork of the Brazos, but upon being relieved of his office became perhaps the deadliest killer of Comanches known to the frontier. Once, in company with four or five other rough-and-ready pioneers, he attacked a band of Indians, took nine scalps, in return for one of a white woman that dangled from a warrior's belt, brought them to Weatherford, and stretched them on a rope for jubilant citizens to dance around. The fervid orgy of vengeance lasted all night and, except that the women "stomped" as freely as the men, was essentially a scalp dance. Then Baylor exhibited the trophies in other towns and, to arouse yet further rage against the Indians, aided in establishing a fire-eating newspaper called *The White Man.*

When the Civil War broke out, he dashed into New Mexico with a detachment of cavalry and proclaimed himself governor of a territory that embraced about half of New Mexico and Arizona. He was also busy with schemes for bringing Chihuahua and Sonora into the Confederacy. After he had poisoned about half a hundred Apaches like so many coyotes and issued orders that all grown Indians should be killed and the children taken prisoners and sold for slaves "to defray the expense [chiefly for whiskey] of killing," the Confederate authorities relieved him of the governorship. Then he fought as a private gunner at Galveston, was a Confederate congressman, and while the war was ending made plans for some sort of expedition that he should lead into Mexico.[3] General Baylor had dreams of empire—but this is the story of a dream-path to gold.

That remark of the trapper about nuggets up the Nueces "as big as a cow's liver," coupled with a report he is said to have received from the noted colonizer Henry Castro, was to cost General Baylor a fortune. Castro, it seems, had just been to Mexico City and there dug out accounts of a Spanish smelter at El Cañon. In detailing to Baylor the results of his researches Castro described how the Spanish miners up the Nueces operated; how, instead of "drifting in" and cross-cutting, they simply followed the vein; how, if it pinched to a narrow width, they made a hole only big enough to crawl through and followed on; how for ladders they used long poles with foot-notches cut into them; how they carried ore out in *zurrones* of javelina skins hung from their heads and shoulders; and how by the use of cheap Indian labor they could work very low-grade ore.

When the Civil War was over, General Baylor filed on some land up the Nueces Canyon—where he could continue to get plenty of action as well as hunt for the Spanish gold. He prospected high and low, in the brush and through rocks. He knew as little about mining as a hog knows about Sunday, but he had his own crucibles and made his own assays.

One day while he was running a test, a neighbor named Stockley, unseen by the General, whittled into the crucible some filings off a perfectly good twenty-dollar gold piece. When the test showed a high percentage of gold, Baylor jumped into the air, yelled, and declared that he had found the famous Spanish lode. Stockley had intended to explain his joke, but now that he saw how happy the General was and

remembered what a temper he had, he was afraid to explain. The General's sons knew of the trick, but they, too, were afraid to explain. So the intrepid frontiersman went on spending his time and hundreds of dollars trying to get another test of gold. An Englishman who claimed to be a mineralogist happened by, and at $150 a month he was engaged to apply his knowledge. He put down a shaft known as the John Bull Mine, and to keep the General's hopes up and his own salary forthcoming, he occasionally rubbed a gold ring against some of the samples turned over for assaying. He kept on working until his ring was worn out.

The gold mines of the Nueces are yet unexploited; when, full of years and experience, Baylor died, he still believed in them. He was buried in the Montell cemetery and his grave was mounded over with the specimens of rock he had spent so much time in accumulating. It was a fitting monument, and it has inspired successive prospectors. Chief among them has been Henry Yelvington, journalist, oil speculator, and charming gentleman.

"When just a boy," said Yelvington, "I went with my father and some other men on a hunt up the Nueces, and was enthralled by the stories of lost mines and buried treasure they nightly told around the camp fire. I resolved then to return when I should be 'a big man' and prospect. I was still not very 'big' when, in 1906, as reporter on the San Antonio *Express*, I received a tip that the records in San Fernando cathedral contained information on Spanish mines of the Nueces. I did not tarry to examine the records; I made for the mines. Throwing in with a trapper, I spent eight months prospecting. I did not find a thing; but as deer, turkeys, javelinas, fish, bee trees, foxes, bob cats, squirrels and ringtails were plentiful and an occasional bear could still be found, I did not miss the gold.

"Then in 1915 I got in touch with George Baylor, a son of General Baylor's, and persuaded him to explore with me. The ruins of the walls and smelter of the San Lorenzo Mission, at what is now Camp Wood, appeared to the casual eye to be nothing but a mound, perhaps an acre in extent, with great trees growing on it. About the mound were many old holes, and one of them revealed a stone-arched door of Spanish masonry; another, a bit of the smelter. Near by I picked up a piece of stray ore that assayed $116 per ton in silver and lead.

"On the Baylor homestead Mr. George Baylor and I undertook to explore what the called 'the round cave.' As we climbed the mountain towards it, I noticed a lead running up. Right on this lead we found the 'cave.' I recognized it at once as an entrance to a Spanish mine—though General Baylor had always regarded the hole as natural. We went inside with candles. The shaft dropped down about ten feet, wall rock on one side and loose formation on the other. After following the drift for about fifty feet, we came to a cave-in that almost blocked our way. But, feet foremost, we crawled through and then entered another fairly open tunnel. As is usually the case in old Spanish mines, the circulation of air was perfect. On the way back we wandered into a branch tunnel, the candles burned out, and we were lost. But three hours later we got back to daylight.

"I took some ore from the lead and had it assayed. It ran from $2.70 to $4.75 gold per ton, which is a good showing for a lead in limestone formation; paying ore in limestone is generally very deep. Although we worked at the old mine in a haphazard way for several months, we never did get back to where the Spaniards had left off. There were too many cave-ins, and reopening the tunnels would have cost too much money. Of course it is possible that the vein may have been worked out.

"Above the San Lorenzo, I found another old Spanish shaft, but all I got from it was a crude pick badly rusted. A cave-in near the entrance of the tunnel blocked us. I expect to go back some day and explore that tunnel to its end. I know that the Spaniards worked mines on the Nueces."

It remains but to say that about two years ago a man hunting sheep in a pasture near the ruins of El Cañon found an antique bell weighing ninety pounds and that the find has caused a fresh outburst of digging.

ESPANTOSA LAKE

Nearly a hundred miles down the Nueces from the ruins of El Cañon is Espantosa Lake. *Espantosa* means *haunted*, or *horrible*, and things have been seen and heard at Espantosa Lake that well warrant the name. The *camino real* between Presidio Rio Grande and San Antonio used to skirt the lower end of the lake, and here was a favorite camping place. They say that the lake used to harbor a peculiar kind of mermen who sometimes seized young women dipping up water for their camps and carried them away.

One night, they say, some freighters with a wagon of money and other valuables camped on the edge of the lake, watered and hobbled their teams, and went to sleep. Suddenly the ground on which they lay sank, their cargo was engulfed, and they themselves were drowned. For generations after that people used to hear in the darkness a strange wagon that left no tracks rumbling down towards the lake from the hills.

Once a cattleman named Cleary and a hired hand were camped beside the old road. They had run out of tobacco and so had the little store near Presidio Crossing, just east of the lake. A wagon load of supplies was expected daily by the storekeeper. One night the two campers heard a wagon clattering down the hill.

"Well," said Cleary, "we'll get some tobacco in the morning sure."

The next morning early he galloped down to the store. "Gimme some tobacco," he demanded as he alighted from his horse.

"Tobacco!" grumbled the storekeeper. "You know I ain't had any for ten days, and if that freighter don't come right away I'll be out of coffee too."

"Now, looky here!" Cleary replied. "I'm as starved fer tobacco as a hay-fed horse fer green grass in April. It's no time fer a joke. We heared that freight waggin pass our camp last night jest about the time we was turnin' in. I had a good mind to step out and hold it up and take some tobacco right then. So shell out *pronto.*"

"You mean you dreamed you heard a waggin," the storekeeper rejoined. "There ain't been any more waggin come to this store than a ghost."

Thus the argument went on for some time. Finally Cleary led the storekeeper out to the road, which was sandy at that place, to show him the irrefutable evidence of a wagon—tracks. There were no tracks. He scratched his head and then loped back up the road to his camp. Not a sign of a track was there on the whole stretch.

A certain man in the country known as Mocho—from the fact that his ear had been gotched, or cropped, by a bullet—was one night camped with a "cow crowd" near the place where Cleary had camped. Soon after supper someone called attention to the rumble of a wagon.

"Maybe it's the ghost waggin goin' down to Espantosa Lake," a man suggested.

"Ghost, the devil," Mocho retorted. "I'll make a ghost of that driver if he don't stop tonight."

The rumble of the wagon was by now a distinct clatter. Mocho with drawn six-shooter walked out into the middle of the road. The night was fairly dark, but the sounds were so distinct that one did not need to depend upon sight. As the wagon approached Mocho, the waiting men heard him bellow out, "Halt!" and then in Spanish, "*¡Párate!*"

For perhaps a minute, not longer, the rolling of the wheels and the tread of hoofs ceased; then they were resumed. They ceased just above Mocho; they began just below him. He stood in the middle of the road; the road was lined with impenetrable brush. Nothing sensible had passed him. The sound of a shot that he directed down the road was not more distinct than the receding clatter of the unhurried wagon. In the morning not a track was to be seen.

No one ever heard the wagon leaving Espantosa Lake; it was always going towards it. In time Peg Leg Tumlinson with much labor put down a shaft at the foot of the lake, where the campers had met their sudden fate, but mud and water prevented anything like a thorough exploration. The precious cargo is still there.

WITCHING FOR SILVER

On the south bank of the Nueces, seventy-five miles below Espantosa Lake, is the site of Fort Ewell. Nothing remains of it now but a trace of adobe foundation and a graveyard overgrown with prickly pear. A year or so ago fortune hunters stepped over the sagging barbed wire about the enclosure and tore open the last clearly marked grave. Fort Ewell used to be a stage stand, a county seat, and a post office. While O. Henry was at the Dull Ranch, fifteen miles away, he used to ride to Fort Ewell for the mail; on those rides he got something that he later put into "Law and Order" and other stories of the Nueces country. But long ago the stage stopped running, the storekeeper and his post office moved away, the wooden bridge across the Nueces rotted down, and the road became a cow trail. Fort Ewell is a place of memories.

Silence and space are kind to memories. The relics of Fort Ewell moulder in a pasture of 60,000 acres. Across the river is the Rancho de la Mota, with 40,000 acres. Joining the Mota on down the river a few miles is Rancho de los Olmos, containing 56,000 acres. Until recently the owner of the Olmos controlled 200,000 acres of uninhabited pasture lands adjacent to his own estate. Thus the country stretches out— a "big country" of no fields, of few people, and of many memories.

Before "bob wire played hell with Texas," as Big Foot Wallace used to say, a hard "layout" of Mexicans hung around El Fortín (Little Fort). Once they waylaid an Englishman and killed him for his horse.

When they were not stealing horses or waylaying travelers, they occasionally looked for a legendary iron safe, full of valuables, that Comanches once took from a *carreta* and dragged out into the tall *sacaguista* grass.

Peg Leg Tumlinson, who sank the shaft in Espantosa Lake, was a "big hombre" among the Fort Ewell Mexicans. One time while he was down on a little *paseo*, a rich old don from below the Rio Grande happened to be visiting in the settlement also. He took a great liking to Peg Leg and one day guided him over to a landmark on the Olmos Ranch known as Estambel Hill, where signs of a mesquite-picket corral are yet visible. At a spot near this old corral the don halted and said:

"I have a *hacienda* with cattle, horses, sheep, and peons a plenty. I need no more. I wish no more. But I wish you to have plenty also. *Por amigo*, I tell you how to get it. Dig here and you will find one burro load of gold money. I know it is here."

Then the old don told Peg Leg Tumlinson specifically what he would find in the hole as he progressed downwards. Peg Leg marked the spot well and went on back up the river to his "stomping ground" around Carrizo Springs. It was twenty years before he returned with a spade and with Doctor Hargus for a partner. If you ask why he delayed so long, Doctor Hargus' explanation will have to suffice: "He was a frontiersman, and those old frontiersmen were peculiar."

Now, according to the directions that the don had given, Peg Leg was to dig down two feet and there he should find some charcoal; two feet under that he should find a saddle blanket; two feet under the saddle blanket, burro bones; two feet under the burro bones, he should come to the bones of a man. And then *"dos pies más abajo y ahí está el oro"* ("two feet on down and there is the gold").

Peg Leg and his partner marked off a hole about ten feet in diameter and began excavation. Two feet down they struck some charcoal. Two feet under that they came to some "dusty dirt" that looked as if it might have once been a saddle blanket. The soil was fairly loose, and a little farther down the diggers struck a pocket of earth, "about the diameter of a barrel," that appeared to have been dug up long before. The loose soil soon petered out, and then they came upon the all but decayed bones of some kind of animal. Two feet under the bones they dug up the knuckle and wrist bones of a man.

"And," Doctor Hargus here interrupted his story, "I ought to know what a human bone is. I drove up the Chisholm Trail before it had a name. When I began practicing medicine down there in the brush below Fort Ewell I was led blindfolded more than once into a thicket to doctor a wounded outlaw. I was with McNelly's rangers while they were cleaning up the border country. I have treated the gunshot wounds of two hundred and fifty-nine men and have seen one hundred and eight men with bullet holes in them that didn't need treating. Those were certainly human bones that Peg Leg and I dug up."

At this stage, the charcoal, the dust of a saddle blanket, animal bones, human bones, all found as the Spanish don said they would be found—the depth only varying a little from his directions—the diggers felt absolutely sure of their burro load of gold. Their pit was now so deep that they could not work in it without a ladder, and they made one by dragging up two poles and lashing short sticks, for rungs, to them with deer skin. That country still abounds in deer.

They dug on down two feet, four feet, six feet. Perhaps the gold had sunk. At the depth of twenty-two feet they crawled out one evening to eat supper. That night the wagon bed caught on fire from a coal that was whiffed into it by the wind. The fire burned up all their provisions. Worst of all, it burned up Peg Leg Tumlinson's vest, which held a pocketful of way-bills to other treasures.

"One of the bills," Tumlinson said, "was without a doubt worth $25,000."

"We intended to come back," Doctor Hargus concluded, "but not long after that old Tumlinson died. I don't know what became of all his charts. He had a lot that were not burned in his vest. He was a strange character. I have decided that when the Spanish don told him to dig *dos pies más abajo* (two feet on down), he probably meant to dig farther down the slope rather than farther down in the hole that contained the charcoal and bones. And instead of *dos pies* he may have said *dos pasos*. A *paso* is a double step, two yards; *dos pasos* would be four yards. I mean to go back down there some fall, when the weather is cool and bucks are fat, hire me a couple of Tonks, and dig a new hole four yards down the slope from where we dug before."

But Doctor Hargus has never seen the enormous hole that envelops the one he helped to put down. Two or three years after he and Peg Leg were burned out, six strangers drove up to Olmos headquarters and asked the owner's permission to dig for a burro load of gold buried on Estambel Hill.

When told that a hole had already been sunk on the site, they responded that the hole was in the right place but that it was not deep enough. Then they set forth the theory that gold sinks in the ground at the rate of six inches every ten years.

"Look," one of the men jubilantly explained, "how far under ground you sometimes find an ordinary Indian arrowhead that you know must have originally been on the surface. How much deeper would a pack load of heavy gold sink in a hundred years!"

The crew enlarged the hole and dug down to a depth of thirty-four feet. Then they struck a seep vein of water and quit.

The hunt for this treasure on Estambel Hill that I took part in a number of years later was perhaps the most successful I have ever made. One day in the summer of 1924 while I was helping the Olmos outfit brand some calves, the boss suddenly said to me:

"Do you know what old George Ray is doing out here?"

"No," I replied, "I do not. I notice that he and Uncle Jim [Dobie] have been riding around a good deal. I suppose they are on a cattle trade of some kind."

"No," he responded, "old George is locating oil wells."

I had known Mr. Ray a long time. He is a cowman of the old school, except that he is not in debt, owns a fine ranch, is president of a bank, and has large interests in a rich silver mine in Durango.

When I got in to the ranch that night, he, his son Haggard, and Uncle Jim were sitting on the gallery.

"Pancho," Uncle Jim said to me, "George has finished locating some oil pools and now he wants to locate those thirty-one mule loads of silver bullion on Estambel Hill."

"Why," I replied, concealing my joy as best I could, "the thirty-one mule loads are down in McMullen County."

"Well, there are thirty-one mule loads in La Salle County too," and Uncle Jim gave me a wink.

Then I learned about the oil pools. The Rays had arrived at the ranch a day or two ahead of me, each provided with a peach switch and an elongated, thin rubber sack. Also, they had a bottle of *fresh* crude oil. Their method of using this paraphernalia was to fill the rubber sack about two-thirds full of oil, tie the open end of it securely around the stub of a forked peach limb, and then to "witch." Thus equipped, they had been riding over the ranch in an automobile locating places to put down oil wells. And they had, to quote George Ray's own words, "located two of the deepest and strongest pools in Texas." As we rode along horseback next morning to Estambel Hill, he told me all about his "gift."

"When I was a boy," he explained, "an old Scotchman, who was the best man to handle horses that I have ever known, showed me how to witch for water. He said that the same principle could be used in witching for minerals. I never seriously applied my knowledge—or gift, as I call it—until two years ago. I went down there to our mine in Durango and arrived just in time to find that the miners had lost a vein of silver and were having trouble in picking it up again. It had 'pinched out,' as they say. I took a regulation switch, fixed a Mexican dollar in a slit at the end of it, and in five minutes' time located the vein. This experience made me realize the value of my gift.

"Oh, I can't explain it. I feel something in me like electricity. When the switch gets over what I am looking for, I simply can't hold it. It will twist itself in two or go down. I can figure out the depths of some veins of water, but I can't tell the depth of oil or metal because I haven't practiced enough. I've been knowing Jim Dobie for forty years. He's needing money and I have come to help him out. I'm mighty glad that I got the oil pools located, and if we can turn up a little ready silver it will be all the better."

We crossed the river six or seven miles above the ranch, plugged through a mile of the hog-wallow *sacaguista* flats, pulled up on top of a small hill, and halted beside the remains of the old Estambel corral.

"This is the place," announced Uncle Jim.

George Ray cautiously slipped down from his horse, Haggard Ray jumped down, and in no time each of them had a half dollar fixed into his switch and was at work.

The divining rod, water switch, caducean wand, or whatever one wishes to call it, and the manner of using it have been described so often and so thoroughly that little explanation is here necessary.[4] Suffice it to say that the switch is Y-shaped, that the prongs of the Y are usually held one in each hand, and that the main stem of the Y, held inverted, "pulls" down towards the object attracting it. If the switch is to be attracted by mineral, it must be "loaded" with mineral; a half dollar is sufficient to make a switch work for any amount of silver.

The two divinators on Estambel Hill were attracted at once—certainly against their desires—into the middle of a very thorny patch of *granjeno* and black chaparral. Finally, after a *granjeno* had torn off most of the elder magician's shirt tail—it had a habit of working out—they got an oblong "box" about the size of a grave marked off on the ground and delivered the joint opinion that the thirty-one mule loads had been buried right there.

Uncle Jim, however, suggested that several of the mule loads had probably been buried separately and that it might be a good idea to explore down the slope. They knew nothing of the great hole which Peg Leg Tumlinson and then the six strangers had put down. A discussion arose as to the space a *carga* of silver bars would occupy. George Ray settled the matter by asserting that in the old days a mule load of bullion in Mexico consisted of six bars, three on each side of the pack, each bar about two and a half feet long and six inches thick. Consequently an entire *carga* could be buried in small space.

A half dozen locations, each over a mule load of silver, were soon made.

"Now mark the strongest deposit and mark it well," Uncle Jim directed.

The Rays both applied the most delicate witchery of their gift. The location was beside a rat's den. To fix the spot beyond any mistake we punched a Spanish dagger stalk into the ground and heaped rocks around it. That afternoon Mr. Ray had to leave to attend a meeting of bank directors. However, he promised to be back in three days with a drop auger, which would greatly facilitate digging. As it turned out, he was detained, but Haggard brought the auger.

The location was not accessible to a wagon, much less to a car, but with the aid of three Mexicans we managed to lug over the auger, block and tackle, some water cans, and other equipment. Three fifteen-foot ash poles, which we "snaked up" from the river at the horn of a saddle and tied together tepee fashion, made a kind of derrick to drop the auger from. Before "spudding in" for the bullion, Haggard switched again and declared that the pull was unmistakable. Discovering that I too possessed a gift, I had learned to hold the switch, and the pull seemed all right to me also. By noon we were ten feet down and the thermometer was about a hundred and ten degrees up.

We rested, poured water in the hole, and dug on. Every once in a while Haggard would manoeuvre his wand, and it never failed to dip straight into the hole. When we were eighteen feet down, Haggard declared that he did not believe it was of any use to dig deeper after the silver bars; something else, he thought, must be attracting his switch. We quit digging.

During the day I had actually spent very little time at the hole but had entertained myself with picking up Indian arrowheads off the hillside. Also I picked up two odd rocks: one that looked to be a petrified oak ball, another that had in it a precipitate of iron. With these specimens I placed three pebbles dug out of the well.

Two evenings later George Ray drove into the ranch posthaste.

"What did you find?" were his first words.

When informed, he became greatly excited.

"Why, there may be radium or anything in that dirt!" he exclaimed. "It pulled so powerfully I know there must be something. Somebody had better ride over and get enough of the dirt for me to test out."

But George Ray never lets his enthusiasm interfere with his rest, and the next morning, after he had had a good night's sleep and was talking again about getting a test of the dirt, I saved somebody a long ride. I pulled out my five rocks. Mr. Ray got his switch, put a half dollar in it, and, squatting on the ground, began testing. Not one of the specimens taken from the well attracted the switch, but when the petrified oak ball came under it, down it went. Then he examined the object more closely.

"Why, this is some sort of old Spanish button," he announced. "The metal in it attracted my switch. It is a great relief to know what it was. I was beginning to doubt my gift. Of course, a man can't listen to all these Mexican yarns about buried treasure. Those people are too durned superstitious."

It was too late for me to explain that the "Spanish button" had come from the hillside a hundred yards away from the well.

The other day an oil company brought in a well on the Ray ranch. It was bored at a spot where Mr. Ray's switch indicated oil. The president of the company, one of the best known and most successful oil men in Texas, has engaged Mr. Ray to make some locations for him in distant sections where he is wildcatting.

> *There are more things in heaven and earth, Horatio,*
> *Than are dreamt of in your philosophy.*

THE GOLD THAT TURNED TO CARBÓN

After our search for the burro load of gold or the thirty-one mule loads of silver bullion—whichever it might be—the ranch Mexicans naturally unlocked their hoards of treasure talk.

One hot afternoon while Uncle Jim and I were sitting on the wide east gallery of the Olmos ranch house, watching whirlwinds down in the *sacaguista* flat and listening to locusts sizz-z-z in the huisache tree—two very bad dry weather signs—Jacinto de los Santos came up. He is about half Comanche, is nearly as black as a negro, and is as good a hand at building dirt tanks and stringing barbed wire as ever tilted a scraper or drove a fence staple.

"Jacinto," I said, "the Madama Burks has been telling me that one morning a long time ago she found under the trees across the lake from her house an empty wooden box beside a fresh hole. Two strangers had camped there the evening before. They left in the night. You have been around here a long time and you used to work at the Mota. What do you know about such matters?"

"Well," responded Jacinto, "I am just a poor ignorant Mexican, and you know very well how little I know, but I will tell you something.

"One night while I was yet *un mediano* [a young fellow], I was coming with the Madama Burks to the Mota from her sheep camp over on the Quintanilla. We were traveling the old Laredo road and it had been raining. Well, when we got on top of that hill about three miles north of the Nueces, we saw a fire burning off to one side. The name of the hill is Loma de Sauce [Willow Hill]. The Madama asked me why travelers should camp in a place so far from water. I told her that the fire was not made by travelers. We drove on into the ranch.

"The next day I had talk with a Mexican named Justo. He was then *caporal* for the Mota outfit. He did not have a good heart. He asked me if I could go to the place where the fire flickered. I told him I could. Then Justo told me that two priests—*pasajeros* on the old road—long time ago were murdered on the hill and buried in a hole with the $25,000 they carried. As every one knows, fire on the ground is a sure sign of buried gold, and Justo said we should all get rich.

"For my knowledge I was to have half the treasure, and Justo and two vaqueros were to divide the other half. We took some tools and I led them straight to the chaparral where I had seen the fire. I knew it was the right place. We set to work and right away we dug up *como un costal de carbón* [about a sack of charcoal]. Yes, sir, *carbón*. Then I knew it was of no use to dig farther; nevertheless, we went on down seven feet.

"That *carbón* was the gold itself! The other men had envy of me, and for that reason God changed it into something else. Had God not done so, the envious men would have killed me for my part of the gold. God protected me. It is possible that the *carbón* later turned back into gold. I do not know. I never went back to see. As I said, I was just *un mediano* then, and as the good God had saved my life once I did not wish to risk putting him to that trouble again.

"Another time some men with a *derrotero* came looking for money on that same old road. The Madama Burks told me if I knew anything I was not to tell them. I told them nothing. They had a kind of machine made out of two iron rods. One man held a rod in each hand and when the points came together it was a sign to dig. They dug by a *coma* tree on the Sauce Creek, but that was the wrong place. I will tell you why I think so.

"Not long after they were gone I was running a wild cow down that Sauce flat, and there, right in the middle of a clump of low mes-

quites, I saw an iron stake with a brass ring in the end of it. I went back later and tried to find it, but cattle had stamped out the tracks of my horse and I could not trail to the stake. I have not seen it since. The treasure was not meant for me. It must have been for the iron stake that the two men with the machine were looking. They were half a mile away from it."

MYSTERIES OF THE SAN CASIMIRO

It is over on the San Casimiro, however, that signs and mysteries have since the mind of Mexicans runs not to the contrary indicated some enormous treasure. The San Casimiro is an old Spanish grant to five

leagues of land now fenced into one of the lonesomest and most formidably thorned pastures to be found anywhere south of the Nueces River. It is incorporated in the Olmos holdings.

A "queer" Mexican *pastor* named Toribio used to pen his goats at the bleak corrals by the *jacal* on San Casimiro Creek. He was always after the *mayordomo* to look for the money that nightly apparitions indicated to him. Sometimes the apparition was a light that flickered back and forth over a hill and then always stopped at a certain place. Sometimes it was *una bruja blanca*—the white ghost of a witch—that with long arms lifted high beckoned him to follow a trail he dared not set foot in. Oftener it was sounds of horrible yelling *como de los indios*—as of Indians. When this yelling set up, the coyotes would cease their howling and listen too. Then there would be groans, and from the mingled sounds one might realize how savages once murdered the rich Spanish rancheros on the San Casimiro—and how the wealth of the *ricos* yet lies there concealed.

Toribio did not like that camp, but Salomé Esparza has never had any uneasiness there, and as pasture man he has lived on the San Casimiro for years. The first night Salomé's bride slept in the *jacal*, she woke him up along about three o'clock in the morning to listen to a strange *tick-tick-tick* of a clock that they did not possess. He could hear nothing. Many nights since then his wife has awakened him to hear the sounds, but always he explains to her that it is the wind or a wire stretched against the house or something like that. She knows better. She knows that the clock has been numbering the hours ever since the treasure was buried, maybe a hundred years ago, and that it will go on numbering them, *tick-tick-tick*, until the treasure is found.

One day I rode over to chat with Salomé's wife. When I arrived, she was turning their little bunch of goats out. She ran into the house, shut the door, presently appeared in a fresh dress, and proffered the inevitable *cafecito*. While we talked and sipped the coffee, it developed that down in Mexico, where she once lived, she had actually located *mucho dinero* by certain strange sounds and sights.

"There," she said, "I used to hear chains rattling and cries coming out of a *chaparro*—a clump of bushes—and at the same time see a light burning. I told a poor family about the matter and very soon they set up a store and had plenty of money. But they never gave me one cent for making them rich."

The most earnest witness of the mysteries of the San Casimiro has been my friend Santos Cortez. During the Madero revolution Santos was a *rural* in Tamaulipas and killed a man. Oxen and log chains could not drag him back across the Rio Grande. I have seldom known him to be without a rifle or pistol; frequently he has both. He is the best hunter I have ever known; indeed, he used to keep a "crowd" of Olmos hands supplied with deer and wild hog meat all through the fall and winter months. He has been a *pastor* too and knows solitude. Many a profitable and happy hour have I listened to Santos tell of wild animals, of his experiences in the revolution, and of the strange things that he has sensed in darkness.

"Oh, it was a lonesome life there on the San Casimiro," he would say, "*una vida muy triste*. I never say anything about some matters except to you. You are my friend, and you will understand.

"I used to sleep with the door well fastened, and sometimes something strange would come and try to shake the door down. I would shout and maybe the thing would go away; if it did not, I would shoot into the door and then it would most certainly leave.

"In the direction where the sun sets, a *corrida* of horsemen used to go galloping by just about the time I was getting to sleep. I could hear the horses trampling and the men seemed to be talking. They were desperate about something, but I could never make out their words. The voices seemed far away and all I could hear was *mum-mum-mum-um-blub-blub-blub*, like that, until they passed. In the morning I would go out to look at the ground but never a track did I see, not even after a rain.

"One time while I was running some cattle over in the direction where the horsemen always went, I saw three long rocks piled together. They were hewn rocks and appeared very peculiar. I was in a hurry and my horse was jumping through the *chaparro* when I saw them, but I marked the place well. The next day I went back to examine the rocks closely. They were gone. Many times I searched for them, always in vain. This is *una seña muy buena*—a most excellent sign of buried treasure.

"You know how the *bandidos* at El Fortín used to waylay *pasajeros* and rob them. Well, one late afternoon, a long time ago, a ranchero who had sold a big herd of steers in Kansas came to the ferry to cross. He had his gold with him in a belt and he wanted to keep away from the *bandidos*, but the river was up so high that he was afraid to swim it. He was alone and he rode a fine horse. After he crossed the river he took the trail to the east. When he got close to the San Casimiro hills, he saw that he was being followed and so he hid his money quickly

71

and went on. The *bandidos* kept following him and before dark they killed him. When they saw that he no longer wore the money belt they had seen at El Fortín, they knew he had hidden it. They tried to find it, but it was too well secured. Nobody has found it yet. It is still out in the San Casimiro hills."

The Martineño is to the south of old Fort Ewell. Santos Cortez used to be *vaciero* on this ranch under the direction of Don Antonio Salinas, and here he had his most intimate experience with creatures of the darkness. A *vaciero* is a kind of overseer and supply agent for sheep or goat camps. One day when Santos went to a certain camp, he found the *pastor* gone and the sheep shut in the pen.

"Well," said Santos, "I had to tend to the sheep, and that night I made my pallet down in front of the *jacal*. After I had been asleep a while, I felt something heavy on my stomach and chest. I tried to raise up and throw it off, but the weight was so heavy I could not lift my shoulders. The thing felt like a great round keg. I could see it, too, and it was white.

"I tried to yell, to speak, but all I could do was pant. My tongue would not move and my teeth were locked. I had a pistol on one side of me and a *carabina* on the other. I strained my hand—for the arm was pinned down—to reach the pistol, and then I touched something icy cold that felt like the hand of a dead man. I worked to breathe like a wind-broken horse—*ha-ha-ha-ha-ha*, fast and hard that way.

"*¡Ah Chihuahua!* There I was pinned down and the white *bulto* on me never budged. I had touched its hand, and yet it seemed to be round without any hands or feet. Then I began to remember how an evil thing against a man will go away if the man puts good thoughts in his mind. So I began to think about El Dios and the Holy Mary. I thought a long time and in myself I spoke to El Dios. Then the weight began to lift slow, slow, and in the time it takes a *paisano* bird to drink water it was gone and seemed to be in the brush. I jumped up with my pistol and shot towards it. I called it many *maldiciones*, but it made no response, and when daylight came I could find not one sign of it.

"Then I became very sick all in my head and stomach. A vaquero came to the camp and took my place and I went to see a *curandero* [a Mexican medicine man]. He asked me what was the cause of my sickness, but I had shame lest he think me a liar, and so I told him I did not know.

"After that Don Antonio Salinas asked me to tell him what was the matter. I was still sick. Again I had shame, but I saw that Don Antonio was an intelligent man and friendly, and so at last I told him of all that had passed. At once I got well. Then Don Antonio took me with him to the camp, and right there across the old road from it he showed me the graves of three *pasajeros* who had been murdered for their money.

"By this time the missing *pastor* had come in. He told of seeing a black dog at his camp with a head as big as a bull's and fiery eyes. Also I learned that something like a skeleton once jumped out of a tree beside the camp and caught on behind a vaquero. It grabbed him about the waist. His horse pitched and screamed like a panther, but the thing held on until the vaquero ran into the corrals at the ranch. Oh, it was a terrible place! They moved the sheep camp away from it. Nobody would stay there any longer."

EL TIGRE

The Tigre Ranch is on one of the long, alligator-gar infested lakes of the Nueces flats about five miles below the Olmos headquarters. For many years now the only inhabitants of the dilapidated house have been a family of white owls. The man who built it and was master of the range about it was Zack Hargus—uncle of the Doctor Hargus who dug at Estambel Hill for gold under human bones—and was as odd a character as ever enjoyed his own oddities. He was something of a reader and very much of a tobacco chewer. His favorite position for reading and chewing was on the gallery overlooking the lake, his chair tilted back against the wall on the left-hand side of a window that opened into the dining room. Here by the hour he would sit, reading and chewing. When he wanted to spit, he merely turned his head slightly to the right and spat inside the window. That took less energy than leaning forward to spit off the gallery. He made it a habit to work harder on Sunday than on any other day. Once he built a chimney to his house, working on it only on Sundays. After the country was fenced up, he invariably left the gates open when he went to Cotulla. He was not much of a lover of horses. Sometimes he kept them tied up for a day or two without water. Year in and year out he kept a horse staked to an old wagon axle driven into the ground out in the *sacaguista* grass; naturally there was not much grass around this stake pin. He had odd names for his horses, too; one of them he called Jesus. One time he told a boy who was working for him to drive the team across the river for some posts. When the horses got into the water, one of them drank himself to death. The boy came back to report the loss. "Oh, Mr. Hargus," he cried, "old Jesus has done went and drank water till he died."

I don't know that Zack Hargus has anything to do with this story, but the man who had most to do with it made his headquarters for a while at the Hargus ranch. His name was Musgraves. One day after having sold a considerable amount of stock, for which he received Mexican gold in payment, Musgraves left the Tigre with $12,000 to deposit in San Antonio. Somewhere between home and Dog Town he ran into a supply of *tequila* and after a night's carouse came back to the Tigre still drunk—and without any money. When he sobered up, he remembered having buried the gold, but to save his life he could not tell where, though he had an idea it might be on a high hill near what is now the line between the Tigre and the Coma pastures. In time he died or left the country.

Years later a Tigre Mexican came into Cotulla and reported to a man—nameless here—that he had found enough Mexican gold "to make them all rich." Shortly thereafter the man gave it out that the Mexican had discovered Musgraves' money and "gone *allá*," or, in other words, had pulled his freight for the tall tules. Now, never before had the man shown any evidence of possessing property, but all at once he appeared to be prosperous. Some people flatly said that the Mexican had found the money all right and had left the country, too, but had left it over a route that no man wants to travel or ever returns by. Maybe this is "just a tale."

It reminds me of a story about a Brownsville man. This man started towards San Antonio with $40,000 in gold. His route would have taken him to Beeville, and somewhere between Brownsville and Beeville—legend has lost all but one particular regarding the place—he discovered that bandits were on his trail. He was in camp at the time; the bandits had to ride across a wide brushy flat before they could see him. He simply pulled the coals of his fire aside, made a little hole into which he inserted the gold, covered it up again, and built a roaring fire over the place, thus obliterating signs of excavation. The fire was between two medium-sized oak trees on the west side of the road.

Leaving it still burning, the man saddled his horse and made tracks. But the bandits overtook him. They tried to make him tell what he had done with the money; he would not tell. They took him back to the Rio Grande and crossed into Mexico with him, swearing that they would hold him prisoner until he should reveal the gold. Still he held out and still he was kept prisoner. He remained a prisoner for long years. When, finally, he got back to Texas, barbed wire had been stretched across the country, brush had covered many of the former prairies, roads had been changed, his own memory had probably been shaken. He set out to go to the two oaks on the west side of the old Brownsville road somewhere south of Beeville. He died before he could locate them, or at least before he could locate $40,000 in gold between any two of the various oaks.

THE ROCK PENS

Austin, Texas
April 17th 1873
About six or seven miles below the Laredo Crossing on the south side of the Nueces River near the hills there is or was a tree in the prairie. due west from that tree at the foot of the hills at the mouth of a ravine there is a large rock under the rock there was a small spring of water coming from under the rock, due east from that rock there is a rock pen or rocks laid around like a pen and due east a few yards there is another pen of rock In that pen is the spoils of thirty one mule loads
[Signed] *DANIEL DUNHAM*

When Daniel Dunham dictated this way-bill he was on his death bed, sole survivor of the little band of men who put the thirty-one mule loads of silver bullion, together with various fine images and other precious articles, under ground. Just who these men were and how they came to have so much wealth is a little hazy, but it is generally believed that they were Texas bandits, that they had raided a Mexican mine and church, and had got within sight of the Nueces on their way north when they became aware of a cloud of Indians or Mexicans, perhaps both Indians and Mexicans, following their trail.

The account from this point on is clear. The guards of the pack train picked the best place within reach to make their stand. It was by a small ravine down which flowed water from a wet-weather spring. Here they threw up some crude breastworks in the form of low-walled rock pens. In one of the pens they buried the bullion, and then, in

75

order to hide all sign of their secret work, ran the mules around and around over the disturbed earth. The fight soon followed; only Daniel Dunham got out alive. Why he never went back himself to claim what was in the pens, I shall not attempt to say.

It is a fact that the Rock Pens have been sought for more widely and by more men than any other lode between the San Saba and the Rio Grande. When the search began it would be hard to say; I cannot remember when I did not know about the Rock Pens. The way-bill just quoted was in the possession of an old Live Oak County settler named Matt Kivlin, who died along in the nineties. He had shown it to his sons a few times, but there was an accompanying paper that he had never shown. This accompanying paper he destroyed shortly before his death, or else his wife destroyed it immediately thereafter. Even to his own sons—and he never mentioned the matter to anyone else, except his wife—Kivlin's attitude towards the way-bill and the treasure and his connection with Daniel Dunham appeared profoundly mysterious. Certainly Matt Kivlin knew Dunham and certainly he held the way-bill to be veracious; certainly, too, he had an inexplicable aversion to following out its directions. Other charts to the Rock Pens cache seem to be in existence also, for various independent parties were searching for it even before the Kivlin document came into circulation.

Those who know anything about the matter never take the "Laredo Crossing" mentioned in Daniel Dunham's testament to be the crossing at Fort Ewell. A very old road of some kind crossed the Nueces on the Henry Shiner ranch—a ranch of forty or fifty thousand acres, in Mc-Mullen County; and this crossing is generally conceded to be the one Dunham had in mind. The country around is hilly, densely thorned, and without springs of any kind. Many a tale tells of early-day travelers perishing of thirst in this drouth-stricken land. Until the advent of the automobile it was indeed a remote country.

So far as is known, no one looking for the Rock Pens has ever found them. Yet they have been sighted time and again—always by men who were not looking for them and who were at the moment ignorant of their significance; when these men, upon being enlightened, attempted to go back to the Pens, they invariably found themselves unable to locate them. The rocks were not piled high in the beginning; very likely they have been scattered.

Along about 1866 Pate McNeill was coming from Dog Town—now called Tilden—down to Lagarto with his young wife. They were in a buggy and were leading a horse, saddled. Somewhere in the Shiner country they glimpsed a fine-looking maverick heifer. McNeill jumped out of the buggy, "forked" his horse, and took after her. After he had roped and tied her, he looked around and saw that he was in a kind of rock pen, the walls of which were low and broken. At that time he did not know that great riches appertained to rock pens in McMullen County; so he calmly ran his famous brand of P A T E on the heifer's ribs, turned her loose, and went on down the country. Years later when old man Kivlin died and Daniel Dunham's way-bill became common talk, McNeill went back up the Nueces and tried to locate the Rock Pens; but the country had changed so much that he could never find the ground he was looking for.

A deer hunter stumbled into the Pens one time and thought he was in a deserted goat camp. Like Pate McNeill and others, he did not at the time realize how close he was to millions. Wiley Williams, a rancher noted for his truthfulness, used to recall how he once ran across the Rock Pens while trailing some horse thieves. He was considered one of the best trailers and woodsmen of the country; yet he could never go back to the Pens.

Pete Staples, an old negro trail cook, told me that one time while he was hunting turkeys with Judge Marcellus Lowe, they came upon some curiously placed rocks.

"Huh, what's this?" Pete asked. "Looks mighty funny to me for rocks in this place. Where'd they all come from and how come this away? Ain't no other rocks like thesen for a mile out."

"Natural rocks all right," said Judge Lowe, "but this is an old pen."

Years later Judge Lowe tried in vain to go back to the place. Had he got Pete Staples to guide him, he might have succeeded. Peter, however, has a firm conviction that it is dangerous to "monkey" with money that some man now dead buried, and he declares that, although he *could* find the Rock Pens, he "ain't a-gwine to." The Pens, according to him, are in the Guidan Pasture, which joins the Shiner ranch and contains twenty or thirty thousand acres of land.

It does look, as Pete expresses it, as if those thirty-one mule loads of bullion "ain't meant" for any of the people who have searched for it. When the man comes along for whom it is "meant," he will "jes' natchly find it without even trying." Nevertheless, some people are still trying. The inspiring thing about looking for the Rock Pens is that even though the search for them be fruitless, one may at almost any time happen upon some other treasure.

WHERE PARALLEL LINES INTERSECT

The southwestern part of McMullen County is quite rough, various elevations rising, in popular speech, to the dignity of mountains. Of these the most noted is San Cajo. Tradition has it that the mountain used to be called Sin Caja (Without Box, or Without Coffin). Certainly enough human bodies have *sin caja* returned to their native element on or around the hill to validate the name.

Along about 1875 a battered old Mexican came in great distress to John Fogg, who ran a livery stable in Corpus Christi. He said that when he was just a boy he enlisted as guard for a *conducta* of silver going from the San Saba mines to Mexico City. In the San Cajo country they discovered that Indians were upon them. They hastily unpacked, cast the silver between some rocks, and prepared to defend themselves. Meanwhile the boy ran down a ravine to see if he could locate water. The enemy cut off his return. Unseen, he witnessed the annihilation of his companions, and then made his way to Mexico, where he related the circumstances of his escape. Before long he was charged with desertion. Authorities seized him and put him in prison, and there for thirty-seven years he was kept. Years after his release he had wandered back to Texas. His one idea was to return to the cache of silver. He needed help.

After hearing the tale, John Fogg got together a party of three or four men to take the old Mexican up to the San Cajo and make search. On the evening of the third day's travel they camped in sight of the mountain. "*Mañana*," said the Mexican, "I shall show you." Deer were plentiful, and for supper the elated treasure hunters prepared some freshly killed venison. Their guide ate more than his feeble nature could stand. He was seized with cramps; before daylight he was dead.

While Joe Newberry was bossing a ranch "down in the Sands" along about 1898, an old Mexican who was headed north to look for the Rock Pens gave him a chart to nine jack loads of silver bullion buried squarely on top of the San Cajo. According to the chart, the bullion was put down under a big rock near a *chapote* (Mexican persimmon) tree. It was being transported from mines up the Nueces Canyon when the escort lost their way. A terrible drouth was on the country; the Nueces River for miles at a stretch was as dry as a bone; the Spaniards had missed the lakes that parallel the river; they and their animals were perishing of thirst. They found a sup of water in some rock *tinajas*, but only enough to tantalize them. They chewed prickly pear, but the slimy juice of it tantalized them ever more. Behind them lay no hope of water; between them and the Rio Grande stretched seven miles of parched desert. To reach this far-away water they must cast aside all burdens. They ascended the San Cajo to get the best bearings possible, left the bullion there, and headed southwest. Only one man endured to drink from the Great River. His experience had been so horrible that he never returned to claim the wealth. Of course, though, he made out a chart to it—the chart that Joe Newberry took.

Yet if one knew how to find the water, there was enough, at times at least, to do a band of brigands who lived in a cave under the San Cajo and preyed on traffic passing over "the lower trail" between San Antonio and Laredo. These brigands used an apartment of the cave to stable their horses in. Back of the stable was their treasure room—*el apartado del tesoro*. Here they stored heaps of bullion, Spanish doubloons, golden candlesticks, bridle bits and spurs of precious workmanship, plated firearms, and all manner of other costly plunder taken from grandees and cathedrals. To these riches they added bullion from a mine—legendary to be sure—in the Lechuzas Mountains not far away.

A more prominent landmark than the San Cajo is Loma Alta. At the foot of this hill an early settler named Drummond had a squat. One time a Mexican—and, true to character, he was as old as the hills—came to Drummond looking for bullion that some of his ancestors had left in the vicinity. His *plata* called for a mesquite tree on the southeast slope of Loma Alta marked by a turtle cut into the bark. It called next for a line of smooth, irregularly oblong rocks bearing a resemblance to *manos*—stones used for grinding corn on the *metate*. These rocks had been culled from the hillside and so laid as to point to the hidden bullion. Drummond and the Mexican found the marked tree but rode around for a whole day without being able to find the rocks. They decided that generations of horses and cattle had scattered them so that they could no longer be recognized as forming a line, and gave up the search.

The Mexican left, Drummond died, years passed. Then one day while John Murphy, who ranches near Loma Alta, was holding down a wormy calf out in his pasture to doctor it, he raised his eyes and saw three or four of the *mano*-like rocks lined up in a clump of thick chaparral. He thought of the tale that Drummond had told him, and, looking about further, he found, badly scattered, yet preserving a kind of line, other such rocks. But he could never "settle on a place to dig and so the stuff must still be there."

So many rumors of treasure in one vicinity are enough to inspire almost anyone, and Snowden was the kind of man to catch inspiration. When one of the two or three negro inhabitants of the region showed him a singular boulder on a little *llano* between the Nueces and the San Cajo, he resolved to act. Before beginning excavation, however, Snowden went to San Antonio to consult a fortune teller.

"I see," said the fortune teller, closing his eyes, "a small plain surrounded by brush, north of it rough hills. I see a curious boulder almost in the middle of this plain. Not far from it and six feet underground I see a kind of chest. Some one will unearth this chest by drawing two parallel lines from the northwest and the southwest corners of the boulder and digging at the intersection of the lines."

The fee was twenty-five dollars. Snowden allowed three friends to join him in digging up the chest. But when they got out on the ground and drew a line from the southwest corner of the boulder and then, according to directions, another parallel to it from the northwest corner, they discovered that the lines would not intersect! Snowden sent the chart back to San Antonio for correction. No corrections came. He was for digging anyway, and, refusing to be played upon any longer by a fortune teller, he and his partners made a second trip to the boulder. They drew the lines now so that, while "not exactly parallel," they would *have to intersect*. They dug and dug. Finally one man flung his grubbing hoe as far as he could fling it and swore that he would sell out all his interest in the treasure for "two-bits' worth of Duke's Mixture." Snowden took him up and presently had bought out each of his other partners on terms equally high.

CASA BLANCA

A chest or something is buried on the west bank of the Nueces at Puente de Piedra, where the *camino real* from Laredo to Goliad used to cross. Fifteen miles or so on down two paltry jack loads of bullion moulder under the great oak trees that mark the ruins of Fort Merrill.[5] At Paso Veleño below that an enormous jag awaits someone. One time a ranchero started from the Veleño to Matamoros with a *morral* of gold; at the Arroyo Colorado he staked his horse, buried the *morral* under one of many mesquite trees about, and went in swimming. The water made him go blind, so that he could not find the gold. It has never been recovered, and very few Mexicans have since its loss bathed in the Arroyo Colorado.

Every old ranch in the Nueces country, every old road, every hollow and water hole has its story of treasure. But between the Rock Pens—wherever they are—and Corpus Christi Bay the most famous resort of the treasure seeker is Casa Blanca.

The land records show that in 1807 the Spanish government granted sixteen leagues of land, known as the Casa Blanca grant, to Juan José de la Garza Montemayor and sons. Before this date, presumably, Casa Blanca (White House), which served as both fort and residence and from which the ranch took its name, had been built. By 1810, according to a rather dubious source,[6] the Montemayors numbered their herds at 60,000 sheep, 24,000 cattle, and 14,000 horses; but in that year Indians overpowered them and razed the walls of their stronghold. The tumbled-down rocks can yet be seen, though prickly pear and mesquite have covered all the land about. Along in the forties, Casa Blanca became, on account of the grassy prairie around and abundant water, a kind of rehabilitation headquarters for great trains of Chihuahua carts freighting between Corpus and points in northern Mexico.

Oh, reader,

> *Forget six counties overhung with smoke,*
> *Forget the snorting steam and piston stroke,*
> *Forget the spreading of the hideous town;*
> *Think rather of the pack-horse on the down.*

In imagination those old freight wagons and Chihuahua carts which rumbled off into silence so long ago, the ruts that they cut long since deepened into gullies, yet creep across the chaparral lands from the Nueces to the Rio Grande. Some of them are drawn by twelve spans of mules and some of them by oxen. The mule trains follow the route leading by the best grass. The ox trains take the road that leads through prickly pear, off which drivers can singe the thorns and thus enable their slow-grazing beasts to get a fill without losing too much time. Many of the wagons are loaded with lumber, unshipped at old Powderhorn or Corpus. Occasionally a Mexican driver gets sick and dies or is killed. His contract has stipulated that in such event his body shall be brought back to Mexico. But embalming fluid is unknown and cremation would be sacrilege. Yonder raised platform of lumber with shallow plank siding and open top is for drying out the body. Buzzards soon strip the flesh, and, unlike coyotes, do not carry off bones. When the skeleton is clean, dry, and bleached, it will be delivered to relatives in Mexico as per contract and the lumber in the platform will also be delivered to its proper owner.

While Casa Blanca was yet a camping place for Chihuahua carts, William Mann took over the ranch. It had already become legendary; people said that the Spanish had here "a kind of sub-mission attached to La Bahia and Goliad." Inevitably all sorts of stories ascribing treasure to the "mission" and to the rich ranchero as well were told, and they are yet believed.

"At a picnic held at Casa Blanca in 1878," Bill Adams, who landed at Corpus Christi in 1852, likes to tell, "I and several other men were seated on some rocks between two mesquite trees near the old *casa*. Before long the talk turned on buried treasure; most of us hooted at the idea of there being anything to the tales, though, as usual, somebody was for digging right there. Well, a man named Brandes was living at the Casa Blanca Ranch, and one morning about a year after our picnic discussion he noticed that the rocks we had sat on between the two trees were all torn up. The signs showed that a wagon had been there in the night, that a hole had been dug, and that a box had been lifted out of the hole. The print of iron bands around the box remained visible in the hole for some time. I saw them myself. What the box contained will never be known."

Had Bill Adams talked to a certain Mexican whose tongue and chart Ed Dubose loosened with *tequila*, he might have been less doubtful about the contents of the box. As the Mexican had the facts, old Montemayor, the ranchero of Casa Blanca, at length sold out his vast herds, acquiring hard cash in payment. He was preparing to transport it and his family to a more civilized place when some Mexican bandits under the leadership of one Carbajal captured him and tortured him until he told where the cash was hidden. Then they killed him. At this juncture they found that they were being spied on by a second band of bandits. Under cover of night they hid their booty in a rock pen adjacent to the Casa Blanca stronghold, burying the body of the murdered ranchero on top of it so that his spirit would act as *patrón*, or guard.

At daybreak the battle between the two bands began. The besiegers far outnumbered the besieged, and in desperation Carbajal and those of his followers who were not killed scattered into the brush. There Carbajal, the chief himself, was shot down, and as he fell he saw his slayer bending over him. That slayer was his own brother. He understood the mistake and, dying, told the brother where the loot was hidden. Even as he told, the last of his companions bit the dust.

But the victorious desperadoes were never to reap the golden benefits of victory. Before they could tend their own dead and wounded, the terrible Texas rangers were upon them. As a matter of fact, Montemayor died or left Casa Blanca many years before there were any Texas rangers—but I follow the story. Ere the bandits could reach the Rio Grande all but one or two of them had been overtaken and, to use a ranger euphemism, been "naturalized."

Just a few miles below Casa Blanca is Lipantitlan, the history of which can be traced back to 1786, but which is now nothing but a thicket of retama and huisache, with an occasional hole at their roots, beside a lake. The story of its treasure, if certain names connected therewith were printed, would certainly provoke a lawsuit. So Lipantitlan will have to remain one of the many, many untold stories down the Nueces.

CHAPTER III

The Facts about Fort Ramírez

I was riding in the country,
My companion said to me:
"A captain killed a bandit
Underneath that tree."

I was riding in the country,
My companion said to me:
"A bandit killed a captain
Underneath that tree."

CAMPOAMOR,
Tradition

Fort Ramírez—or, more properly, Rancho del Ojo de Agua Ramireña—also belongs to the Nueces country. As a boy I knew it well, for it was situated on our ranch. Frequently I rode by it, and sometimes with legs stiff in leather *chivarras* climbed its walls, there to gaze long at the serpentine winding of Ramireña Creek below and the oak-fringed hills beyond. Often I listened to tales the Mexicans and ranch people told.

The walls that I used to stand on are all down now; treasure hunters are responsible for that, and insensate workmen for a pipeline company recently hauled away most of the rocks. Lines of thorned *granjeno* bushes—those markers sown by birds along old fences all over Southwest Texas—made irregular by more than a hundred years of drouths and sproutings, yet delineate the quadrangular picket corral; but only a native eye can discern those lines. In another generation Fort Ramírez will hardly be more than a name, and treasure hunters may even debate on what hill to sink their holes. Let it be recorded that it is the hill in the southeast corner of what is known as the Primm Pasture overlooking Ramireña Creek to the north and Ramírez Hollow to the west.

The land records in the county seat recite a history that gives to the

Ramírez legend a fitting background. Undoubtedly the ancient landmark was the first of any permanence to be erected within the confines
of what is now Live Oak County, though when it was built no record
tells. Undoubtedly it served for fortification as well as for residence. In
1829 the heirs of Don José Antonio Ramírez and of Don José Vic-
toriano Ramírez entered, from the state of Tamaulipas, a plea to the
Mexican government for title to eight leagues of grazing land "known
as the Rancho de los Jaboncillos but more commonly as Ojo de Agua
Ramireña." On these *sitios*, according to the plea, the Ramírez
brothers had cleared land for fields, built a tanyard, erected corrals
and ranch houses, made other improvements, and were living in peaceable possession of the estate, though for some reason they had not yet
received a grant to it, when in 1813, as a result of the Mexican uprising against Spain, all frontier troops (*presidiales*) were withdrawn.
This withdrawal released hordes of Indians to prey on the few scattered rancheros. The Ramírez people were forced to leave their ranch
in such haste "*que nada se saco de la casa, ni de los muchos bienes
de campo que había*" ("that nothing was taken from the house nor of
the extensive herds on the range").

The Texan war of independence found the Ramírez suit still unsettled. For years after the war the claim was prosecuted, but neither
the republic nor the state of Texas ever confirmed title to the land, the
Señores Ramírez, however just may have been their pretension, having
failed to procure a clear grant from either the Spanish or the Mexican
government.

While the country was still "all open," Tol McNeill settled on the
Ramireña a few miles above the Ramírez stronghold, and in time the
talk was that he had dug up $40,000 of the money buried there. It was
not until a year or so before his death (in 1927) that I mustered sufficient courage to ask him about the treasure. He told me something,
but, so far as interest goes, his story can in no way compete with the
man himself, for he was "a character," during forty full years of his
own lifetime the theme of crescent speculation and yarn.

He used to be pointed out as a man who had killed "two or three
white men and no telling how many Mexicans," and there were other
tales—all utterly without proof so far as I know—about the "wide
loop" he had swung back in the early days. His right arm terminated
in a stub about halfway between wrist and elbow, and on account of
the defect he was often referred to as "El Mocho." All sorts of ex-

planations were current as to how he lost the hand. Despite the absence of it, he could roll Bull Durham cigarettes as facilely as anybody, and during his years of activity he was an expert roper both on horseback and in the pen, where he cast the loop with his foot. How he could manage a team of fiery buggy horses! He had a fine ear for music—hymns, dance tunes, Mexican waltzes—and it was a joy to see him at the piano dashing from treble to bass and keeping both going with that one hand.

His cattle were about the wildest in the whole brush country, and many a time I have ridden down Ramireña Creek through his pasture without sighting an animal, though I could hear *ladino* cows popping the bushes a half mile away. He believed in "natural water," but the water holes on the creek always went dry along in the hottest part of the summer and at the same time his two or three little tin windmills quit pumping; then some of his cattle would die of thirst, but the wilder ones survived on prickly pear. A cow that had to be supplied with water by a gasoline pump and couldn't "chaw" it out of prickly pear wasn't worthy of an old-time Texian cowman anyhow.

I remember going over to the Buena Vista—that was the name of his ranch—one time while his vaqueros were gathering to ship. They had been working for a month and had caught only about a car load and a half of cattle. Most of these were in a big corral built of pickets ten feet high. They were existing on singed prickly pear with a modicum of cotton-seed cake mixed in. Every animal in the pen had been roped and led in necked to an old brindle ox. They looked "as gant as a bunch of gutted snow birds." I did not see them when they were finally driven to the shipping pens, but I heard they were "a sight." Some of the steers were necked together; some had heads tied down to a front foot; some were belled; one or two were hamstrung. They had to be "fixed" somehow so that they could not get away in the brush. Tol McNeill never owed anything on his land or stock, never bought on credit, and he did not have to raise many cattle in order to keep himself and family supplied with such necessities as Bull Durham, frijoles, salt pork, kerosene oil, calico, and a good buggy.

When "Old Man Tol" was converted at a camp-meeting, his conversion was counted as about the greatest victory for the Lord that the Ramireña country had ever witnessed. It was not long, however, before he "backslid." But whatever his spiritual state might be, he always had the blessing asked at his table, and those people who understood him knew that he had a heart "as big as an ox."

The last time I saw him, which was at a meeting of trail drivers in San Antonio, I asked him if oil-leasing was very lively down in his country.

"A fellow was over to my ranch not long ago," he replied, "wanting to lease my land."

"Did you close with him?"

"Well, I don't know. He asked me about an abstract. I just pointed to my old forty-four Winchester over in the corner and told him that was my abstract. 'It has protected me on this land for forty-six years,' I says, 'and nobody ain't ever questioned the abstract yet. It's the only one I'm going to furnish.' The fellow agreed that my abstract must be good, but we haven't signed any papers yet."

While we were talking, a ranger captain walked by.

"I know that man," old Tol remarked, "but he don't seem to know me. If they don't know me, Pancho, I never bother 'em. I never say anything. I'm that way.

"Now, about that old Ramírez Mission down there on your pa's land, I'll tell you all I know. When I first saw it, the walls were all standing and everything about it was good except the roof. They say it was one of a line of Spanish missions extending all the way from Corpus Christi to San Antonio.

"Of course all these old ranch missions and the like were on Spanish grants. I can remember when some Mexkins down in Tamaulipas were trying to establish a title to my own land and all the other land between the Lagarto and Ramireña creeks. They claimed eleven leagues out of the Ramírez grant, but the acreage they wanted to take in would have amounted to twenty leagues. You know how those old grants were surveyed, I guess. They didn't bother with stakes and chains. Two men got on horseback with a forty-foot reata tied from stirrup to stirrup, and they rode in a trot all day counting the rope lengths, throwing in plenty of extra ones so as to have full measure. The man ahead was supposed to halt and hold his position until the other man came up beside him, their stirrups touching, but oftener than not they were both riding at the same time, the second rider merely marking with his eye the starting point of the first. When they came to a creek, they crossed it without marking anything, and it was the same way when they had to go through a bad thicket.

"Well, along after the Civil War brother Pate and I heard of an old Mexkin woman who was said to know all about the Ramírez Mission. People were talking about the treasure buried there and some were already digging. We were interested and we went to see this woman. She lived on Captain Kennedy's Lapara Ranch down on the coast. She was old, old, maybe ninety or a hundred years old.

"Yes, she said she'd been at the Ramírez before it was abandoned. That was when she was a little girl, hardly more'n big enough to carry water from the creek. One day she was just starting up the hill with an *olla* of water on her head, she told us, when a vaquero galloped up and yelled for her to get on behind him, that the Indians were coming. He had sighted them at the big Ramírez water hole, which, you know, is only a mile or so above the old Ramírez house, and about the time he saw them they took after him. I guess he figgered there were too many Indians for the people at the Ramírez ranch to stand off. Anyway, he stopped just long enough for the girl to jump behind him. She rode astraddle, hanging on to him, until they crossed the Lagarto. Then they went on down to Casa Blanca. It was deserted and half destroyed. The Indians had started their raid at Corpus and come on up the country, making a clean sweep of everything in front of them. They killed every soul on Ramireña Creek.

"Well, after telling us all this, the old woman claimed she didn't know a thing about the money in the Ramírez house, but she said the *dueño* was *muy rico*. She said also that somewhere between Casa Blanca and the Ramireña the Indians had wiped out a wagon train hauling some pretty valuable freight.

"I guess it must of been about a year after picking up all this ancient history that I was running wild horses over south of the Picachos on Lagarto Creek. I was going lickety-split, hell-bent for breakfast, trying to head off a gotch-eared brown stallion and his bunch when all of a sudden I ran into a lot of human bones. I stopped right there to examine them. I knew the other boys would get the horses. There was heads and arms and legs scattered all about. They were as white as bones can bleach. That night I told Oliver Dix about what I had seen and we rode back next day to take another look at the bones. He had been in the country longer'n I had and he just knew those bones were the remains of the Mexkin freighters who'd been killed by the Indians on their big clean-up.

"One time out on that long hogback running south from the Ramireña water hole I found a wheel belonging to an old-time Mexkin *carreta*. Somebody had been digging around it; it was claimed that the Spaniards had buried a store of money there.

"Of course no such digging went on at this place as has always been going on about the Ramírez Mission itself. It was along in the early seventies, I guess, that I hitched my bridle reins to a *granjeno* bush one day and stepped into the Ramírez building. Right there on the ground were pieces of a *jarro* [an earthen pot] that had been dug out of one corner. The print of some of the coins was still fresh and plain on the caked earth sticking to pieces of the *jarro*. I don't know how much was found. If the Ramírez outfit didn't put all their money in one place, some of it is still there to find. I know damned well I never got any of it."

There is a sequel to this story of the *jarro*. George Givens told it to me thus:

"In 1874 I went to Abilene with a herd of steers, and that same year, I remember distinctly, a saddle, blanket, and bridle were found in a hole pawed up by bulls on the prairie east of the old mission on Ramireña Creek. A little later a man's body was found half buried at the head of the hollow just above the mission. Strange lights had been seen about the old house, and some claimed that a Mexican *jarro* had been dug up inside it. People talked about the saddle and the dead man and the *jarro* a lot. The general supposition was that two men had dug up the treasure and that then one of them killed his pardner and hogged the whole find."

East of the Ramírez ruins there was and is a big field. The Mexicans who cultivated this field lived in a *jacal* from which at night they were always seeing mysterious lights flickering and flitting between the rock walls and the creek, but never around the fort itself. Many people have held that a tunnel once ran from the fort to the creek; the lights indicated treasure hid in the tunnel. Several shafts have been sunk in attempts to probe the tunnel, but none has succeeded.

One Mexican used to tell how as a child he came with his parents to the Ramireña. They had a little money, and, as land was then very cheap and as the fort was still in tolerable condition, all that it needed to make it habitable being a thatch of beargrass, they considered buying it. One day while they were approaching it to examine it more closely, a white panther leaped out; then when they got inside, they saw many curious coins on the walls and dirt floor. But they were afraid to touch the coins and abandoned the idea of purchasing the place. The white panther was the soul of the dead *dueño* of the treasure, there to watch it.

Yet taking the money would very likely have brought no harm, for a white object—*un bulto blanco*—usually signifies a good spirit; a

white cat, a white calf, a white dog, a white mule, a woman dressed in white, or any other form of whiteness may at times appear for the purpose of leading people to buried treasure. It is *un bulto negro* that one had better beware of.

One time a man from East Texas drove up to our ranch in a buckboard. He had a Mexican with him. He asked permission to dig at the fort, and the permission was readily granted. This Mexican claimed to have been digging at the south wall once ten years before when all of a sudden, just as he was sure his *talache* had struck the lid of a chest, he heard an unearthly yell and the rattle of trace chains behind him. It was night. He had enough presence of mind to kick a few clods back into the hole, which was a small one; but he was so frightened that he left in a run and had never been back. He had never even told of his experience until he found this *amo*, whom he could trust. I went along on horseback to guide the treasure hunters. When the Mexican got to the fort he appeared to be a stranger to it. He and his *amo* moved very little dirt.

Not long after this we ourselves had an experience in digging. While looking for the Casa Blanca treasure, Ed Dubose and Stonewall Jackson Wright met with a Mexican sage who gave them "the true facts" about Fort Ramírez. They must look for the treasure in "a secret cell." They possessed a "gold monkey"—a mineral rod—and this instrument they took to the fort; it oscillated towards the west and made two locations. After excavation proved futile at both places, Stonewall Jackson Wright quit, but Ed Dubose kept on. Fort Ramírez "just looked too good" to abandon.

The next step was to consult a noted mulatto fortune teller at Victoria. He described Fort Ramírez satisfactorily and said that for $500 he could and would locate a chest of money buried near it. The agreement was made and one night Dubose drove the mulatto to the fort. He stepped off a few paces, planted his foot down, and said: "Here it is. Dig a round hole here ten feet in diameter." When the two got back to Wade's Switch about daylight, the mulatto demanded his $500. Dubose told him that he would have to wait until the money was dug up and offered to allow him to be present at the ceremony, but he refused to stay. He declared that unless he was paid his fee at once, "spirits would move the box," and it would be useless for anyone to try to find it.

He was not paid at once, but despite the threats of malignant spirits, Ed Dubose persuaded my father to help him dig. I believe that my father had as little superstition and was as little given to extravagant fancies as any man I have ever known; yet there is something about the lure of buried treasure that will cause almost any man to "take one trial." It happened that work was slack about this time, and so one morning in a wagon loaded with tools, bedding, chuck, a lantern, a gun or two, and three Mexican laborers, we all set out for Fort Ramírez. A big hole was to be dug and it was to be guarded until completed.

When the diggers got down six or seven feet, they came upon some loose soil that was quite different in color and substance from the contiguous earth. It appeared to be "the filling" of some old hole. Hopes became feverish, but after about a barrel of the extraneous earth had been removed it petered out. At the depth of twelve feet the men quit digging. Evidently the spirits had moved the box. I saw the old sink the other day. On four or five acres of ground around it are many other holes, some of them freshly dug.

"If I just knew where the big door to the fort was," said the Mexican with me, "I could send for a friend of mine who has a map and get plenty of *dinero*."

All I regret now is that the stones of Ramírez Fort have been carried away. I should like to stand on them once more in April and gaze across the winding Ramireña upon the oak-fringed hills beyond. Yet the hills could hardly be so lush with buffalo-clover—as we used to call the bluebonnet—and red bunch grass, so soft and lovely, as they are in the eyes of memory.

CHAPTER IV

The Circumstance of War

I have remarked that the stories
of treasure buried by the Moors which prevail
throughout Spain are most current among the poorest people. It is thus
kind nature consoles with shadows for want of substantials.
I R V I N G , The Alhambra

A politician "hunts not the trail of policy so sure" as the seeker after buried treasure hunts chests of "pay money," stuffed cannon, and other valuables hastily secreted by marching armies. A cannon that the Hessians are supposed to have blocked full of gold and pitched into the Delaware River during the Revolutionary War is still looked for.[1] In Sweden, farmers plow with the hope of turning up some of the tribute money paid by Anglo-Saxon kings to a Danish army a thousand years ago. More than any other military people, however, the Spaniards and Mexicans have been given to prodigal abandonment of riches along the path of glorious war. The route pursued by many an armament over the Southwest is kept in mind nowadays solely by accounts of treasure left behind.

RELICS OF DE SOTO

In the year 1539 Hernando De Soto embarked from Cuba with two thousand followers to explore for gold and silver in Florida. For three years the yellow *ignis fatuus* lured him north and west, he and his men killing, pillaging, and baptizing with Christian thoroughness the savage heathen of the wilderness. In 1541 he discovered the Mississippi, and the next year he was buried beneath its waters. "He had crossed a large part of the continent in search of gold, and found nothing so remarkable as his burial place."

One find, however, that has helped immensely the cause of legend was "three hundred and fifty weight of pearls, and figures of babies and birds made from iridescent shells." The quotation is from one of

94

the Spanish chroniclers who accompanied the expedition. The place was in Georgia.

On the long march that followed, one of De Soto's foot soldiers, Juan Terrón by name, grew so weary that he drew from his wallet a share of the pearls and offered them to a cavalryman if he would carry them. They weighed six pounds and were in a linen bag. The cavalryman told his comrade to keep them. Then Juan Terrón opened the bag, whirled it about his head, and scattered the pearls in every direction. The chronicler estimates that in Spain they would have been worth over $12,000. "There are no pearls for Juan Terrón," became a Spanish proverb, meaning that a fool makes no profits. But little did Juan Terrón care for pearls or proverbs when, finally, he and three hundred other survivors out of the original two thousand crawled, naked, starving, broken, empty-handed, into Tampico, Mexico.

Such was the fate of De Soto's search for an El Dorado to the north. And now through the enchantment of distance people who inhabit lands that De Soto by the remotest possibility may have traversed go out with sanguine hopes after a plethora of riches that he is supposed to have buried. It cannot be proved that he did not pass through Searcy County, Arkansas. A few years ago an Oklahoma man who had some business respecting a zinc deposit in that county engaged the services of a local surveyor. After the required lines were run, the surveyor said:

"Come over here, and I will show you the oldest mark of civilized man to be found in America." Then the surveyor led the way to a mound that had been dug out so as to give it the appearance of a crater.

"In 1900," he continued, "a Mexican priest came here from a monastery in Mexico. With him he had a chart that he claimed had been made by De Soto and preserved in his own monastery all these centuries. The chart called for a silver mine in a cave, and the location of it was given in degrees and minutes both of latitude and longitude.

"The priest offered me half the silver if I would locate it for him, and the agreement was made. The chart was dated 1541. So I figured to a fine point what the declination of the needle would be for the time elapsed since that date. Then I made my location.

"It was on top of this mound and right in a big oak tree. Well, when the priest saw that I was running into an oak hundreds of years old, he got disgusted. But there had been plenty of time for an oak to grow, and my own theory is that the Spanish set out a sapling as a kind of marker. Anyway, we got a couple of hands, grubbed up the oak, and began to sink a hole.

"When we got down twelve feet we came to a slab of limestone rock. We dug this away and then we found ourselves at the mouth of a kind of cave. And there as fresh as if they had been left yesterday were two or three sticks of zinc and some old clay retorts. De Soto's men made retorts out of native clay in order to control the distillate. I don't know why they called it a silver mine, but they did. Another thing we found was a pearl, scorched like the Indians used to scorch them when they burnt them out of mussels."

THE STUFFED CANNON OF THE NECHES

Any party planning to hunt or fish down the Neches River, in East Texas, will do well to secure the services of "Uncle Jimmie" Clanton. He is pretty old but no older than he was twenty years back. As a cook he is not noted for cleanliness and as a handy man he has a remarkable aptitude for letting George do it, but as a recounter of what has happened in the piney woods he is without peer.[2]

"Boys," he began one night, after he had comfortably propped his back against a tree, lighted his pipe, and dismissed from his mind the supper dishes which the "boys" were paying him to wash—"Boys, I want to tell you that my paw helped old Sam Houston whop Santa Anna back in 1836.

"Well now, after the treaty of peace was signed at San Jacinto, or maybe it was just afore, Paw went under Colonel Burleson to smoke the Mexicans out of the fort at Nacogdoches. You all have likely read about this in history, but I'm going to tell you something that never gets into history at all.

"It was early one morning when Burleson's bunch made the charge. Not a soul was inside the walls. They nosed around a little, found the Mexicans' trail leading due south, and struck out to follow it. It was fresh and as the Mexes were traveling with waggins, to haul all their plunder in, Burleson's men figgered they'd probably catch them by dark.

"Well, they rode all day without seeing the enemy, but the trail kept getting fresher. When they camped at dark they was fifty miles from Nacogdoches. About ten o'clock next morning they came to a couple of abandoned waggins. The Mexes was getting scared and cutting loose from their plunder. They pushed on without stopping for dinner, and about three o'clock sighted some Mexes at Boone's Ferry. That ferry wasn't two miles up the river from where we are camped.

"As soon as the Texians saw the Mexes, they made a dash, hoping to cut them off. Just as they got in comfortable shooting distance, the ferry-boat landed on the opposite side with a waggin and three men. The waggin drove on off, but the Texians were too busy to foller it just then. Some of the Mexes took to the timber on the near side and fired back and there was a right lively little scrap. Paw used to tell me all about it, and he said he was laying kinder behind a log firing away when he looked up and noticed three men rolling a cannon toward the river. They rolled it to a high bluff and shoved it right off into the deepest hole in ten miles. He said he wondered what the idear was, but about that time he was too interested in number one to investigate cannons.

"Well, about fifteen of the Mexes were killed and the rest captured. That is, they was all captured except the three that got across the river with the waggin. A detachment took after them. Not more'n a mile and a half from the river they found the waggin, as empty as a last year's bird's nest with the bottom punched out, and one dead Mexican, but the other two got away. Burleson reported with his prisoners to General Houston, and that was the end of the expedition.

"Well, the things that happened in the next few years wouldn't interest you any. Then in the spring of 1875 a slick-haired young Mex showed up in our neighborhood. He didn't appear to have any pertic'lar business—just seemed to be nosing around. After he'd been here for a month or so, he comes to me one day and says that as I seem to be pretty well posted he'd like to make a proposition. We went behind the pen where nobody could see us. There he pulled out an old map. It was in Spanish, but it wasn't no trouble for me to make out the lay of the land. It showed a road beginning at Nacogdoches and running due south. It showed the Neches River and it showed Boone's Ferry. Just below Boone's Ferry—a mile and a half, he said—the road stopped. Well, I was right interested.

"Then he asked me if I knowed where Boone's Ferry used to be.

" 'Shore,' I says.

"Then he opened up. His grandfather, so he says, was at Boone's Ferry when Burleson arrived with the Texians. He was one of two

men that got away. The young Mexican wants to know if I am acquainted with the details of the battle.

" 'I certainly am,' I says. 'My paw was in the fight and has told me about it many a time.'

" 'Did he ever tell you about seeing a cannon shoved off into the river?'

" 'Many a time,' says I.

" 'Well, Mr. Clanton,' he says—for he was perlite as a basket of chips—'did it ever occur to you to wonder why that cannon was shoved into the river?'

" 'Why, yes,' says I, 'I've wondered about that lots of times.'

" 'I'll tell you why,' he says, and he was getting excited, I could see mighty plain, but he didn't let his voice get up. 'That cannon was filled with gold from breech to muzzle.'

" 'Gold!' I whistled. 'So that's it.'

" 'Yes, that's it,' he says. 'Not only that, but I have in my pocket another map giving the exact location of more gold, just on beyond the ferry. You see, the waggin that crossed the river carried a chest of money. The three men with it went on till they got well out of sight; then they buried it. They had a quarrel over it, and one Mexican shot another to shut him up. Then he and my grandfather took down some landmarks on a piece of paper, and pulled for Mexico. On the way the other Mexican died, leaving my grandfather with the map. He died before he could come back and get the money. My own father was killed by bandits; so I was left with the one and original map of the buried treasure.'

"If ever I saw a man that believed he was telling the truth, that young Mexican was him. He didn't ask me for a penny. He just came out flat and said he'd give me half of everything we found providing I'd help him.

"You all can guess I jumped at such an offer. We looked for the cannon first, because I knowed exactly where it ought to be. I still know, for that matter. We dredged and dredged and fished and fished for the blamed thing, but never could locate it. You see, it took about a forty-foot jump off into the river and it had had about forty years to settle in.

"Well, we finally stopped fishing for it and went after the chest. The map called for a triangle with the chest in the center. Without any trouble at all we found the first of the three corners of the triangle. It was a big rock, kinder queer shaped. The other two landmarks were supposed to be pine trees. But all the big trees in the country had been cut off and rafted down the river. There just wa'n't no trees to sight from. We sighted off triangles from every old stump in the neighborhood, but I guess we didn't hit the right ones. Anyhow, we hunted gold for two months and never dug up a penny. The Mexican finally got discouraged and went back home. But he gave me a copy of his maps and I've been looking for money off and on ever since he left.

"That's about all there is to the history connected with Boone's Ferry, I guess. If any of you all want to see where the cannon was rolled off into the river, we'll go up to Boone's Ferry in the morning."

SANTA ANNA'S CHESTS

How many chests of "pay money" designed for Spanish and Mexican troops were dropped into Texas streams and left there, it would be impossible to say. Reliable testimony discloses at least one.[3] According to the venerable chronicler Noah Smithwick, a Mexican officer who was taking pay money to the garrison at Nacogdoches found the San Bernard River so high that he had to cross it in a dugout. The dugout tipped over, and the box of money—"a large sum"—sank to the bottom. After trying in vain to recover it, the Mexican left. During a low stage of water, some time later, a negro who belonged to a settler living near the ford found the box and delivered it to his master. He, as rarely honest as his slave, promptly notified authorities of the Mexican government and turned over the property.

This chest was dropped before the time of the Texas Revolution, but it set an example. At what is known as the Rock Crossing on the Nueces River a detachment of Santa Anna's invading army, so tradition runs, was fording the river in great haste when the "pay cart" broke down, toppling a chest into the channel. It was too heavy to pull out; the cart could not well be repaired to transport it farther even if it were pulled out; the river was turbulent; the commanding officer was in a hurry to annihilate the Texans at Goliad. He decided to leave the chest in the river, where, after speedy subjugation of the revolutionists, the Mexicans could get it on their way home. Fortunately it had a chain attached to it—a log chain. A diver brought up the loose end of the chain and fastened it around the trunk of a tree growing on the bank. As everybody knows, those of Santa Anna's forces who made their way back to Mexico did not tarry anywhere in Texas long enough to haul out a heavy chest. Forty-seven years after it was anchored, a cowman noticed a piece of chain around the trunk of an elm growing on the bank at Rock Crossing—a crossing even then abandoned. When a long time afterwards he learned the purpose of the chain, he took a team of horses to hitch to it and drag out the chest. The tree had washed away.

Now, it is a matter of history that when the Texans captured the commander-in-chief of the Mexican army at San Jacinto in 1836, they found $11,000 in his military chest, not counting the "finery and silver" which were auctioned off for $800. Was that all the treasure Santa Anna had in Texas?

Neal Russell and two fellow "brush poppers" were down in the Nueces country catching wild cattle. They had plenty of horses, plenty of supplies, and a pack outfit. I do not know when this was; it was years ago. Their camp was beside water.

One morning while they were "chousing" a bunch of outlaw cattle, Russell caught a hurried glimpse of two very old Mexicans. In those days any stranger on the range was a curiosity, but there was no time for parley now. However, after the cowhands had "fought brush" for three hours, roped and tied down a *ladino* apiece, and then ridden to the river to water their exhausted mounts, they came again upon the Mexicans. They looked shy and acted rather peculiarly, but they were so thin and worn that Neal Russell had nothing but pity for them. After passing a few remarks, he told them where camp was and invited them to go up and get a fill of beef. The only baggage the old men had was in a couple of frayed serapes carried by a burro.

When, after the usual afternoon hunt, the "white men" rode into camp, the Mexicans were already there, standing respectfully to one side and sucking at some cigarettes that had considerably less tobacco than corn shuck in their "makings."

The Texans talked "Mexican," or "cowpen Spanish," as fluently as though they were natives, and after supper the ancient strangers, evidently feeling at ease, asked if anyone present could tell where the old "War Crossing" on the Nueces was.

"Why," Neal Russell replied, "it's not a mile down the river from our camp. I'll show it to you in the morning."

The Mexicans now seemed to think that they had as well take the

The Mexicans now seemed to think that they had as well take the Texans into confidence, and one of them began a long explanation.

"I was here on the Nueces," he said, "in the spring of 1836. I was with thirty-eight other soldiers of the Mexican army. We were taking a cart load of money to San Antonio to pay off soldiers. One day's ride north of the Nueces a courier met us and told of Santa Anna's defeat at San Jacinto. We knew that it was foolish to go on and so turned back. We expected to be overtaken at any time by the Texans. Just before we reached the Nueces on our back trail, the axle of the pay-cart broke square in two. The only thing to do was to cut a tree down and hew a new axle. We dragged out of the road a little way and set to work.

"As I told you, we were expecting the Texans at any moment. The captain was a discreet man. He made us dig a trench beside the cart; he spread two cowhides in the bottom of it, and then emptied the money on the hides. We had to unload the cart anyhow. Then we cut down the straightest mesquite we could find and carried it to the cart. Barely done was all this when we heard a galloping in the distance as if a whole troop of cavalry was coming. *Pronto, pronto,* we threw the log in on top of the coin, spread another cowhide or two over that, and then threw in dirt. It took but a minute to turn the cart over on top of the fresh earth and set fire to it. It blazed up. We mounted our horses and spurred south. I believe now that what we heard running was mustangs instead of cavalry. Anyway, we left the signs of our digging concealed by the fire.

"So far as I know, I am the only survivor of that escort of Mexicans. I do not believe that one of them has ever been back to get the money. Poor fellows, most of them were killed in the war with the United States that came a few years later. I am come now with my old *compadre* to claim what I helped save. You see how we are. We started out poorly prepared. Now we are almost afoot and have no provisions left. If you will help us, we will share with you."

The next morning Neal Russell, the other two cow hunters, and the Mexicans started out with axe and spade. They went to the War Crossing, and then out a short distance on the north side. The elder Mexican led them to three little mounds—knolls common to that part of the country. Beyond these three knolls was a stump, and beyond the stump another knoll.

"That is the place," half panted the Mexican, while they were yet fifty or sixty yards away from it.

The cowboys rode slowly, for the old men on foot almost stumbled at every step. When the party got fairly around the knoll they saw a pile of fresh dirt. Pitched across it was an old log. Mesquite lasts a long time beneath the soil of Southwest Texas. The men looked down into the hole. It was not very deep and had evidently been dug about a week before. A few tags of rotten rawhide lay about.

The Mexicans did not say a word. They were a week too late. The last Neal Russell saw of them they were tottering back towards the Rio Grande, their burro loaded with jerked beef and what other supplies the cow hunters could spare them.

PALO ALTO AND RESACA DE LA PALMA

The battles of Palo Alto and Resaca de la Palma, which began the war between Mexico and the United States, were fought on Texas soil May 8 and 9, respectively, 1846. A *resaca* is a kind of marshy lake; the Resaca de la Palma is about three miles out from Brownsville (old Fort Brown). The Palo Alto battlefield is something like twice that distance. After a demoralizing defeat at Palo Alto, some of the retreating Mexicans made a stand at Resaca de la Palma, where they were completely routed.

Many years after the war was over, a Mexican named Ramón used to ferry passengers across the Rio Grande. He claimed to have been a ferryman when the Mexican troops crossed to halt General Taylor's army. This is the way he used to describe his experience:

"It took me three days to ferry all the Mexican army over, crossing and crossing back, day and night, night and day. And, oh, I had much desire to go with the troops. There was *música*, oh so lively, and there were the *banderas* all flying bright in the air, and the men were all happy and singing. But I did not go, and in three days more here they were back, but without any *música* or *banderas* and not needing any ferry-boat. They came in flocks, running and crawling like *tortugas*, and they fell into the water flat on all fours like *tortugas* and never stopped till they were in the brush of the República Mejicana.

"They had been at the fight of what we call Resaca de la Palma, and I was very glad that I had not been with them. They did not have time even to bring back the *señor* general's chest of money or any of the silver that he ate out of. They left it all where three tall palms make a triangle; in the middle of that triangle it is buried. They dug a hole and put the chest and the silverware and a golden cross in it, and then they filled up the hole and made a great fire on top of it so it would look as if some military stores had been burned. And then they came back here like so many *tortugas,* and the gringos were so *bravos* that no one of those who helped hide away the treasure ever would recross the Rio Grande to get it. Besides, most of them were killed at Monterrey."

It was at the Palo Alto battlefield that Santiago's father helped bury army money. Taylor's men were pressing the Mexicans. In order to escape with their lives, the Mexicans must lighten their baggage. The officer in command of the pay-carts received orders to bury the money and retreat. He told off a detail and put them to opening a trench. When the trench was made, he commanded that the money be dumped into it. The place was well hidden by brush. While the last cart load was being dumped, Santiago's father, who had been throwing dirt out like a badger, slipped into the mesquites. He well knew that the poor peons who were doing the work would go into the trench next—for the dead tell no tales. No sooner was he out of sight in the brush than the sound of shots told him how prudent he had been in leaving. He never went back to the place, but he liked to tell about the fine treasure, and his loquacious son has guided several parties of men to the Palo Alto battlefield.[4]

In connection with treasures of the Mexican War a veteran[5] used to tell this tale. After the capture of Monterrey two American soldiers slipped down the San Juan River and robbed an old priest of $10,000. General Taylor discovered the crime—but not the money—and sent the soldiers to New Orleans to be tried. One of them died in prison; the other made his way back to the home of Wash Secrets on the Colorado River in Texas. There he became very ill and on his death bed told "Old Wash" that he and his accomplice had buried the ten thousand dollars in gold at the root of a pecan tree thirty steps from Walnut Springs, where Taylor's army was camped. After the fellow was buried, Wash Secrets went to Mexico to dig up the money. He found Walnut Springs all right, but as Taylor's men had for military purposes cut down all the trees, he had no pecan to go by. He searched for many days among the stumps without finding the gold. "It is there yet."

STEINHEIMER'S MILLIONS

One of the flashy figures of the filibustering era in Texas—vivid like a darting cardinal but too swift to permit of analysis—was Louis Aury, slave smuggler, privateer, and for a time ruler of Galveston Island. History has neglected to delineate Aury's vari-colored accomplices, but concerning one of them at least legend is explicit, even to the date of his birth.[6]

Karl Steinheimer, according to the most knowing of the many men who have dug for his gold, was born near Speyer, Germany, in 1793. At the age of eleven he ran away from home, became a sailor, and by the time he was grown could speak ten languages and had become a renowned captain of pirates. He threw in with Aury and for a while throve in the traffic of "black ivory"; but the days of Aury's prosperity were numbered, the two quarreled, and then Steinheimer withdrew into the mountains of Mexico, where he carried on extensive mining operations. Disappointment in an early love affair made such retirement congenial.

He had mined for nearly ten years when, in 1827, he learned that Hayden Edwards, the noted Texas empresario, had revolted against Mexico and established the Republic of Fredonia. Steinheimer decided at once to make his way to the Edwards' forces and offer his assistance in person and money. He considered himself powerful enough to become ruler of the new country. However, when he reached Monterrey, he learned that the revolt had been put down. Steinheimer returned to his mines and prospered for ten more years. Then he learned something that caused him to close out his business and head north.

He learned that the woman he had wooed but not won or forgotten was living in Saint Louis, still unmarried. His fortune, after he had sold out all his interests and paid all his debts, amounted to ten jack loads of silver and gold. He evidently had little doubt of his ability now to win the one woman. At any rate, he determined to take the fortune with him. He picked two Mexicans to assist in the transportation.

Meantime Texas had become a republic, though Mexico was still claiming it. When Steinheimer arrived in Matamoros, he found a Mexican officer named Manuel Flores with a few followers preparing to invade Texas for the purpose of instigating an Indian uprising. At this time he had no interest in Texas events, but knowing how hostile

105

the Apaches and Comanches were along the San Antonio road, he threw in with the Flores expedition as a means of protection. A few hours before a band of Texans engaged with the Mexicans near the Colorado River, Steinheimer separated himself and his loaded burros from the military party and cut across the country.

His situation was now perilous indeed, for he had not only Indians to avoid but, as a Mexican citizen, the hostile Texans. In order to travel safely he must travel light. He decided to bury all his riches but one package of gold, which would suffice for immediate uses. Accordingly, in the hill country sixty or seventy miles north of Austin, near a place "where three streams intersect and combine into one," he unpacked his ten burros and concealed their freight. The only mark made to designate the spot of concealment was a large brass spike driven into an oak tree some forty or sixty feet away, the spike being of that

type formerly used in the construction of boats. The burros were liberated to shift for themselves; then with his two trusted men Steinheimer took a southeastern direction. That was an illogical direction for him to take, it must be admitted, but he took it.

When they had traveled, as he judged, some twelve or fourteen miles, they came to what he termed "a bunch of knobs on a prairie," from the tops of which they could see a valley skirted with trees several miles to the west. At these knobs they were attacked by Indians, the two aides were killed, and Steinheimer himself escaped with a bad wound. He hid for a while in the brush on the central knob of the group, and there he buried the package of gold he had retained from the packs. He had lost his horse and all his supplies, but he still had a gun and some ammunition.

Choosing a northern direction, he now set out afoot. By the time he

got far enough away that he was not afraid of being betrayed by the sound of his gun, he was almost starving. His wound had become very painful and gangrene had set in. At this juncture he fell into the hands of some travelers.

They were evidently well disposed and evidently respected the trust that Steinheimer placed in them. Realizing the threat of death, he made a crude map of the region about his buried millions, directed it to his former sweetheart, and sealed it with a letter in which he gave a concise account of his activities during their years of separation down to the moment of writing. He explained that the strangers to whom he was entrusting this message knew nothing of his name or history and that they would get nothing of his but a few coins on his person. Finally, he requested that she keep his message secret for three months after receiving it. If he recovered, he would, he said, reach Saint Louis by the expiration of that time; if he did not arrive, she was to understand that he was dead and that his fortune was hers. These are the last tidings of Steinheimer.

The letter was delivered. A number of years passed before relatives of the lady addressed felt that conditions in Texas would permit of a thorough search for the treasure. They came, and then after months of scouting concluded that the three small streams at the confluence of which the ten burro loads of gold and silver were buried must be the Salado, the Lampasas, and the Leon, which unite below the present town of Belton to form what is called Little River. Between twelve and fifteen miles southeast of this junction a prominent "bunch" of hills known as the Knobs overlooks the tortuous valley of Little River; here amid these Knobs it may be supposed that Steinheimer buried his package of gold and received his death wound.

The men whom the Saint Louis woman sent to secure her strange inheritance found nothing. They were careful not to reveal her name, but, while making their prolonged search, they were naturally obliged to reveal their motives. Thus the story of Steinheimer and his millions became known to the inhabitants of the country. For more than three quarters of a century now the quest has been prosecuted.

CHAPTER V

Tales of the Cow Camp

*Did you ever notice how much better a pipe smokes
when it's lit by a coal out of a camp fire?*
Brushy Joe's Reminiscences

THE RIDER OF LOMA ESCONDIDA

"Boys, ever' time I camp at this crossing I think of the way Jeff Cassidy got waylaid and murdered between here and Loma Escondida."[1]

The speaker was Captain Crouch. He was with his outfit at the old Presidio Crossing on the Leona River near the border. Supper was over.

"Yes," Captain Crouch went on, "that was a long time ago, and tough hombres in this country were thicker'n fiddlers in hell. Horse thieves was so bad that a man couldn't hardly keep a gentle saddle horse without hiding him in a thicket after dark and then sleeping by him. Money was safer'n horses, but a man with a good horse and money both had better be keerful.

"Now, about Jeff Cassidy. He was representative for the 7 D's, a big outfit. Well, he left San 'tonio one day for the old H-Triangle Ranch below here to receive a herd of steers and start 'em up the trail. Like the custom was at the time, he carried money to pay for the stuff in his saddle pockets. He had five thousand pesos, gold, the balance to be paid when the cattle were sold in Kansas and the money brung back.

"The second night out Jeff slept in Friotown. He left there at daylight next morning, coming this way. He was alone, and was riding a little creamy dun pony that I'll tell you about d'reckly. He'd got into Friotown after dark and somehow had failed to learn that the sheriff was going down to inspect brands on the herd, or he might have had company. The sheriff left Frio 'long latish in the morning. When he got about halfway between Loma Escondida and this crossing where we're camped, he found Jeff and his dun horse in the middle of the road both deader'n thunder.

"He hit the trail in a high lope, struck a couple of cowboys that joined him, and together they overtook the murderers somewhere this side of Eagle Pass. Everybody knowed them Newton boys wasn't no 'count and was rustling cattle, but nobody would have suspicioned them of killing a man in cold blood like they did Jeff Cassidy. The case was plain as daylight and the Newtons owned up. Still, they didn't have any of the gold with them, though the pockets had been stripped off Jeff's saddle. Furthermore, neither Jim nor Tom Newton could be forced to tell where the stuff was. They was hung, of course, and————"

But at this point the Captain's narrative was interrupted by an unceremonious announcement from the cook, Alfredo, that the camp was out of coffee.

Alfredo was a new *cocinero*, and in terms free and vigorous Captain Crouch expressed his opinion of a cook who would leave headquarters without enough coffee and not say anything about the shortage until it was nearly time to cook breakfast. The fact that Alfredo had carefully put his coffee in a big can and then loaded on in its place a similar can containing frijoles did not remedy the mistake.

"Well," concluded the Captain, "there ain't but one thing to do, and that's for somebody to ride to Charlie Trebes's commissary and get the coffee."

It was ten miles to the Trebes ranch. Twenty miles on horseback will not leave the rider much of a summer's night for sleeping. None of the hands said anything. It was not for them to say.

Otis Coggins, who had been working on the Crouch ranch since boyhood, was patching a stirrup-leather. He was a tall, swarthy man under thirty.

"Otis," the Captain went on, "I reckon you're the man to go for the coffee. You know old man Trebes better'n anybody else, and if you get back here by breakfast time you can stay in camp and sleep all morning. Better get about ten pounds, I guess."

"All right," said Otis.

Then, addressing a Mexican, he ordered, "Go get me that Trigeño horse. It's lucky I staked him."

"Guess I taught you never to be caught afoot, even if your back was broke and you couldn't fork a pillow," remarked Captain Crouch. "That reminds me————"

"But, Captain," Otis broke in, still mending on his saddle, "don't you reckon them Newton boys must 'a' buried that gold around somewhere clost to where they killed Jeff Cassidy? They shore aimed to make use of it some day."

"Yes, I guess they did hide it somewhere," Captain Crouch agreed, his mind brought back to the story he was telling when the *cocinero* interrupted. "I don't know as anybody's ever looked for it much. There never was anything that hurt me more'n Jeff's death. He and me had been side pardners—reg'lar yoke mates, you might say—for years. I guess we broke enough horses together to furnish a dozen outfits going up the trail. There was still some mustangs in the country, and one day we laid into a little bunch that had their bellies too full of water to run much and roped one apiece. Mine was a purty black filly; I broke her neck a-trying to get the saddle on her. Jeff's was a creamy dun stallion with a black stripe down his back about the width of your hand—a *bayo coyote*, as the Mexicans call a horse of that color. He was all life and bottom, and Jeff got so he didn't want to ride anything else. He was riding him when he was killed. I always figgered one of them Newton boys made a misshot and killed the horse accidentally. They'd 'a' been mighty glad to take him as well as the gold."

The Mexican had arrived with Otis' horse. The saddle was thrown on him, and a sack for the coffee was tied on the saddle. With an *adios* the rider was off.

Otis Coggins was a silent kind of man. He liked to be alone. His route lay through a vast flat country of mesquite, catclaw, *huajilla*, *chapote*, prickly pear, and other kinds of brush common to Southwest Texas. The only break on the plain that his brush-lined road traversed was a solitary hill known far and wide as Loma Escondida. It is *escondida*—hidden—because the brush is so high and thick around it that a rider cannot see it until he is almost upon it.

The moon was full; as usual the sky was flawlessly clean; one might have read ordinary book print in the moonlight. As he approached Loma Escondida, not a sound but the pad of his horse's hoofs and the squeak of saddle leather breaking the silence, Otis Coggins noticed an object, or, rather, two objects, in the road some distance ahead of him. They were partly in the shadow of high brush, and at first he took them to be a cow and calf. Cattle in a brush country often bed down in open roads. But presently Otis saw that the larger of the objects was a horse and that the lesser was a man apparently humped over on the ground. The man soon straightened, mounted, and started up the hill ahead of Otis.

Now, the road that Captain Crouch's most trusted hand was traveling was a private ranch road. It was his business to know who was riding around in his employer's pasture at night. He hailed the rider. There was no response. He set spurs to his horse to overtake the trespasser, and, without hard running, was soon close upon him. He saw—saw plainly—that the horse ahead was dun-colored with a black stripe down his back. "He's a *bayo coyote*, like Jeff Cassidy's mustang," Otis reflected.

Near the top of the hill he was actually by the stranger's side; neither spoke a word and Otis could not get a view of the rider's face. Then suddenly the stranger pulled out of the road into some half-open ground and headed straight for a stark, dead mesquite tree, the trunk of which was exceptionally large. Otis knew that tree; he recalled how late one evening while he was driving a bunch of saddle horses over Loma Escondida, something—he did not see what—jumped out of this very tree and stampeded the remuda so that they ran two miles before he could get around them.

He saw something now that he did not believe. He saw horse and rider head into the tree—straight into it—and disappear. The ground beyond was open enough that anything traversing it would have been plainly visible.

He pulled up his horse and looked, just looked. Like most other range men, he had a prosaic head that absolutely refused to harbor ghosts and other such superstitions common among the Mexicans. He guessed maybe he had been half asleep and did not know it. Yet he could not have been mistaken about seeing the man down by his horse back in the road, the man mounting and riding off, the dun horse with a black stripe down his back. All the details were clear.

He rode on now to get the coffee, got it, answered a few questions about the cow work, and started back.

He rode absorbed in contemplation of the strange rider and horse. He determined to investigate the mesquite tree into which they had vanished. Once he turned in his saddle to look behind him, and down a straight stretch of the road saw a coyote following. Off in the brush he heard now and then the lonely wail of other coyotes; he liked to hear them.

True to its name, Loma Escondida did not reveal itself until he was at it, and then Otis saw something that made him know he had not dreamed the rider on the *bayo coyote*. There he was, trotting his horse leisurely up the hill, going in the opposite direction from what he had been going when seen earlier in the night. Otis reined up. He heard distinctly the sound of the dun's hoofs on the dry, hard ground. Those very material sounds made him realize that some trick had been played on him, and he resolved to end the mystery. He knew that his Trigeño horse could put up a hot race, even if the race led clear to camp on the Leona; and if it came to running in the brush, he wore his regular protection of ducking jacket and leather leggins and he considered himself second to no man in skill as a "brush popper."

¡Vámonos! The stranger was a full hundred yards ahead, up the hill. For a minute he continued the leisurely trot, but when Otis had lessened the interval by half he saw the man ahead of him strike into a run. Now the squat top of the hill was reached; Otis was gaining. He was not more than twenty yards behind. They were coming to the half-opening into which the mysterious rider had before turned out of the road. Here he suddenly turned again. Otis was not surprised. In less time than it takes to draw a six-shooter he had the horn string around his rope loose and a loop shaken out.

"*¡Ojalá!*" he yelled. "Damn you, if I can't catch you, I'll rope you." But he was too late. Just as he prepared to cast his loop, the pursued rider and horse disappeared into the dead mesquite. There was no sound of impact. Otis himself dodged under a low-hanging limb of the old tree so as to be upon the tricky stranger on the other side. On the other side was nothing but bush, moonlight, vacancy, and silence.

Otis got down and led his horse up to the old mesquite. The first episode had been a surprise. The second, with every sense of the observer alert and expectant, was overwhelming.

"Have I eaten some *raíz diabólica*² to be seeing things?" Otis asked himself aloud, for he was determined not to be awed. Then he answered the question with "No I ain't, and I haven't been smoking *marihuana* weed either." There is a vague belief among some of the more ignorant Mexicans that after death their souls enter the mesquite—the mesquite that feeds them such good beans during life. As he rolled a cigarette, Otis Coggins remembered this superstition with contempt. The mesquite had never been sacred to him; he had cursed its thorns a thousand times.

He determined to give the tree a thorough examination. First he bent over to look at the ground around it. The moon, still high, revealed nothing but his own horse's tracks. The tree itself, though dead, was far from rotten. However, his eye caught a long groove in it. He felt the groove with his hands. It had been made with an axe long ago.

With face averted, he was slowly circling the old trunk when his boot caught on a flat rock. It was in shadow and he lit a match to examine more closely for other marks on that side of the tree. Glancing down, he noticed a dull glint of metal. He picked it up, lit another match; it was a twenty-dollar gold piece.

If there was one coin, there must be several. In order to clear the ground for closer inspection, Otis lifted the rock out of place. He hardly needed the light of a match to see what now lay exposed. It was a pair of old saddle pockets. They were so rotten that they almost fell apart when he picked them up. Several coins fell out.

"Jeff Cassidy's gold right where the Newton boys hid it!" Otis exclaimed aloud.

He was not excited. He never got excited. Calmly he went to his saddle, took down the sack, tied the coffee into one end of it, and then secured his find in the other end. Counting it could wait.

When he got into camp on the Leona, Captain Crouch and the *cocinero* were already up.

"I've shore been wanting that coffee," the Captain greeted him. "The water's been bilin' half an hour."

"Well, here it is," Otis sang out, at the same time dismounting and untying the sack, from which he brought to view only a part of the contents. "Hurry up, *cocinero*, I'd like a sip of coffee myself."

BUMBLEBEES AND SKILITONS

The vaqueros had unrolled their blankets, but with backs propped up against a comfortable old log over by the simmering bean-pot, Pete Staples and I were thoroughly awake. His tones were strictly confidential. Pete's "people" brought him to Texas from Mississippi before the Civil War. He was raised in the border country, and he used to cook and rustle horses for outfits going up the trail. For a while he lived down in Mexico, where he married a native woman.

"One time," Pete pursued the subject under discussion, "there was a white man who got wind of a lot of Mexican dollars buried down below Roma. He had the place all located, and was so sure of hisself that he brung in an outfit of mules and scrapers to dig away the dirt.

114

He was making a reg'lar tank digging down to that money when a Mexican what I've knowed all my life comed along.

"This Mexican stopped a minute under a mesquite tree to sorter cool off, and right there he seen a hoe laying on the ground half covered up in the dirt. He retched down to pick it up and then he seen a whole *maleta* of coins. A *maleta*, you know, is a kind of bag made out of hide. This one was old and rotten, and when he turned it over with the hoe it broke open and the gold money jes' rolled out in the dirt.

"D'reckly the Mexican went over to where the white man was bossing the scrapers, and he asked him what he was doing.

" 'Oh,' says the white man, 'I'm jes' digging up some buried money.'

" 'Well, you's digging where it ain't no use to dig,' says the Mexican. 'The money ain't there; hit's over here. If you want to see it, come along and I'll show it to you.'

"The white man laughed like he didn't believe what the Mexican was telling him, but he come along. When they got to the mesquite there wa'n't no money in sight, but there was a hole down at the root of the tree kinder like a badger hole, and bumblebees was going in and out making a roaring sound, and the dirt was fairly alive with great big bugs, humming and making a sizzling noise and working round awful like.

" 'Huh, is this what you call money?' says the white man, stamping down on the tumblebugs.

" 'That's all right,' says the Mexican. 'There was dollars right here —dollars of gold and silver too. But there ain't now, I admit, 'cause they dollars is evidently not intinded for you. White man didn't hide that money and it ain't meant for white man to find it. No matter how much you dig or where, you won't find nothing.'

"Shore enough, the man kept on digging and he didn't get nothing. One time I asked the Mexican why he didn't go back and take out the money.

" 'I didn't want none of it,' he says. 'I never put it in the ground. 'Twa'n't mine any more'n that white man's.'

"A few days after he saw the money, though, he went back and scratched around in the dirt a little and picked up an old Mexican square dollar. He brung it to Roma and bought some flour and some coffee and some candy, and give some of the candy to my wife. She was living down there and knowed the man well and she's told me many a time how she et some of the candy the Mexican bought with that old square dollar. I always have thought the money was intinded

115

for him, but you know how some people are, and I can't say as I blame him for not teching what he hadn't a right to. If buried money like that is intinded for a human, he'll come by it jes' easy and nach'al. But if it's not intinded, he won't come by it, no matter how much he hunts. Even if he did find it and it wa'n't intinded for him, it ud prove a curse. I'd be afraid of it myself.

"Lemme tell you something. Down there som'er's below Realitos in one of them sand mottes is an old dug well with six jack loads of Mexican silver in it. Nobody ain't a-going to get it neither. When the bandits captured it, they found the rangers was right on top of 'em; so they jes' pitched silver, dead burros, dead men, and all right down in the well. Then they got cleaned up theyselves.

"Well, one of the rangers a long time afterwards got on to the stuff somehow. So he went and bought the land what the well was on and set a bunch of Mexicans to clean it out. After a while they struck bones. They hollered to the white man, who was bossing on top, and he hollered for them to come on up and let him down. They wa'n't a bit slow coming up.

"When the white man got down there, the first thing he done was to grab holt of a corner of an old *maleta* what he seen sticking out among the bones. He jerked it out and it had the dollars in it all right. Then he looked up and yelled to the Mexicans to pull. He hadn't more'n got the words outen his mouth when he seen a tall skiliton standing alongside the wall of that well. Its toes was right next to hisen and it must of been forty feet tall. It retched clear up to the top, and its face away up there was a-looking down at the white man. He couldn't take his eyes offen it, and all the way up while them Mexicans was a-pulling him slow and jerky he had to look that skiliton in the face. He forgot all about the *maleta* of money and dropped it back, and when he clumb out he was so weak they had to help him on his horse. They managed to get him home and put him to bed, and that night he died. Ain't nobody what I know of undertook to get them six jack loads since."

Pete arose to tinker with the coals around his bean-pot and put a little more water in it before going to bed.

"None of these new-fangled shiny pots cain't make frijoles black and sweet like an old iron kittle," he said.

"That's right, Pete. Hear that owl?"

"Owl in August, rain shore. Gonna be some juicy calf ribs this fall."

THE MEASURE OF A WAGON ROD

Belas Carter has a right to certain shady spots in Wichita Falls, where nowadays he can be found. Seven times through sun and storm he drove up the trail; then for years he was a hand on the three-million-acre X I T Ranch. Before he quit riding, he had this story to exchange around the chuck wagon.[3]

"While I was working for the X I T's in eighty-six, another feller named Jackson and me were sent to rep[4] with the L F D roundup over on the Pecos. With eight good horses apiece and a pack mule, we left Spring Lake before sunup, camped out that night, and the next afternoon about two o'clock came in sight of the Pecos River. We were making for a crossing about twenty miles above Roswell and expected to find the L F D wagon somewhere on the other side.

"It was all prairie country and we could see for a long piece. There was a crowd of horsemen down clost to the river, and directly we saw two of them light out in a neck-and-neck race. Then we saw them go back to where the others were. Next come a shot, one of the riders fell, and the rest of the outfit clumb the hurrikin decks of their ponies and took out. I never saw nor heard of them again.

"When Jackson and I got to the place, there lay a man shot through the neck and bleeding something turrible. We carried him over into the shade of a little abandoned 'dobe hut clost by, and then Jackson roped out the best horse in our string and headed for Roswell to fetch a doctor. The way he lit out I could see there wasn't any grass going to grow under his horse's feet.

"Meantime I'd clamped my thumb and finger on the artery where the blood was flowing from the wounded man. He begun to cough and jerked the artery loose, and the blood spurted so bad I thought he'd die the next minute. He thought so, too, and as soon as I clamped the artery back begun to talk about himself. Said as how he'd been a pretty bad man, that the jig was up now, and he wanted me to have his horses and guns and what money he had. He seemed awful grateful to me. He was a lone wolf, and, though I didn't know his name or he mine, I was the only friend he had in the world.

"He told me that he and four other men had robbed the bank at Monterrey, in Mexico. Before they could get across the Rio Grande, two of them were shot by *rurales*, and after they crossed over, some Texas officers got two more of them. That left him with a pack horse loaded with eighteen thousand dollars. Most of it was in gold dou-

118

bloons worth about twenty dollars apiece. He decided that the safest place for him was Montana.

"But he was a hunted man, and traveling that way with a pack of gold was ticklish business. He had to keep dodging and couldn't course straight. When he got up on the Brazos about the mouth of the Clear Fork, he decided he'd better hide the money and get it later. So in the night he goes to a ranch house and stole the bean-pot and wagon rod from a chuck wagon. Then he buried the money.

"It took him a long time to tell me all this, for he kept having coughing spells and was awful tired. He got weaker and weaker, until about sundown I saw he was going. All the time I was a-holding his neck trying to stop the blood. Then he pulled me down and whispered: 'Cut open the handle of my war bag and you'll find a written description of where the money is buried. It's sure there and it's all yours.' Then he died.

"Well, before he got cold and while I was still sorter straightening him out, I heard a horse a-galloping. But it wasn't the doctor. The man introduced himself as the sheriff of Lincoln County. Lincoln County at that time took in about a fourth of New Mexico. It turned out that when Jackson got to Roswell and told that a man was shot, this sheriff got the word quicker than the doctor. In them days a man with a bullet hole in him generally didn't need a doctor nohow.

"It was about dark; so I pulled the saddles off mine and the dead man's horses, hobbled them, and turned them loose to graze. I laid the saddles beside the door of the old 'dobe house. Then after we'd et supper I told the sheriff the man had given his things to me.

" 'No,' says the sheriff, 'you ain't got no witnesses to that deal, and the law will have to take charge of the dead man's property.'

"I didn't say anything, but I was determined to have the description of the buried money. I'd already noticed that the dead man's war bag was something unusual with a fancy handle. We generally used just an old sack to carry our duffle in, you know. Along in the night I slipped up, cut the handle of the bag open, and pulled out a piece of paper that was rolled into a tight wad. I just stuck it down in my breeches to wait for daylight to read by.

"The doctor and Jackson rode in during the night. The next morning we got a spade from the L F D wagon, which was about five miles away, and buried the dead outlaw. Then the sheriff took his property and left.

"This is what the paper read: 'Buried one mile of Fort Belknap. 256

steps North of a little creek and 86 steps West of a prickly pear marked swallow-fork. $18,000 is in a bean-pot, the depth of a wagon rod with half the ring sticking out of the ground and three small rocks piled against the ring.'

"Fort Belknap, on the Brazos, was at that time abandoned. A wagon rod is forty-two inches long. So the money was buried pretty deep. I figgered the ear-mark in the prickly pear leaf would be easy to find. There was another description.

"It read: '2½ miles up that branch on the West bank under a large mesquite tree with a limb projecting West, buried 2½ feet deep in the crevice of a rock and wrapped in a Mexican blanket is a Winchester, a six-shooter, and 50 dollars Mexican gold. The crevice is filled up with loose gravel.'

"Well, this last wad of stuff I found. I had to look over a good many prickly pear bushes before I found a leaf marked swallow-fork. The ring on the end of the wagon rod was barely exposed above the surface of the ground. I had actually kicked away the three little rocks piled against it and was about to dig, when I saw a horseman. He saw me too. I gave the ring a stamp with my boot heel so as to drive it out of sight, and then moved to one side. The stranger riding up claimed to be the owner of the land. He did not want any trespassing and he followed me clear out of his range.

"I figgered that I'd go back in a day or two when he was off guard and dig up the money. The first time I went back was at night and I couldn't locate the wagon rod ring. The next time was in broad daylight, but I still couldn't locate it. I played hob when I kicked those rocks away and stamped it down. Still, I thought I'd get the bearing easy enough from that swallow-fork in the pear leaf. The leaf was gone. I guess some cow ate it up, for that was a hard year and cattle were chewing pear lots. You can figger out for yourself how many years back this was. I've been trying off and on ever since to locate the place. I made investigation and found out that the Monterrey bank was really robbed in the way the dying outlaw told me it had been. Within a mile of old Fort Belknap the $18,000 is still down in the ground at the end of a wagon rod waiting to be dug up.

"As the outlaw said when he gave it to me, it's all yours."

CHAPTER VI

Post Hole Banks

*I used to hear the early settlers tell how a cow and calf was legal
tender for ten dollars. Even if a man paid in gold—say forty dollars
for a horse—he might say he gave "four cows and calves" for it. So the
banks were logically just cowpens.*
Brushy Joe's Reminiscences

"The methods of business were in keeping with the primitive conditions of society," says a chronicler of the open range of southern
Texas.[1] "There were no banks in the country. Consequently every
ranch home was the depository of more or less money. The coin, if of
considerable amount, was put in saddle bags, *morrals*, etc., and secreted in remote corners of the house or up under the roof or it was
buried; it could be brought forth from its hiding place as occasion
demanded. . . . In buying stock the ranchmen brought the money in
gold and silver to where the animals were to be received and there
paid it out dollar by dollar. They generally carried the gold in leather
belts buckled around their waists, but the silver, being more bulky,
was carried in ducking sacks on a pack horse or mule. . . . It was a
matter of current knowledge that one thousand dollars in silver
weighed sixty-two and one-half pounds. . . .

"One time a rancher near the line between Karnes and Goliad counties decided to bury a considerable amount of money that he had on
hand. Choosing an especially dark night, he went down to the cowpen
and, after removing one of the fence posts, dropped his bag of gold in
the post hole. He then replaced the post and went to bed satisfied that
he had put his treasure where moth and rust could not corrupt nor
thieves break through and steal. After a year or two had gone by, he
needed the money and went to get it. He had failed to mark the particular post under which it was buried and time had obliterated all
trace of his work. There was but one thing for him to do and he did it.
He dug up post after post until he came to the right one, and by that
time half his pen was torn down."

I don't know whether old Tolbert forgot his post hole or not. He ranched on the Frio, and, as the saying goes, was "stingy enough to skin a flea for its hide and taller." He would never kill a maverick no matter how hungry he was for meat, but would always brand it. He never bought sugar or molasses; "sow bosom," even of the saltiest variety, was a rare luxury; he and his men made out on "poor doe"— often jerked—javelina meat, and frijoles. When he "worked" and had an outfit to feed, he always instructed the *cocinero* to cook the bread early so that it would be cold and hard, and thus go further by the time the hands got to it. He distrusted banks, and during a good part of his life there were no banks to trust. The practice of keeping money on the premises suited him finely.

When he died, none of his money could be found. So, even till this day, people dig for it around the old ranch house. One evening about twenty years ago a man who was working on the place saw two strangers in a wagon go down a ravine that runs near the ranch. He thought they were deer hunters; but when they passed him on their way out next morning, he noted that one of them had a shotgun across his knees and that they avoided conversation. While riding down the ravine a few days later, the ranch hand found that the wagon tracks led from a fresh hole under a live oak tree and that near the hole were pieces of rusted steel hinges with marks of a cold chisel on them. However, not many people believe that the two strangers got Tolbert's money.

Berry got that—and he never hunted for it either. Years ago Berry bought the Tolbert ranch and went to live on it. One day when he had nothing else for his Mexican, Pedro, to do, he told him to put some new posts in the old corral fence. Pedro worked along digging holes and putting in new posts until near ten o'clock. Then at the third post to the east from the south gate he struck something so hard that it turned the edge of his spade. He was used to digging post holes in rocky soil with a crowbar to loosen it and a tin can to dip it out, and so he went to a mesquite tree where the tools were kept and got the crowbar.

But the crowbar would no more dig into the hard substance than the spade would. The sun was mighty hot anyhow; so the Mexican went up to the house where *el señor* Berry was whittling sticks on the gallery and told him that he couldn't dig any more. "Why, *señor*," he said, "in that third hole from the south gate the devil has humped himself into a rock that nothing can get through."

Berry snorted around considerably at first, but directly he seemed to think of something and told his man, very well, not to dig any more but to saddle up and go out and bring in the main remuda. Now, only the day before they had had the main remuda in the pen and had caught out fresh mounts to keep in the little horse pasture. By this time the released horses would be scattered clear away on the back side of the pasture. The Mexican wondered why his *amo* wanted the remuda again. But it was none of his business. Well, the ride would take him all the rest of the day, and at least he would not have to dig any more post holes before *mañana*.

After Pedro had saddled his horse and drunk a *cafecito* for lunch and fooled away half an hour putting in new stirrup-leather strings and finally had got out of sight, Berry slouched down to the pens. He came back to his shade on the gallery and whittled for an hour or so longer until everything around the *jacal*, even the road-runners and Pedro's wife, was taking a siesta. Then he pulled off his spurs, which always dragged with a big clink when he walked, and went down to the pen again. The spade and the crowbar were where the Mexican had left them fall. Berry punched the crowbar down into the half-made hole. It almost bounced out of his hand, and he heard a kind of metallic thud. No, it was not flint-rock that had stopped the digging.

Berry went around back of the water trough to the huisache where his horse was tied and led him into the pen. Then he started to work. He began digging two or three feet out to one side of the hole. The dry ground was packed from the tramp of thousands of cattle and horses. He had to use the crowbar to loosen the soil. But it was no great task to remove a patch of earth two or three feet square and eighteen or twenty inches deep. Berry knew what he was about, and as he scraped the loosened earth out with his spade he could feel a flat metal surface that seemed to have rivets in it.

It was the lid of a chest. When he had uncovered it, Berry placed one of the new posts so that he could use it as a fulcrum for the crowbar. With that he levered up the end of the chest. As he suspected, it was too heavy and too tightly wedged in the soil for him to lift. He worked a chunk under the raised end of the chest and then looped a stout rope over it. Next, he mounted his horse and dallied the free end of the rope around the horn of his saddle. He had dragged cows out of the bog on that horse, and he knew that the chest was not so heavy as a cow. He had but fifty yards to drag it before he was in the brush, where undetected he could pry the lid off.

When the Mexican got back that night his *mujer* told him that Señor Berry had gone to San Antonio in the buckboard and that he had left word for the remuda to be turned back into the big pasture and for the repair of the corrals to be continued.

"They say" that the deposit Berry made at the Frost National Bank was a clean $17,000, nearly all in silver.

Will McNabb, of Matagorda, on the Gulf coast, while digging post holes a few years ago had a chance at a fortune probably greater than Berry's, but he did not realize it until too late—until he had lost the right post hole. In a certain hole about two feet deep he uncovered eighteen Spanish dollars dated from 1752 to 1814, all neatly stacked one on top of the other and held together by rust from what had probably been an iron brace. The land where he was running the fence is marshy, and six inches below the dollars McNabb hit soil spongy enough "to bog a saddle blanket." He knows now that he found only a few coins out of a heavy, iron-bound chest that sank long ago; at the time he found them, however, the idea of a whole chest of dollars far beneath them and the possibility of sinking a well to recover the fortune did not occur to him. When the idea did occur, he could not even guess what post marked the right place to dig. Putting a well down at every post in a fence line across a marsh would be altogether too expensive a gamble against even a chest—perhaps a pirate chest—of money.

"Uncle Jack" Wilkerson came to Texas from Mississippi in the early days and began ranching in Menard County. Before long he and his partner, Wat Key, were raising cattle by the thousands and were trailing them to New Orleans, Kansas, and other places where they could find a market. Each had a family and they lived close together. Wilkerson was banker for the firm. He would have nothing but gold; he kept it buried in an abandoned smokehouse made of adobe.

When in 1872 he left for New Orleans with a trail herd, Wat Key having gone to Abilene, Kansas, with another herd, Mrs. Wilkerson remained in charge of the ranch. One day a cow dog looking for a cool place in which to take a nap entered the old smokehouse and scratched up the money, scattering it over the floor. When Mrs. Wilkerson discovered the mischief, she called Mrs. Key and together they picked up the coins. It took them some time to do this; the gold amounted to about $10,000. After it was all gathered, they put it in a

fruit jar; then, saying that she would go bury it in a place where it would not be disturbed, Mrs. Wilkerson went off alone towards the corrals.

Shortly after this Mrs. Wilkerson became very ill—so ill that she remained most of the time in a state of coma. She rapidly grew worse. Several times, however, she roused into a kind of dim consciousness, at which times she said to Mrs. Key, her constant attendant, "It seems there is something I want to tell you." That was as far as she ever got in telling whatever was on her mind. In a few days she died.

It was weeks later that Jack Wilkerson received word of his wife's death, and then he was nearly home. All Mrs. Key could tell him about the $10,000 in gold was that his wife had carried it in a fruit jar towards the corrals. First and last he dug up most of the posts, but only a few years ago he stated that, so far as he knew, the money had never been found. Other people have been searching for it ever since he moved away from the old ranch quarters.

"One day," relates a young ranchman of the Menard country, "I passed the Wilkerson ranch site while I was gathering some steers. The yard in which the house once stood looked as if it had been plowed. Every inch of dirt inside the ruined foundation had been spaded up. Some distance from the house I came upon a trench about twenty feet long. The upper end of it was shallow, but at the lower end it was perhaps three feet deep. There I noticed a thin flat rock lying on the floor of the trench. I got down off my horse and picked it up. Under it was a hole about the size and shape that a half-gallon fruit jar would occupy. When I told Uncle Jack about it, he said that it was too far away from the house to have been the place where his wife buried the money. That's all I know; there are people in the country who talk as if they knew more."

CHAPTER VII

Midas on a Goatskin

High on a throne of royal state, which far
Outshone the wealth of Ormus and of Ind.
Paradise Lost

"He's the second sorriest white man in Sabinal," my host said. "The sorriest white man keeps a Mexican woman without marrying her, but Dee Davis lawfully wedded his *pelada*. He's town scavenger, works at night, and sleeps most of the day. He'll probably be awake 'long about four o'clock this evening and more than ready to tell you the kind of yarns you want to hear."

We found Dee Davis just awaking from his siesta. He occupied a one-roomed shack and sat on a goatskin in the door, on the shady side of the house.

"I'm a great hand for goatskins," he said. "They make good settin' and they make good pallets."

I sat in a board-bottomed chair out on the hard, swept ground, shaded by an umbrella-China tree as well as by the wall. The shack was set back in a yard fenced with barbed wire. Within the same enclosure but farther towards the front was a little frame house occupied by Dee Davis' Mexican wife and their three or four half-breed children. The yard, or patio, was gay with red and orange zinnias and blue morning-glories. Out in a ramshackle picket corral to the rear a boy was playing with a burro.

"No, mister," went on Dee Davis, who had got strung out in no time, "I don't reckon anything ever would have come of my dad's picking up those silver bars if it hadn't of been for a surveyor over in Del Rio.

"You see, Dad and Uncle Ben were frontiersmen of the old style and while they'd had a lot of experiences—yes, mister, a lot of experiences—they didn't know a thing about minerals. Well, along back in the eighties they took up some state land on Mud Creek and begun trying to farm a little. Mud Creek's east of Del Rio. The old Spanish crossing on Mud was worn deep and always washed, but it was still used a little. Well, one day not long after an awful rain, a reg'lar gully-washer and fence-lifter, Dad and Uncle Ben started to town. They were going down into the creek when, by heifers, what should show up right square in the old trail but the corner of some sort of metal bar. They got down out of their buggy and pried the bar out and then three other bars. The stuff was so heavy that after they put it in the buggy they had to walk and lead the horse. Instead of going on into town with it, they went back home. Well, they turned it over to Ma and then more or less forgot all about it, I guess—just went on struggling for a living.

"At that time I was still a kid and was away from home working for the San Antonio Land and Cattle Company, but I happened to ride in just a few days after the find. The Old Man and Uncle Ben never mentioned it, but Ma was so proud she was nearly busting, and as soon as I got inside the house she said she wanted to show me something. In one of the rooms was a bed with an old-timey covering on it that came down to the floor. She carried me to this bed, pulled up part of the cover that draped over the floor, and told me to look. I looked, and, by heifers, there was bars as big as hogs. Yes, mister, as big as hogs.

"Nothing was done, however. We were a long ways from any kind of buying center and never saw anybody. As I said in the beginning, I don't know how long those bars might have stayed right there under that bed if it hadn't been for the surveyor. I won't call his name, because he's still alive and enjoying the fruits of his visit. My dad was a mighty interesting talker, and this surveyor used to come to see him just to hear him talk. Well, on one of these visits he stayed all night and slept on the bed that hid the bars. One of his shoes got under the bed, and next morning in stooping down to get it he saw the bars. At least that's the explanation he gave. Then, of course, he got the whole story as to how the bars came to be there and where they were dug up.

" 'What you going to do with 'em?' he asked Dad.

" 'Oh, I don't know,' Dad says to him. 'Nothing much, I guess. Ma here figgers the stuff might be silver, but I don't know what it is. More'n likely it's not anything worth having.'

" 'Well,' says the surveyor, 'you'd better let me get it assayed. I'm going down to Piedras Negras in my waggin next week and can take it along as well as not.'

"The upshot was that he took all the bars. Two or three months later when Dad saw him and asked him how the assay turned out, he kinder laughed and says, 'Aw pshaw, 'twan't nothing but babbitting.' Then he went on to explain how he'd left the whole caboodle down there to Piedras Negras because it wasn't worth hauling back.

"Well, it wasn't but a short time before we noticed this surveyor, who had been dog poor, was building a good house and buying land. He always seemed to have money and went right up. Also, he quit coming round to visit his old friend. Yes, mister, quit coming round.

"Some years went by and Dad died. The country had been consider'bly fenced up, though it's nothing but a ranch country yet, and the roads were changed. I was still follering cows, over in Old Mexico a good part of the time. Nobody was left out on Mud Creek. Uncle Ben had moved to Del Rio. One day when I was in there I asked him if he could go back to the old trail crossing on Mud. The idea of them bars and of there being more where they come from seemed to stick in my head.

" 'Sure, I can go to the crossing,' says Uncle Ben. 'It's right on the Spanish Trail. Furthermore, it's plainly marked by the ruins of an old house on the east bank.'

" 'Well,' says I, 'we'll go over there sometime when we have a day to spare.'

"Finally, two or three years later, we got off. First we went up to the ruins of the house. About all left of it was a tumble-down stick-and-mud chimney.

"Uncle Ben and Dad, you understand, found the bars right down the bank from this place. Just across the creek, on the side next to Del Rio, was a motte of *palo blanco* [hackberry] trees. The day was awfully hot and we crossed back over there to eat our dinner under the shade and rest up a little before we dug any. About the time we got our horses staked, I noticed a little cloud in the northwest. In less than an hour it was raining pitchforks and bob-tailed heifer yearlings, and Mud Creek was tearing down with enough water to swim a steamboat. There was nothing for us to do but go back to Del Rio.

"I've never been back to hunt those bars since. That was close to forty years ago. A good part of that time I've been raising a family, but my youngest boy—the one out there fooling with the burro—is nine years old now. As soon as he's twelve and able to shift for himself a little, I'm going back into that country and make several investigations."

Old Dee shifted his position on the goatskin.

"My eyes won't stand much light," he explained. "I have worked so long at night that I can see better in the darkness than in the daylight."

I noticed that his eyes were weak, but they had a strange light in them. It was very pleasant as we sat there in the shade, by the bright zinnias and the soft morning-glories. Pretty soon Dee Davis would have to milk his cow and then in the dark do his work as scavenger for the town. Still there was no hurry. Dee Davis's mind was far away from scavenger filth. He went on.

"You see, the old Spanish Trail crossed over into Texas from Mexico at the mouth of the Pecos River, came on east, circling Seminole Hill just west of Devil's River, on across Mud Creek, and then finally to San Antonio. From there it went to New Orleans. It was the route used by the *antiguas* for carrying their gold and silver out of Mexico to New Orleans. The country was full of Indians; it's still full of dead Spaniards and of bullion and bags of money that the Indians captured and buried or caused the original owners to bury.

"Seminole Hill hides a lot of that treasure. They say that a big jag of Quantrill's loot is located about Seminole too, but I never took much stock in this guerrilla treasure. But listen, mister, and I'll tell you about something that I do take consider'ble stock in.

"Last winter an old Mexican *pastor* named Santiago was staying here in Sabinal with some of his *parientes*. He's a little bit kin to my wife. Now, about nine-tenths of the time a sheepherder don't have a thing to do but explore every cave and examine every rock his sheep get close to. Santiago had a dog that did most of the actual herding. Well, two years ago this fall he was herding sheep about Seminole Hill.

"According to his story—and I don't doubt his word—he went pirooting into a cave one day and stepped right on top of more money than he'd ever seen before all put together. It was just laying there on the floor, some of it stacked up and some of it scattered around every which way. He begun to gather some of it up and had put three pieces in his *jato*—a kind of wallet, you know, that *pastores* carry their provisions in—when he heard the terriblest noise behind him he had ever heard in all his born days. He said it was like the sounds of trace-chains rattling, and dried cowhides being drug at the end of a rope, and panther yells, and the groans of a dying man all mixed up. He was scared half out of his skin. He got out of the cave as fast as his legs would carry him.

"An hour or so later, when he'd kinder collected his wits, he discovered three of the coins still in his *jato*. They were old square 'dobe dollars like the Spanish used to make. As soon as he got a chance, he took them to Villa Acuna across the river from Del Rio, and there a barkeeper traded him three bottles of beer and three silver dollars, American, for them.

"Well, you know how superstitious Mexicans are. Wild horses couldn't drag old Santiago back inside that cave, but he promised to take me out there and show me the mouth of it. We were just waiting for milder weather when somebody sent in here and got him to herd sheep. Maybe he'll be back this winter. If he is, we'll go out to the cave. It won't take but a day."

Dee Davis rolled another cigarette from his supply of Black Horse leaf tobacco and corn shucks. His Mexican wife, plump and easygoing, came out into the yard and began watering the flowers from a tin can. He hardly noticed her, though as he glanced in her direction he seemed to inhale his smoke with a trifle more of deliberation. He was a spare man, and gray moustaches that drooped in Western sheriff style hid only partly a certain nervousness of the facial muscles; yet his few gestures and low voice were as deliberate—and as natural—as the flop of a burro's ears.

"What I'd rather get at than Santiago's cave," he resumed, "is that old smelter across the Rio Grande in Mexico just below the mouth of the Pecos. That smelter wasn't put there to grind corn on, or to boil frijoles in, or to roast goat ribs over, or anything like that. No, mister, not for anything like that.

"It's kinder under a bluff that fronts the river. I know one ranchman who had an expert mining engineer with him, and they spent a whole week exploring up and down the bluff and back in the mountains. I could of told them in a minute that the mine was not above the mouth of the Pecos. If it had of been above, the trails made by miners carrying *parihuelas* could still be seen. I've peered over every foot of that ground and not a *parihuela* trace is there. You don't know what a *parihuela* is? Well, it's a kind of hod, shaped like a stretcher, with a pair of handles in front and a pair behind so two men can carry it. That's what the slave Indians carried ore on.

"No, sir, the mine that supplied that smelter—and it was a big mine—was below the mouth of the Pecos. It's covered up now by a bed of gravel that has probably washed in there during the last eighty or ninety years. All a man has to do to uncover the shaft is to take a few teams and scrapers and clear out the gravel. The mouth of the

shaft will then be as plain as daylight. That will take a little capital. You ought to do this. I wish you would. All I want is a third for my information.

"Now, there is an old lost mine away back in the Santa Rosa Mountains that the Mexicans called El Lipano. The story goes that the Lipan Indians used to work it. It was gold and as rich as twenty-dollar gold pieces. El Lipano didn't have no smelter. The Lipans didn't need one.

"And I want to tell you that those Lipan Indians could smell gold as far as a hungry coyote can smell fresh liver. Yes, mister, they could smell it. One time out there in the Big Bend an old-timey Lipan came to D. C. Bourland's ranch and says to him, 'Show me the *tinaja* I'm looking for and I'll show you the gold.' He got down on his hands and knees and showed how his people used to pound out gold ornaments in the rock *tinajas* across the Rio Grande from Reagan Canyon.

"Now that long bluff overlooking the lost mine in the gravel I was just speaking about hides something worth while. I guess maybe you never met old Uncle Dick Sanders. I met him the first time while I was driving through the Indian Territory up the trail to Dodge. He was government interpreter for the Comanche Indians at Fort Sill and was a great hombre among them.

"Well, several years ago an old, old Comanche who was dying sent for Uncle Dick.

" 'I'm dying,' the Comanche says. 'I want nothing more on this earth. You can do nothing for me. But you have been a true friend to me and my people. Before I leave, I want to do you a favor.'

"Then the old Indian, as Uncle Dick Sanders reported the facts to me, went on to tell how when he was a young buck he was with a party raiding horses below the Rio Grande. He said that while they were on a long bluff just south of the river they saw a Spanish cart train winding among the mountains. The soldiers to guard it were riding ahead, and while they were going down into a canyon out of sight, the Comanches made a dash, cut off three *carretas*, and killed the drivers.

"There wasn't a thing in the *carretas* but rawhide bags full of gold and silver coins. Well, this disgusted the Comanches mightily. Yes, mister, disgusted them. They might make an ornament out of a coin now and then, but they didn't know how to trade with money. They traded with buffalo robes and horses.

"So what they did now with the rawhide sacks was to cut them open and pour the gold and silver into some deep cracks they happened to notice in the long bluff. Two or three of the sacks, though, they brought over to this side of the Rio Grande and hid in a hole. Then they piled rocks over the hole. This place was between two forks, the old Comanche said, one a running river walled with rock and the other a deep, dry canyon. Not far below where the canyon emptied into the river, the river itself emptied into the Rio Grande.

"After the Comanche got through explaining all this to Uncle Dick Sanders, he asked for a lump of charcoal and a dressed deerskin. Then he drew on the skin a sketch of the Rio Grande, the bluffs to the south, a stream with a west prong coming in from the north, and the place of the buried coins. Of course he didn't put names on the map. The only name he knew was Río Grande del Norte. When Sanders came down here looking for the Comanche stuff, of course he brought the map with him and he showed it to me. The charcoal lines had splotched until you could hardly trace them, but Sanders had got an Indian to trace them over with a kind of greenish paint.

"Uncle Dick had some sort of theory that the Comanche had mistook the Frio River for the Rio Grande. Naturally he hadn't got very far in locating the ground, much less the money. He was disgusted with the whole business. Told me I could use his information and have whatever I found. I'm satisfied that Devil's River and Painted Cave Canyon are the forks that the Indians hid the *maletas* of money between, and the long bluff on the south side of the Rio Grande where they poured coins into the chinks is the same bluff I've been talking about."

Dee Davis got up, reached for a stick, squatted on the ground, and outlined the deerskin map that Uncle Dick Sanders had shown him. Then he sat down again on the goatskin and contemplated the map in silence.

It was wonderfully pleasant sitting there in the shade, the shadows growing longer and the evening growing cooler, listening—whether to Dee Davis or to a hummingbird in the morning-glories. I did not want the tales to stop. I remarked that I had just been out in the Big Bend country and had camped on Reagan Canyon, famed for its relation to the Lost Nigger Mine. I expected that Dee Davis would know something about this. He did.

"Now listen," he interposed in his soft voice, "I don't expect you to tell me all you know about the Lost Nigger Mine, and I know some things I can't tell you. You'll understand that. You see I was *vaciero* for a string of *pastores* in that very country and got a good deal farther into the mountains, I guess, than any of the Reagans ever got. You may not believe me, but I'll swear on a stack of Bibles as high as your head that I can lead you straight to the nigger who found the mine. Of course I can't tell you where he is. You'll understand that. It was this away.

"One morning the Reagans sent Bill Kelley—that's the nigger's name—to hunt a horse that had got away with the saddle on. A few hours later Jim Reagan rode up on the nigger and asked him if he had found the horse.

" 'No, sah,' the nigger says, 'but jes' looky here, Mister Jim, I'se foun' a gold mine.'

" 'Damn your soul,' says Jim Reagan, 'we're not paying you to hunt gold mines. Pull your freight and bring in that horse.'

"Yes, mister, that's the way Jim Reagan took the news of the greatest gold mine that's ever been found in the Southwest—but he repented a million times afterwards.

"Well, as you've no doubt heard, the nigger got wind of how he was going to be pitched into the Rio Grande and so that night he lit a shuck on one of the Reagan horses. Then a good while afterwards when the Reagans found out how they'd played the wilds in running off, you might say, the goose that laid the golden egg, they started in to trail him down. No telling how many thousands of dollars they did spend trying to locate Nigger Bill—the only man who could put his hand on the gold.

"I've knowed a lot of the men who looked for the Lost Nigger Mine. Not one of them has gone to the right place. One other thing I'll tell you. Go to that round mountain down in the *vegas* on the Mexican side just opposite the old Reagan camp. They call this mountain El Diablo, also Nigger-head; some calls it El Capitan. Well, about half way up it is a kind of shelf, or mesa, maybe two acres wide. On this shelf close back against the mountain wall is a *chapote* bush. Look under that *chapote* and you'll see a hole about the size of an old-timey dug well. Look down this hole and you'll see an old ladder—the kind made without nails, rungs being tied on the poles with rawhide and the fibre of Spanish dagger. Well, right by that hole, back a little and sorter hid behind the *chapote*, I once upon a time found a *mecapal*. I guess you want me to tell you what this is. It's a kind of basket in which Mexican miners used to carry up their ore. It's fastened on the head and shoulders.

"Now, I never heard of a *mecapal* being used to haul water up in. And I didn't see any water in that hole. No, mister, I didn't see any water.

"As I said, as soon as my boy gets to be twelve years old—he's nine now—I'm going out in that country and use some of the knowledge I've been accumulating."

Dee Davis leaned over and began lacing the brogan shoes on his stockingless feet. It was about time for him to begin work. But I was loath to leave. How pleasant it was there! Maybe Dee Davis is "the second sorriest white man in Sabinal." I don't know, but it seemed to me then, and it seems to me still, that there are many ways of living worse than the way of this village scavenger with a soft goatskin to sit on, and aromatic Black Horse tobacco to inhale leisurely through a clean white shuck, and bright zinnias and blue morning-glories in the dooryard, and long siestas while the shadows of evening lengthen to soften the light of day, and an easy-going Mexican wife, and playing around a patient burro out in the corral an urchin that will be twelve *mañana*, as it were, and then————. Then silver bars out of Mud Creek as big as hogs—and heaps of old square 'dobe dollars in Santiago's cave on Seminole Hill—and Uncle Dick Sanders' gold in the chinks of the long bluff across the Rio Grande—and somewhere in the gravel down under the bluff a rich mine that a few mules and scrapers might uncover in a day—and, maybe so, the golden Lipano out in the Santa Rosas beyond—and, certainly and above all, the great Lost Nigger Mine of free gold far up the Rio Bravo in the solitude of the Big Bend.

Dee Davis is just one of Coronado's children.

CHAPTER VIII

The Lost Nigger Mine

Gold is where you find it.
Prospectors' Proverb

After twisting southward all the way from its source high up in the Rocky Mountains of Colorado, the Río Grande del Norte veers southeast at El Paso as if to shoot straight for the Gulf of Mexico. For three hundred miles—measuring as the crow flies and not as the stream winds—it keeps this general course; then it turns sharply to cut northeast for more than a hundred miles before it resumes its gulfward trend. The great bow thus made, its string the Southern Pacific Railroad and its arc the Rio Grande, is known as the Big Bend country of Texas.

It is a land of mountain, canyon, and mesa grown over with greasewood, coarse chino grass, dagger, and thorned brush. There are, too, stretches of fine grazing land. Here ranching still is—and forever will be—undisturbed by the plow; here land is measured by the section rather than by the acre, and anything less than forty sections makes "a little ranch." Although a majority of the pastures are abundantly watered, certain far-stretched areas are devoid both of surface springs and of underground veins within tapping distance of the drill. A solitary *tinaja* called Pata de Venado, at which a man and his horse can barely get a drink, is famed two hundred miles away.

Like all soil that has not been transformed by so-called improvements, the Big Bend is a land of traditions. Outlandish pictures painted on the sides of caves by aborigines tell a story that no white man can now decipher; rings of blackened rocks show where Apaches roasted sotol for food. Somewhere in this jagged and gashed land legend has placed a lost canyon, its board floor carpeted with grass that is always green and watered by gushing springs, its palisaded walls imprisoning a herd of buffaloes—the only buffaloes in all probability that ever entered that rough, thirsty region. Somewhere in this land credulity has fixed a petrified forest with tree trunks "seven hundred feet long."

Down in the most remote rincon of the Bend, the Chisos (Phantom) Mountains hide a Spanish mine, the entrance to which was once visible at sunrise from the ancient church of San Vicente across the river. The Big Bend is a strange country where strange characters have lived and yet live—characters like Alice Stillwell Henderson, who single-handed dared fifty Mexican cow thieves, and like "Don Militón" Favor, whose ranch on the Chihuahua Trail was a fort and who alone made treaties with savage tribes. It is a country where strange things have happened and where anything may yet happen.

Across the awful gorge that bounds the Big Bend, the wild, broken country belongs to the deer, the javelina, the panther, and the bear. A great stretch of it a hundred miles long and sixty miles broad has not since the Madero Revolution twenty years ago desolated northern Mexico contained enough cattle or horses to tempt even the bandits. Vacant and silent, it, too, is a land where many strange things have happened and where anything may happen—a land of stories.

And the greatest story of all the Big Bend country and of all the Mexican wasteland across the river is the story of the Lost Nigger Mine. It is not an old story like that of the San Saba Mine; some of the chief contributors to it are still living. The mine is supposed to be either above the mouth of Reagan Canyon, in Brewster County, on the Texas side, or else across the river in the Ladrones (Robber) Mountains, the odds favoring Mexico. From the railroad it is seventy-five miles, with only one house to pass, to the mouth of Reagan Canyon.

I have led a pack mule down the trail that follows Reagan Canyon and I have camped where the dark waters of the Río Bravo swishing under the stars make that part of the world seem as remote as it was when Cabeza de Vaca wandered across Texas.

"How far is it up the river to your next neighbor?" I asked Rol Rutledge, who had guided me down to his camp.

"Well," he answered, "it's about fifteen miles on up to where Juan Español lives. He killed his goat-herder not long ago because the herder wouldn't tell him where he had picked up a strange rock."

"How far is it down the river to your next neighbor?"

"There ain't no neighbors down the river. The way a man has to ride, you go on down for fifty miles without finding a crossing. Then you come to where three trails just pitch off the bluff—Las Veredas Coloradas, the Mexicans call them. This is the famous Shafter Crossing."

Along about 1884 the four Reagan brothers, John, Jim, Frank, and Lee, moved their cattle from the Pecos down San Francisco Creek, through Bullis Gap, and against the Rio Grande. The country was all open and unclaimed. The canyon near which they made headquarters camp soon became known as Reagan Canyon. Here the river could be forded, and here it was forded quite frequently. There was stock to drive into Mexico from Texas and there was stock to be driven into Texas from Mexico—and there were no inspectors. Occasionally the Reagans used also the *paso* at the mouth of Maravillas Canyon fifteen miles up the river. The Southern Pacific Railroad connecting San Antonio with El Paso had just been completed. Sometimes the Reagans went to Sanderson, sometimes to Dryden; either place afforded shipping pens, groceries, and liquor.

On one trip to Dryden, one of the Reagan boys saw a Seminole negro who wanted a job and hired him. He had been raised in the Santa Rosa Mountains below Del Rio; he spoke only a few words of English, and his Spanish was very corrupt. His name was Bill Kelley, but he passed variously as Seminole Bill, Nigger Bill, and Santa Rosa. This was in 1887.

One night, while the outfit was sitting around the camp fire, Seminole Bill announced that he had that day found a gold mine. The announcement produced nothing but scornful jeers from the white men. Probably not one of them had ever in his life given a moment's thought to mining.

The next morning Lee Reagan and the Seminole went across the river to hunt a couple of horses that had got away on that side. The horses were valuable, they had been missing several weeks, and the Reagans had already put in considerable time trying to find them. The two men separated in order to cut for sign and did not see anything of each other until along in the shank of the afternoon. Then they pulled up together on a little ridge a few miles out from the ford, dismounting to shift saddles and exchange observations. Neither had found the horses.

"But, Mr. Lee," Seminole Bill said with animation, "we's right heah clost to that gold mine. It's not more'n half a mile ovah yander. Please lemme show it to you." And he gave a sweep with his arm towards the east that Lee Reagan many a time afterwards wished he could recall more accurately. Here the story prongs.

Lee Reagan's own version[1] is that he asked the nigger why he did not bring some of the gold with him.

141

The reply was, " 'Cause I'se always heared that if you's out by yer-self and finds gold and takes some of it, you's sure to die befo' you gets in."

The more common version of the story—said to be the nigger's version—is that the nigger reached into a *morral* (a fibre bag commonly carried on the horn of the saddle by horsemen of the South-west), drew out a rock, and handed it to Reagan.

"Damn your gold," Reagan is reported to have growled, hurling the rock as far as he could. "We're not feeding you to hunt mines. What you're to hunt is horses."

At any rate, Reagan did not go with the nigger to see the mine and nothing more was said concerning it. Also, as developments will reveal, the nigger evidently defied the superstition of death by carrying away a piece of ore.

A few days later, when the Reagan outfit was in Dryden with a bunch of cattle, Seminole Bill hopped a freight train for San Antonio. He knew Lock Campbell, conductor on the passenger train between San Antonio and Sanderson, for he had once given Campbell a deer ham, and had found out that he was interested in minerals. In San Antonio he tried to find Campbell but missed him. However, he met a friend of Campbell's and turned over to him a piece of ore to give the conductor.

Then Bill returned to Dryden. There he found the Reagans, who had got back from delivering their cattle to the north. The outfit went on down into the Big Bend. In a week or two somebody rode up to Sanderson to get the mail. He brought back a letter addressed to Bill Kelley. It bore a San Antonio postmark. Here again the story prongs.

According to a widespread belief, one of the Reagans opened the letter during Bill's absence and read that a sample of ore furnished by him was very rich. All that the nigger had to do in order to become immensely wealthy was to reveal the mine. As the story goes on, the Reagans, now thoroughly aroused and very much averse to any stranger's "horning in" on a gold mine in their territory, shot the nigger that night and pitched his body into the Rio Grande. They felt sure, it is claimed, that they could go to the mine, Lee Reagan having been very near it and having seen the direction in which the nigger pointed. But this oft-told tale is not true—not all of it at least. About this time a dead negro was pitched into the Rio Grande of the Big Bend all right, but that was because the Flint gang, for whom he was working, were preparing to forsake the business of smuggling stolen cattle in order to rob a train. They intercepted a letter showing that their negro was planning to give them away, and so they "pecosed" him in the Río Bravo.

No, the Reagans most assuredly did not kill Nigger Bill, but one night, about the time the letter came, he took the first horse he could get hold of, a plug staked out to wrangle the remuda on, and "pulled his freight for the tules." Why he left so secretly and suddenly has never been satisfactorily explained. Lee Reagan's story is that his brother Jim read the letter to Seminole Bill and then joined the other white men in laughing at him. "The idea of there being any gold in that God-forsaken country and the idea of Bill's knowing anything about gold even if he saw it!" And it was the morning after this laughing bout, according to Lee Reagan, that the nigger turned up missing.

A more commonly believed explanation is that the Mexican *cocinero* (cook), a friend of Bill's, warned him that the Reagans had read a letter about gold and that he had overheard them planning to have the nigger show them the mine and then kill him. This hardly jibes with the surprised manner of the Reagans at a later date when Lock Campbell told them what he knew. Yet another common explanation is that the Reagans had a quantity of "wet" stock on their range, that they knew Nigger Bill was going to "roam" pretty soon, and that in order to rid themselves of a dangerous witness they planned to put him out of the way, with the result that the *cocinero* overheard them and warned the intended victim.

At any rate, the nigger left suddenly on a "borrowed" horse and left in the night.

"When Bill did not show up with the remuda after big daylight," says Jim Reagan in a letter, "we figured he had made a run at a horse and maybe got crippled by his own pony's falling with him. So we all got out and caught some horses and began looking for Bill. The other hands scattered and I took the trail. To my surprise I soon saw that the nigger was headed for Dryden. I trailed him to what we called Dinner Creek. There the tracks turned off down a draw towards the Shafter Crossing on the Rio Grande. I figured that this was just a blind on the nigger's part to throw somebody off his trail and so rode on to Dryden to catch him. But no Bill came there."

The Stillwells were at that time ranching at the Huerfanito in northern Coahuila about a day's ride south of the Shafter Crossing. According to a story they later told, Seminole Bill came to their ranch afoot soon after he had left the Reagan camp. He had a *morral* full of rocks, which he showed, explaining that he had picked them up out of something like an enormous "ant bed." The elder Stillwell had been a mining engineer and at once recognized in the rocks gold ore of a very high grade. The nigger described in a rather vague way where the outcropping was to be found and then went on towards his people in the Santa Rosa Mountains. The Stillwells were interested enough to take several looks for the mine. Indeed, as will appear in its place, one of them may have found it many years later.

The real story of the hunt for the Lost Nigger Mine, however, will always be associated with the name of Lock Campbell, the railroad conductor. He alone of all the hunters seems to have known what he was about; he alone was both persistent and consistent. He was an extraordinary character. I am glad that I got his story from his own lips before he died, in 1926, less than a year after I visited him.

I found Lock Campbell living in a great house out on Broadway, San Antonio, set deep back from the street with fine trees in front and fine pictures within. He had collected a number of original paintings and his interest in art was genuine—but it was not a passion as was the Lost Nigger Mine. I derived from his beautifully correct speech that he was foreign-bred, and upon question he told me that he was born of Scotch parents and educated in Canada. In the course of our conversation I learned that he had made a neat profit on some Florida lands; that he owned some oil leases in South Texas—"right where the biggest field in Texas is due to come in"; and that he possessed a lot of stock in a dormant copper mine near Lordsburg, New Mexico—a mine "as rich as the famous Number 85 in the same vicinity." Mr. Campbell had passed his seventieth birthday and was retired from railroad duty, but neither age nor retirement had withered his sanguine nature.

"And yet," Campbell went on, "it looks as if something fatalistic hounds every man who follows after these mines. Take that Lordsburg mine. The only reason our company never struck the vein is that we did not go deep enough. Finally one man proposed to advance enough money to sink the shafts on down—and the day after the proposition had been agreed upon, a woman killed him in Mexico. Years passed; another man took up the work and operations were about to be resumed. Then a saddle galled the inside of the man's leg and in a week's time he was dead from blood poisoning.

"A dozen times in my life I have been on the verge of making an immense strike only to have fate step in and thwart me. In 1877 I was mining in Nevada. One day an old-time friend hobbled into camp and said to me: 'Down on the Sitka River in Alaska the Indians are carrying out free gold by the bagful and trading with it. Wait until I get well and we'll go up there together and get rich in one month.' I knew that he could never get well and that there was no use of my waiting. I struck north, was held up at Victoria for months, and then in disgust came back to the States. Ten years after that I picked up the paper in San Francisco one morning and read a headline story about how free gold had just been discovered on the Sitka.

"Even while I was looking for the Lost Nigger Mine, I missed getting rich by a hair's breadth. Another man and I had hired a prospector to look for the mine. The prospector took cold feet about going across the Rio Grande—was afraid of bandits—and in consequence spent all his time on the Texas side, going as far up the river as Terlingua—clean out of the Reagan nigger's range. I did not see him for six months, but my partner did.

"Well, one day years afterwards, when the Terlingua quicksilver mines were making their owners rich, this former partner casually remarked to me: 'You and I could have had those quicksilver mines if we had had sense enough to take them.'

" 'How's that?' I asked.

" 'Why,' he answered, 'didn't that old prospector ever tell you about finding cinnabar around Terlingua?' Then he went on to tell me how he had met our prospector right after he had found all kinds of cinnabar and had instructed him to leave it alone. I asked why in the world he had let such an opportunity go by. His explanation was that one day in a Denver hotel he had overheard three strangers agree that cinnabar was no good. That is the way chance works."

But to get to Campbell's fatalistic search for the Lost Nigger Mine itself. In the first place, when Seminole Bill left a piece of ore in San Antonio to be delivered to Campbell, he explicitly stated that he had found it on the Mexico side of the Rio Grande. He described the ore as being in a canyon among rocks sticking up so close to each other that if a man tried to ride to it he would break his horse's leg. He was hunting horses, he said, when he saw the sun from the west shining upon it. A shower had fallen not long before and there was some water in the canyon. Some of the gold was shining under the water, which was very shallow.

After Campbell got the rock, he had a piece of it assayed. It ran "about $80,000 to the ton." When it is remembered that ore running $20 to the ton is considered good pay, one will realize what even a small quantity of the nigger's rock would be worth. At the time I talked with Campbell, he still had a piece of the rock. It was iron-stained quartz closely sprinkled with fine gold.

For two years after he had the assay made Campbell kept his counsel while he searched. The Reagans, it seems, had about quit the Big Bend. Campbell himself went down into the Maravillas and Reagan canyons. He grubstaked prospectors and kept them looking. Above all, he tried to trail Seminole Bill down. Then one day he saw Jim Reagan on the train going to the cattlemen's convention at San Antonio. He told Jim how he had secured the ore from the nigger, how it had assayed, and how for two years he had been prospecting on the quiet. He went to his grip and pulled out the piece of ore for Jim to see. Jim Reagan was so excited that he could hardly wait to catch the next train back west. He was desperately afraid that somebody would find the mine before he could reach the Big Bend.

"Why, I never believed before that Bill had a thing!" he explained. "I can go to it in an hour's time after we cross the Rio Grande. I know where we were camped when the nigger found the mine. I know that Lee can go straight to the hill he stood on when the nigger tried to show him the mine and pointed towards it. I know the canyons of that country as well as I know the feel of my own boots."

Reagan offered to take Campbell along on the hunt, but the conductor could not get off, and, besides, horseback riding "tore him all to pieces." It was agreed, however, that he should have an interest in the findings.

As soon as the train pulled into San Antonio, Jim Reagan went to the telegraph office and wired his brother Frank at Del Rio to ship eight good horses to Dryden and have an outfit ready. Jim did not tarry even long enough to bet on the horse races out at the fair grounds. Two days later Lee, John, and Frank Reagan, together with Henry Ware, a kind of jack-leg prospector, were riding towards their old stamping ground in the Big Bend.

When it came to mining, not one of these men knew split beans from coffee, but they were all armed with hammers, and for a day and a half they went about hammering on the boulders (float) that litter the gravel ridges east of where the nigger met Lee Reagan on that memorable afternoon. It seems strange that they should have looked anywhere except in canyons, but there was no canyon due east and within half a mile of the hill that Lee designated as the place where he talked with Bill Kelley. Perhaps Lee had forgotten. Anyhow, the hunters decided that the only sensible thing for them to do was to get back out and try to find Bill Kelley.

They got out. And now began a concerted search for the gold-finding nigger that Lock Campbell joined in and kept up almost as long as he lived and that the three living Reagan brothers have not yet abandoned. Two of the Reagans went to the Seminole settlement in Coahuila, learned that Bill's mother was a hundred miles away, and went there. The old woman said that her son had come home with some rocks rich in gold, that the rocks had become lost, for the family had moved around two or three times, and that soon after his return Bill had left again. She did not know where he had gone. After he went away, she had never heard a word either from or about him.

Meantime Lock Campbell advertised far and wide, offering a reward for accurate knowledge of Seminole Bill's whereabouts. He had several letters about a negro living with the Creek Indians in Oklahoma and claiming to be Bill Kelley; Campbell offered to pay this negro good money if he would come to San Antonio and prove that he was Bill Kelley. The negro never appeared. Another negro asserted that for fifty dollars he would produce Bill Kelley in Brackettville—where some of the Seminoles live now. Campbell told him to produce Kelley and he would pay a hundred dollars. The negro never came to claim the money. He did not have to produce Kelley in order to get money; several men advanced him various sums on the mere promise to produce the one living being who knew the whereabouts of the Lost Nigger Mine. Campbell and the Reagans were by no means alone in their hunt for the nigger.

One day a strange negro brought some gold nuggets to a man named Dickey living in Eagle Pass and for pay offered to show him where he had secured them. Dickey had just lost about a thousand dollars looking for some wildcat mine and he came near kicking the negro out of his place. Later he felt sure that the negro was Bill Kelley—but he could not find him.

While Wes Burton was in Monterrey years ago, he came to know a negro who went by the name of Pablo; and in Burton's mind Pablo was undoubtedly Seminole Bill. He had a peculiar scar on his face, was a desperate drinker and gambler, and, whooping and shooting, frequently rode a fine horse down the street at full speed. He always had plenty of money, and it was well known that he got it by bringing in about every three months a pack horse loaded with gold ore.

On the other hand, it is asserted that when the Spanish-American War broke out Bill Kelley enlisted in the United States Army and was eventually killed in the Philippine Islands. Somebody trailed Bill Kelley to Louisiana and found that he had died there. I have a letter, written in April, 1930, from a man in Marietta, Ohio, assuring me that he has Bill Kelley located in Arizona. A month after this letter came to hand, a man appeared in my office with a communication from a Spanish lady in Durango reciting how a Mexican who worked on her hacienda before the Madero Revolution swore that he had killed Bill Kelley near Del Rio for attempting to steal a horse—after the negro had shown him the mine, on the Texas side. Bill Kelley has become as much a legend as the gold he found, and his vanishing is as uncertain as the vanishing of his mine.

One of the prospectors that Campbell grubstaked was known as

"Old Missouri." He is remembered principally for the number of burros he let stray off, and people got to saying that Campbell had stocked the Big Bend with burros. Old Missouri had instructions to scout out from the Reagan camp site only as far as a burro could go and come in a day. Solitary, often not seeing a human being for weeks and months at a time, Old Missouri examined ledge after ledge, canyon after canyon. He was looking for a kind of blue stone, he said. Then one day he found it. He put some of it on his pack burro, loaded on his blankets and a little grub, and started for Sanderson.

On the road he became very sick. He was feeble anyhow. When he reached Sanderson he was too sick to talk. What the "blue" stone in his pack meant or where he had found it, nobody ever ascertained. Old Missouri died before he could explain.

The years passed. Jim Reagan went out into Arizona, "where there are sure enough prospectors," and engaged the services of an expert who "knew rocks from A to izzard." However, when this expert prospector got down into the Big Bend, he swore that he would be ashamed for any mining man who knew straight up to catch him looking for gold in such a country. His liquor played out before he reached the Rio Grande; he was very fond of liquor; and he refused absolutely to prospect.

But "gold is where you find it." And, after all, there are granitic outcrops in the Reagan Canyon country, and the Chisos Mountains are well mineralized. If ever there was any doubt concerning Seminole Bill's gold, old Finky put that doubt to rest.

On July 19, 1899, five men signed a written agreement to hunt and develop the Lost Nigger Mine. The signers were Lock Campbell, railroad conductor; J. G. (Jim) Reagan, who at that time ran a saloon in Sanderson; D. C. Bourland, who was ranching down in the Reagan Canyon country; O. L. Mueller, a German who had taken out naturalization papers in Mexico and was ranching across from Bourland; and John Finky, prospector. Finky was to be grubstaked by the other four men while he looked for the mine and was to have a fifth interest in it.

And Finky found the mine. He made his headquarters with the Bourlands, who lived close to the river. He hunted consistently across the river in the Ladrones Mountains, which at that time were occasionally visited by Mexican bandits. Every evening, the Bourlands said, Finky would come in from his search dead tired, absolutely worn

149

out. Then one evening, earlier than usual, he came in with his face all lit up, a joyous spring in his step, and a rusty old rifle in his hand. He said that he had found the rifle by the side of a dried-up skeleton of a man and that in less than an hour, not three hundred yards away from the skeleton, he had found gold. He said that he had taken about ten pounds of the ore in his *morral* and started back with it but buried it before he reached the river. He did not tell why he buried it. That he had reason enough for not producing it will come out later. No phrenologist or archaeologist was by to examine the skull of the skeleton, but in the opinion of Finky it was a negro's skull.

It happened that about the time Finky arrived at ranch quarters that afternoon, Bourland rode in to get a fresh horse. A drouth was on the country, his cattle were dying, and he was working desperately night and day to save them. Finky pleaded with him to go right then to see the mine he had found. "And we had better take along an extra hand and all the artillery we can raise," he said.

But Bourland simply could not leave his cattle. The mine had waited there ten thousand years, he figured, and it could wait a day or two longer. He often declared later that had he known how things were going to turn out he would have let all his cattle die rather than have delayed an hour in going across the river with Finky.

The rest of the story can best be told in Lock Campbell's own words.

"The next morning Finky's face was swollen as if it had been poisoned. Mrs. Bourland doctored it with potato poultice, prickly pear poultice, bread and milk poultice, applications of kerosene oil, and every other remedy she could think of, but it got no better. They brought Finky to Sanderson. When my train ran into the station, Jim Reagan was there to meet me.

" 'Old Finky has found the mine and is going to do us,' was the first thing he said. 'He's here. You can go see him and talk to him yourself.'

"I went over to the rooming-house to see him. Swollen and painful as his face was, he had nevertheless the happiest look I have ever seen on a human countenance.

" 'I have found it, Mr. Campbell! I have found it!' he said. 'I could break the rock with my hammer, but after I had broken it I could not pull the pieces apart, they were so woven together with wire gold.'

"Now the nigger's ore was not wire gold and, therefore, it would seem that Finky found an entirely different deposit. One thing is certain: granting there are two deposits, there is no lead to either of them; each is a 'chimney,' or 'spew.'

"Well, Finky would not tell me or anybody else where he had made his location. He impressed me as having a kind of secret fear, but he said openly that he had been beat out of a fortune more than once and that he was not going to be beat out of this one. He particularly distrusted Jim Reagan, and had it not been for Reagan we should have gotten the mine all right. According to the laws of Mexico, no foreigner could denounce or operate a mine in that country nearer than sixty miles to the border. With this law in mind we had taken in Mueller so that, as a Mexican citizen, he could denounce the mine. But no, Jim Reagan got on a horse and rode clear down to Mueller's ranch in order to tell him not to make a move until old Finky should show us the place. Meantime, Finky recovered and went to the upper Bourland ranch in the Haymond country to await developments.

"The game was blocked. Then Finky became restless and declared he would go to Mexico City himself and see President Díaz. He got as far as El Paso. Now old Finky had one great weakness; that was whiskey. In El Paso he got on a high lonesome and told the barkeeper his business. The barkeeper told him to wait a few days and he would go with him to Mexico and help him fix matters up. The barkeeper seems to have turned the saloon over to Finky. In less than two weeks Finky was dead and his secret was buried with him."

The years went on. John Reagan had died; the other Reagans had moved to Arizona; Lock Campbell had about quit grubstaking prospectors. Then one day in 1909 a man from Oklahoma by the name of Wattenberg drifted into the Big Bend country. He made Alpine his headquarters and stayed around there several weeks, learning what he could about the Mexican border land and picking up details regarding the Lost Nigger Mine tradition. Finally he took into his confidence an old-timer named Felix Lowe and told him his tale. Lowe advised him to see John Young, who has been on the frontier all his life and who has generally been "willing to take a chance." Why Finky did not produce a sample of his wire gold is now to be explained.

Wattenberg had with him a map, and he had a story as to how he had come by that map. According to his story, a nephew of his in the Oklahoma penitentiary, condemned to death, had called him in and, without asking for a cent of remuneration, had told him of an immensely rich gold mine in the Ladrones Mountains across in Mexico about opposite the mouth of Reagan Canyon.[2]

This nephew had been one of a gang of horse thieves operating all the way from Mexico to Oklahoma. While they were on one horse-stealing expedition across the border, they learned that the Mexican *rurales*, a force corresponding to the Texas rangers, were on their trail. The horse thieves were making tracks for the Rio Grande when they came upon an old prospector lugging a rust-eaten gun and a *morral* full of rocks.

The prospector, as the condemned horse thief described him to Wattenberg, must have surmised that the gang was after him. Consciousness of the wealth he had suddenly become master of no doubt made him suspicious. At any rate, he went down on his knees and before they had even searched him told the fleeing bandits that if they would spare his life he would show them the richest gold mine in Mexico—the mine from which he had secured the samples in his *morral*. They took the samples. He showed them the mine. Then the bandits swore that if he should ever tell another soul of the location or come back into Mexico from the Texas side, they would "hound his soul to hell." Before they left the country, the bandits drew a rough sketch of the region, marking plainly the site of the mine.

When John Young examined the sketch presented by Wattenberg, he found the landmarks of it all correct—the Ladrones Mountains, Las Vegas de los Ladrones, Ladrones Canyon, which runs into the Rio Grande above and across from the mouth of Reagan Canyon, Maravillas Canyon, and other features. One of the other features was a dot in the Ladrones entitled "MINE." In short, the map from Oklahoma showed that the maker of it was familiar with the country.

Wattenberg's story dovetailed exactly into Finky's incomplete account. It explained the strange reticence of old Finky, his failure to bring in any ore, his refusal to tell where he found the mine, his hesitation in returning to it.

John Young, Felix Lowe, and Wattenberg now entered into a partnership to explore for the Lost Nigger Mine. As a preliminary step John Young went to the City of Mexico, saw President Porfirio Díaz personally, and secured a permit to operate a gold mine anywhere in northern Mexico, no matter how near the border. Next he went to Múzquiz and made arrangements to denounce certain mining claims, at the same time engaging for $200 the services of a Múzquiz surveyor. This was early in 1910—on the eve of the great Madero Revolution.

The surveyor came to Alpine and the whole party set out. When they got to the mouth of Maravillas Canyon, where they intended to cross, they found the Rio Grande on a big rise. The surveyor and John Young's son Johnny crossed it on a crude raft, but once across they could do little scouting on foot. The country was so immense and the speck in the Ladrones Mountains marked "MINE" was so little that they knew not where to go. It was like looking for a needle in a haystack—but they looked for two days. Getting into the country at that time in a wagon was a trial; getting out was worse. Everybody was disgusted and John Young's partners quit him.

He, however, did not give up. Thirty days after the first attempt to cross the river, he and his son went down again. This time they took a little flatboat on their wagon. The Rio Grande was up higher than ever. In crossing over, Johnny Young got the Wattenberg map so soaked that it came to pieces. Again he was afoot, the river too swift to put horses into it. The revolution was now going on and nobody who knew anything about Mexico wanted to make permanent camp on the south bank of the Rio Grande.

"I came out and quit the search forever," John Young says.

Then, no longer having any reason for secrecy, he told a newspaper man of his hunt. And, beginning with the beginning—that is, with Seminole Bill and Lock Campbell—the newspaperman wrote the story of the Lost Nigger Mine for the San Antonio *Express*. It was printed September 7, 1913.

A miner named Jack Haggard, who had been living in Mexico for many years, saw the article and immediately wrote a letter that is here produced verbatim.

Múzquiz, Coahuila, Sept. 10 de 1913

Sr. John Young
Alpine, Texas

Dear Sir
The article in the S. A. Express of Sept. 7th attracted my attention. Whether it is a coincidence or a lost mine story, I do not know. But, anyway, about twelve years ago I had a Seminole negro working for me at the mine at Las Esparzas, and he told me a tale of a wonderful rich gold mine that he had found in the Big Bend country. But as I had heard such stories before and spent money and time looking for such mines (without results) I paid very little attention to him.
However, one of the mine foremen named Harry Turner did believe

him and from the description given by the negro, Turner and I made
a rough sketch of the country in which the mine is supposed to be.
Then about five or six years later Turner went on a trip to that locali-
ty. He brought back some samples with him and after getting assays
made of them he was very much excited. He never showed me the
assay reports, stating that anyone who saw them would think he had
sent away a twenty-dollar piece and had an assay made of it. He
began making hasty preparations to wind up his business as soon as
possible. At the time he was contractor in the mine at Rosita, making
$2,000 per month. He was in a great hurry to finish his contract and
tried to persuade me to go with him, saying that in a year's time we
could buy all the coal mines in the state of Coahuila. But as I had a
contract for two years I could not leave.

About a week before Turner was to finish his contract at Rosita
(Mine No. 3) an explosion of gas killed every man down in the mine,
Turner with the balance. Having been a personal friend of his for
years, I was called to his house and asked to help settle his affairs. In
going through his papers I came across the old sketch we had made
according to the Seminole negro's description, also a lot of notes in
cipher, which I have not been able to read.

I know where the Seminole negro is. He had some trouble and had
to leave Mexico but came back during the Madero Revolution. If
there is anything to the newspaper report of the Lost Nigger Mine and
you wish any further information, you can write me here. I'll have
another talk with the negro.

Very respectfully yours,
Jack Haggard.

John Young immediately replied to this letter and considerable correspondence passed. Then Jack Haggard came to Alpine. He wanted
the Youngs to go with him. After all, he had not been able to locate
the Seminole negro, and he seemed to prefer a copy of the Wattenberg
chart to the one he and Turner had made. Neither of the Youngs was
willing to make another trip. Haggard went back to Múzquiz. According to one story he later told, he found the negro. At any rate, he made
a pack trip into the Big Bend from Múzquiz, hunted around, crossed
the river at the old Stillwell Crossing, and came again to Alpine solicit-
ing the aid of the Youngs. The Youngs still refused to go.

When Haggard left, he said, "If you don't hear from me in fifteen
days, you may know that something has happened. The Villistas are

chasing all over the country and no man's life is now safe in Mexico."

More than fifteen days passed and nothing was heard of Jack Haggard. Then John Young learned that the revolution had run him out of Mexico. The next news was that he had drowned in Medina Lake.

William B. Cloete of the Cloete coal mines in Coahuila believed in the Lost Nigger Mine so thoroughly that he offered to put up $10,000 for Lock Campbell to spend in hunting it. Campbell told him that all had been done that could be done and that the money would be wasted. Cloete asserted that he was going to spend it anyhow. He went down with the *Lusitania*.

One day in 1918 Charlie Stillwell, then in California, received a letter from his brother Will, a Texas ranger on border duty. In part the letter read:

At last I have located the Lost Nigger Mine. The samples I have correspond with those given to Father by Nigger Bill when he was running away from the Reagan camp and passed our ranch. The distance of the deposit from the river corresponds to the distance described by Nigger Bill. As soon as conditions are so we can work, you must come and we will denounce the mine according to the laws of Mexico. A fortune awaits us even if the ore does not extend to any great depth.

Several months elapsed, and Charlie Stillwell was preparing to return to the Big Bend to help work the mine. A few days before he was to leave, he received a message saying that Will had been killed in Mexico while trying to apprehend a Mexican outlaw. Whatever he may have known about the mine died with him.

Thus those who seek the Lost Nigger Mine may expect to be foiled by fire and water and to meet sudden death.

Many people say that there has never been a mine and that the Reagan nigger merely stumbled on a piece of ore salted out by a certain old California prospector with a sense of humor. As Don Pedro Salinas, the sagest sage in Coahuila, has the facts, three Mexican men and one woman who had been stealing high-grade ore from the gold mines south of Las Cienagas fled with some *morrals* full of it towards the refuge across the Rio Grande. In the Ladrones Mountains they were so hard pressed that they dropped the ore. A little later *rurales* killed them—and the crude gold cast away remained unseen until Seminole Bill found it. Despite such explanations, most border men—men familiar with the character of the Big Bend country—are of the opinion that the nigger found native gold under a cliff and that the cliff soon afterwards caved off, covering all signs so that they can no longer be detected. Another theory, assuming that the nigger found his gold in a canyon, is that gravel has washed over it, hiding it from view. Not many people doubt that it is hid.

The Lost Nigger Mine—what is it? It is the spell of the Big Bend of unsurveyed mountains and the Lost Canyon, the spell of vast solitudes where men with strange tales have lived strange lives and died strange deaths. It is the lure of unknownness. It is Mystery—Romance. And it is Reality—the Imagination of men of the earth.

There will be other stories of the Lost Nigger Mine.³ The mine will in all probability be found again—and lost again. But my own story, in the gathering of materials for which I have spent so many vivid hours, is done and, having finished it, I am poignantly conscious of extraordinary scenes and extraordinary characters connected with it that can never be realized on paper. Often and often I recall some of them:

A low camp fire down in the willow *vegas* of the Rio Grande at the old Reagan ford and dark waters swishing under the stars while Rol Rutledge of the border and Carl Raht, historian of the Big Bend, argue low and gravely for and against the possibility of gold in that region.

Another camp, at the mouth of Heath Canyon on the Rio Grande, where customs officers hardly ever come and where red Jim Manning, cowman, ranger, borderer, boils *candelilla* into wax and tells of the Seminoles who used to bring ore to Brackettville. While he is talking, a Mexican rides up on the other side of the river and shouts. We go over. The Mexican wants us to visit his *jacal*. There we see panther skins, and he shows us the flesh and head of an outlaw steer, branded before the revolution, that he has just shot after having trailed it for three days out in the Sierra de los Ladrones. The horns are not the biggest I have ever seen but they have the wildest expression that horns can possibly assume.

And then a cow camp by the famed *tinaja* called Pata de Venado in Bullis Gap and one of Asa Jones's vaqueros telling a long story about an ancient Indian and an ancient *rural* and gold up the Cañon de los Leones, so difficult of access that no gringo prospector ever gets there, though the vaquero draws me a sketch of the whole land.

And then old Dee Davis, seated on a goatskin in his cabin door at Sabinal, unlocking his hoard of lost-mine traditions while a humming-bird sucks at a morning-glory near by.

And John Young in his friendly land office in Alpine going into a steel safe and bringing out documents from the Mexican government, Wattenberg's testimony, a yellowing copy of the San Antonio *Express*, and letters from a miner by the name of Jack Haggard who wrote from Múzquiz, Coahuila.

Then Lee Reagan in the corner of a café at El Paso telling of hunt after hunt he and his brothers made for the Lost Nigger Mine and protesting against "wild tales" concerning their abuse of the nigger.

But oftenest of all characters recollected is Lock Campbell. His portly frame rests comfortably in a great cushioned chair in his big house that sits back amid fine trees. He goes over to the mantel to get Seminole Bill's sample of ore, and in a ray of sunlight entering through one of the tall windows holds it up for me to see the myriad flecks of color. Lock Campbell is dressed as an old Scotch gentleman should be dressed, and a great gold watch chain rests on his ample front. His talk is of free gold on the Sitka, prospectors in Frisco, assays in Denver, copper in Lordsburg, land in Florida, oil in South Texas; of Seminole Bill with a deer ham at Dryden and then of Seminole Bill in San Antonio with a rock and a description of the western sun shining on millions in gold beneath a canyon cliff; of booted Jim Reagan rushing from the train to telegraph for horses to carry him and his brother into the Big Bend; of blind old Felix Lowe being led up the high steps to the Campbell gallery and begging for a grubstake on "just one more hunt" that is sure to lead to the gold; of "Old Missouri" and his burros; and of Finky with swollen face and joyous voice crying, "I have found it, Mr. Campbell, I have found it."

Lock Campbell is saying that he has "quit," but over and over he repeats, "I know it is there."

"And remember," he concludes, "remember that, no matter what the geologists say, *gold is where you find it*."

CHAPTER IX

On West

"Begging your pardon, sir," says Joe, "what sort
of wonders might them be?"
"Why, all sorts of wonders," says the parson. "Why, in the west," he
says, "there's things you wouldn't believe; not till you'd seen them,"
he says. "There's diamonds growing on the trees. And great,
golden glittering pearls as common as pea-straw. . . .
Ah, I could tell you of them."
MASEFIELD, A Mainsail Haul

THE ENGINEER'S LEDGE

When the Southern Pacific Railroad was building west of Devil's River, back in the eighties, one of the construction engines was driven by an engineer named Hughes. Hughes had a mania for picking up samples of rock along the right of way—and the four hundred miles between Del Rio and El Paso afford plenty of rock to pick up. The engineer's work often allowed him a deal of free time, for when his train brought up supplies to the slowly advancing railhead, it might be hours before the cars were unloaded. Then he would get out and look for rocks.

Hughes had a wonderful memory and he depended on it. He did not label a single one of his scores of specimen rocks. He boasted that he could tell offhand where each came from. He knew the ravines, the bends, the mountains, every cut and canyon from Del Rio to El Paso "like a book."

Thus he went on collecting and remembering for three years. Then one day the railroad construction was ended. The East and the West had run into each other. Engineer Hughes got a pass that took him to Denver for a brief vacation. He carried some of his rocks with him.

He was the kind of man who loves rocks and mountains more than money. He was like old Henry Warren, who, after he had spent a lifetime teaching little Mexican schools along the Rio Grande, was offered a farm by his rich brother in Mississippi if he would come back there and live. "You can't offer me a Western sunset," Warren replied, and remained in the Big Bend. Still, when Hughes got to Denver he became quite interested in having his specimens assayed. All but one proved worthless. The exception was so wonderfully rich in gold that the engineer at once regarded himself as a wealthy man.

He remembered in a flash the black ledge over a ravine where he had found the sample. It was located not very far west of Paisano Pass and just south of the railroad; chips from the ledge were scattered out from it for a hundred yards. The picture in his mind was like a photograph: the angle of clustered sotol above; a gnarled piñon in the ravine below; the curve of the railroad at exactly the point where he would walk southwest.

Before he resigned his position, he had plans all made. First, he must get possession of the land. Then he would need water to work the mine. He had heard that there was an Indian spring ten miles up the ravine; he could pipe the water down. The railroad would put in a switch when the time came.

In El Paso he got a light camping outfit and crawled into the engine cab with an old crony who was headed for Del Rio. It would be a good idea, he thought, to stake his claim before he talked. Besides, he wanted to get out among the mountains. His crony promised to let him off at Paisano Pass, and as they puffed up the grade, it pleased Hughes to see how well he had remembered all the details of the location.

He stood looking after the train until it was out of sight; then he walked back. There were the rusted spikes he had remembered. Of course, there could be no mistake now. But what if there were? After he had crawled up out of the deep railroad cut he sat down to get his breath. He hadn't remembered that the air was so light at Paisano Pass.

Then he went on. He looked first for the angle of sotol; there it was. He swept his eye down the ravine; there was the gnarled piñon. He stumbled. His heart certainly was beating hard. He had gone two hundred yards. Where was the black ledge?

He ran. He ran so far that he got out of sight of the sotol and was away below the piñon. That certainly was wrong. He ran back. He came against the railroad cut before he knew it. Then he zigzagged.

Night found him walking aimlessly about. He had forgotten that he was either thirsty or tired. When he sat down, his feet seemed on fire. At least he could sleep. And he did sleep.

When he awoke, his mind was clear. This was evidently the location of another sample, not the gold one. If he could find a rock to match that other sample, he would try to remember what place he had been associating it with. That other place would be the right one. His memory had simply swapped locations with the rocks.

In ten minutes he found a familiar rock. It was in a pothole and was of a gray color speckled with black quartz. The quartz glistened in the sun, worthless. Where now had he remembered this speckled rock as belonging? He hesitated, but only for a minute. He knew. It was a half mile above the crossing on Eagle Nest Canyon. That was a hundred and seventy miles east. He would go there and find the black ledge he had mistakenly remembered as being at Paisano Pass.

Hughes flagged a freight and rode it to Eagle Nest Canyon. He walked up it a half mile. No black ledge was there!

The only thing to do now was to revisit every place from which he had ever taken a rock specimen. East and west, up and down the railroad, he traveled, sometimes on foot, sometimes on a freight. At first the trains would pick him up. Then his old acquaintances dropped away and strangers did not want to bother with a "cracked pebble hunter," even if he had been a trainman.

Years passed. Engineer Hughes told his story often. He told it in great detail. Occasionally some old prospector would join him for a week or so. He has been dead thirty-odd years now, but people out on the S. P. still talk about the Engineer's ledge.

THE LOST PADRE MINE

The guide tapped the ponderous old bell with the clapper so that I might hear its tones. We were in the church of Nuestra Señora de la Guadalupe in Juárez, across the river from El Paso. His own tones gave the guide—and me also—as much pleasure as those of the bell; he had reason to be proud of his precise English. "Why, sir," he clattered on, "that bell swings from the very same rawhide that was stretched up there when this church was built in 1659."

The rawhide does look weathered. A guide so well informed on Juárez bells must, I thought, know something about the Lost Padre Mine. I was not mistaken.

When he was only a boy, he knew an Indian in Juárez—a "pure quill," as the gringos down in Mexico call an aboriginal of undiluted blood—who, although he never did a lick of work, was always well provided. Once a year, regularly, this Indian would absent himself a few days and then return with a small *carga* of gold and silver ore. It was well known that he got it from the Padre Mine, but he would never tell a soul where the Padre Mine was.

The tradition of this famous mine was hoary long before guides became the chief functionaries of the church at Juárez.[1] By standing either at the front portal of the church or else in the tower—authorities differ—exactly at sunrise and looking to the northeast, one should be able to see the black opening of a tunnel in Franklin Mountain across the Rio Grande in Texas—the entrance to La Mina del Padre. Since the sun rises at a different angle every morning of the year and since it is occasionally obscured by clouds, I doubt if of the hundreds who have strained their eyes toward the northeast from the church a single matutinal watcher has ever given the direction for locating the Padre tunnel a thoroughly scientific test. Anyway, the tunnel was filled up over a hundred and fifty years ago.

In the year 1888 a man by the name of Robinson and an old government packer known as Big Mick began business in a sensible way by starting with the mountain instead of the church. They located the Padre shaft and set to cleaning it out. Backing them was a man who had examined the records at Santa Fe sufficiently to conclude that in addition to working the Padre Mine the Jesuits had secreted three hundred jack loads of silver bullion at the bottom of the shaft. The Jesuits were expelled from Spanish America along about 1780—and when they left the country, they left their mines and their bullion all well hidden. They say, also, that Oñate, founder of the province of New Mexico, walled up in the Padre tunnel 4336 ingots of gold, 5000 bars of silver, nine mule loads of jewels pilfered from Aztec treasure houses, and four codices—smuggled from Spain—each as precious as the Codex Vaticanus itself and, therefore, worth their weight in diamonds.

The prospectors got down into the shaft leading to all this wonderful booty only far enough to clean out about twenty feet of "very peculiar filling." It was of a reddish cast and appeared to be river soil. Certainly it could not have come from the mountain side. Thirty years after this abortive attempt to open the shaft, an old, old Mexican woman told Clabe Robinson, nephew of Big Mick's partner, that before she was born a priest from Ysleta had his people carry river dirt— red river dirt—up the mountain and fill a shaft with it. Singularly enough, about the same time a retired railroad engineer from Mexico produced a chart, presented to him by a Tarahumare centenarian, that recited how a valuable mine in Mount Franklin had been filled at the top with twenty feet of red silt from the Rio Grande.

Clabe Robinson is a logician as well as a plainsman. Incidentally, he has put together the most interesting collection of facts about mustangs that has ever been printed. He is out in the mountains above El Paso now, and news of his project for getting to the bottom of the Padre shaft may be expected at any time. He has the spur of rivalry to urge him on.

Not a great while ago an Italian came to El Paso with a chart as fresh and "hot" as were the contents of the Pardoner's wallet. He elicited the interest of an aviator, and this aviator, fired probably by Lindbergh's success in locating lost Mayan cities, attempted to locate the old mine from the air. He discovered something that calls for a vast amount of work, but whether he will have faith enough to remove a mountain remains to be seen.

Although I have ridden clear across the Sierra Madre on a mule in order to view the Lost Tayopa Mine so dramatically rediscovered by C. B. Ruggles, and although I intend to go in search of the Lost Adams Diggings in New Mexico—for a wonderful story is attached to it—I should not spend a minute looking for the Padre shaft. This is why.[2]

Upon one of the peaks of Mount Franklin there stands out against the perennially clear sky the distinct outline of an Indian's head. "The spinsters and the knitters in the sun" and the mantilla-muffled old women who squat in the plaza with palm outstretched and a mumbled *"pido por Dios"* to every passerby know how that head came there and what it means.

It is the head of Cheetwah, chief of an ancient tribe of Indians. For two hundred years he held the mountain land of his people secure against all invaders. Then came a new enemy, pale of features, pompous of manner, commanding all Indians to deliver up their gold and silver. The order so incensed Cheetwah that he climbed to the top of the mountain and there cried out a great summons to all the warriors in the spirit world to rally for exterminating the enemy. The warriors of the spirit world heard. History sets the date as 1680, when every Spaniard in New Mexico was either killed or driven south.

After this victory Cheetwah and his people vanished into the mountains, there to keep vigil forever that no alien with pick and shovel should prosper from the mineral wealth of the land. As a symbol of this watch, the peak of the mountain took on the features of Cheetwah's face. The white men returned. They own the country now, but they can never possess its gold and silver. The decree is written in the sky, as whoever looks up to the immutable outlines of that peak of Mount Franklin may read. No, the Lost Padre Mine is lost forever.

CHAPTER X

Los Muertos No Hablan

*"There is something in a treasure that fastens upon a man's mind.
He will pray and blaspheme and still persevere, and will curse the
day he ever heard of it, and will let his last hour come upon him
unawares, still believing that he missed it only by a foot. He will see it
every time he closes his eyes. He will never forget it until he is dead—
and even then—Doctor, did you ever hear of the miserable gringos
on Azuera, that cannot die? There is no getting away from a
treasure that once fastens upon your mind."*
CONRAD, Nostromo

*Red Curly's bandits made a raid
One night in Monterrey;
They put the loot under granite rock
And they put it there to stay.*

*They killed their Mexkin pardners all,
Next shot a poor stranger;
A mob then hung Red to a joist
In the town of Shakespeare.*

*Now, just before they strung him up,
Red offered, so I'm told,
To show them at El Muerto Springs
A wagon load of gold.*

According to Bill Cole, the ballad—and it has twenty verses—should
be sung to the tune of "The Drunkard's Hiccoughs." Bill knows, for
Bill has not done much the last fifteen years but think about "the
Monterrey holdup stuff," as it is called, sing about it to himself, talk
about it to anybody who will listen, and dig, dig, dig after it—out by
El Muerto Springs in Jeff Davis County on the Texas border. They are
digging for it, too, the identical loot, five hundred miles farther west in
Skeleton Canyon on the Arizona line. It is the most magnificent booty,

not even excepting Pancho Villa's, to have been buried in modern times.

Valentine, in Jeff Davis County, where Bill Cole lives, is noted chiefly for its shipping pens and a lunch room for freight crews. North and east of it lie the Davis Mountains. I went to Valentine to see Bill Cole.

"Just follow them whittlings," one of the railroad men replied in answer to my query, pointing at the same time to the ground beside a shaded section of the depot platform, "and you'll find ole Bill."

I followed the whittlings and found Bill comfortably chewing tobacco in his mother's lodging house. She was a very old woman, and he was, I judged, about fifty-five, with a drooping black moustache and a drawl that drooped in harmony. Few men have ever welcomed me with more warmth than Bill. For two nights and one day we talked, meanwhile visiting his workings at El Muerto Springs, where he has been digging since 1917. As "the wad," according to Bill's calculations, amounts to "a fraction over $800,000," he was naturally very much worried over the income tax laws.

"In 1914," he began, "I was sitting in my pool hall talking with Preacher Bloys. He wasn't too damn good to come in and see a pool hall man or shake hands with a saloon keeper. Well, while we were chatting, a man and a boy who said they were from Oklahoma stepped in to ask me where they could get burros for a trip into the Davis Mountains. In them days I was considerable of a hunter, and somebody had advised them to come to me to get outfitted. They said they wanted to go on a hunt for bear and black-tails.

"I told 'em where to get burros and packs, and after they left, old Preacher Bloys turned to me and said, 'Those men are not hunters. What they are hunting is that pack train money. It's out there in the Davis Mountains all right, but the man who finds it will have to have a true map.'

"That was all he said on the subject. I knew, though, that Preacher Bloys never talked idly and from that day I began looking for the true map. The Oklahoma man and boy were out ten days and came in without a thing. They were back the next year and then gave up the search for good. I don't know what kind of map they had, but they had one. I began piecing evidence together from first one place and then another. After the state closed my business, I was free to go after the stuff right and I have been after it ever since."

167

The quest for evidence led Bill Cole to the Pacific coast, down into Mexico, and up into the Rocky Mountains of Arizona and Colorado; and it has caused him to spend many a long day whittling on the depot platform while receiving "authentic tidings of invisible things." The result of all these researches Bill told with many jerks and cutbacks. I have tried to put the story into connected form.

It begins with a band of nineteen Mexican bandits, led by Juan Estrada, who at one time were the terror of the Big Bend. Frequently they dressed themselves up like Indians, and many a foul act of their doing was laid to the innocent Apaches. With feathers in their hair, they robbed the stage coach and chased Big Foot Wallace. Painted like savages, they raided across into Mexico. They were inordinate cattle thieves, and even old Milt Favor, the biggest cowman at that time on the Rio Grande, with a hundred and fifty vaqueros under him,

a ranch that was a fort, and an orchard that supplied peach brandy to every traveler over the Chihuahua Trail, was helpless against their depredations.

In 1854 the United States government had established Fort Davis in the Davis Mountains. After the Civil War the fort was rehabilitated. In 1879—the very year that Victorio and his Apaches broke out—a detachment of Fort Davis troops was camped near Lobo in the wide Van Horn valley. The detachment consisted of ninety-nine negroes and a white lieutenant. Their business was to cut toboso grass to be used for hay by the Fort Davis cavalry.

While the negroes were haying and the lieutenant was commanding, four American outlaws came into the country from the west. Their names were Zwing Hunt, Jim Hughes, Red Curly (called also Sandy King), and Doctor Neal. Hughes was the leader. Some of them had

been mixed up in the Lincoln County War, wherein Billy the Kid won his fame. Following John Ringo, the gang had raided cattle off the Sonora ranches. They had all helped materially in giving Tombstone the reputation of being the rowdiest and roughest mining town in the West. They were desperate men and they had a desperate plan. It was to throw in with the Estrada bandits, seize a quota of mules and supplies from the United States troops, and, thus outfitted, make a flying swoop upon the riches of Monterrey.

They had no trouble in making an alliance with the Estrada gang. Then one fine morning when the ninety-nine negroes and the white lieutenant fell out unarmed to the picket lines, the twenty Mexican and the four American desperadoes arose from their concealment in the tall grass near at hand and opened fire. Only one negro escaped alive.

"The official report sent to Washington," says Bill Cole, "gave sixteen negroes killed by Indians, but those government reports are always wrong. The officers were afraid to report the cold facts. I myself have seen enough old .44 Winchester shells on the ground of that Lobo camp to fill a sack."[1]

The desperadoes took an ample supply of provisions, ammunition, horseshoes, blankets, saddles, and other goods and picked out twenty-five choice mules—one around and an extra. They headed south for Mexico. At Paso Viejo in the San Antonio, or Lost, Mountains they paused to shoe their animals in a thorough manner.

A day's ride below the Presidio del Norte crossing on the Rio Grande, Estrada of the Mexicans and Hughes of the Americans halted their followers to load the mules with guano from the immense bat caves still to be found in that mountainous region. Posing as traders, they then went on into Monterrey and sold their guano at a hundred dollars per ton.

Their character thus established, they pitched camp near the edge of the city and opened a monte game, in which they at times lost heavily. One night, after the mules were well rested from the trip, Estrada's men were sent out with explicit directions to toll the guards of the mint and smelter to camp. The bait was to be free *tequila* and a game of monte in which the banker was losing thousands. No peon soldier could resist the allurement of monte and *tequila*. But as the truant sentinels slipped into camp, they found instead of a monte game a death trap. Twelve guards in all walked into it. The proverb that guided the greatest ruler Mexico has ever had, Porfirio Díaz,

president of the republic at this time, was *Los muertos no hablan*—
The dead do not talk. So Hughes and company had good precedent.
No one of the twelve guards ever talked after entering the bandit
camp.

Meantime a picked crew looted the mint, raided the smelter, and
sacked the cathedral. The combined bandits now loaded their jag on
the twenty-five government mules and pulled for the Davis Mountains. They knew that they would be pursued and they lost no time.
By the map it is three hundred and ninety miles from the rich city of
Monterrey in the state of Nuevo León to El Muerto Springs in Jeff
Davis County, Texas. The desperate bandits traveled this distance
without once taking the packs off their mules!

"I have been disputed on this point," Bill Cole explains. "Three
hundred and ninety miles is a long ways for any animal loaded down
with a dead weight of gold and silver to travel. But it is possible.
Those were picked mules. Tom Bybee rode from Cisco to Fort Stockton, over three hundred miles, without once taking the saddle off his
sorrel horse."

Anyway, the raiders made a forced march, and it was well that they
did so. As soon as their depredations were discovered, dispatches were
sent to the Mexican troops at Monclova. The Monclova cavalry made
for the Presidio del Norte crossing, where they expected to intercept
the robbers. The robbers, however, in anticipation of just this move,
crossed the Rio Grande at the mouth of Reagan Canyon nearly two
hundred miles below. According to international agreement, troops of
either country could at that time cross the border between Mexico
and the United States, but only *on the trail of marauders*. The Monclova pursuers lost a week riding back down the river to strike the
trail.

So far as testimony has come down, only one man on the Texas
side saw the mule train as it forged on to its destination. This may
well be, for the Big Bend is a wide and lonesome country now and it
was a great deal wider and a great deal more lonesome back in 1879.
That one witness was a Mexican *pastor*, or shepherd, named Quintana.

As Quintana told the story to Cole, he was herding a little flock of
goats near Barrel Springs, seventeen miles east of El Muerto Springs,
when he saw the first *mulero* coming up the draw. The bandit train
was strung out for nearly a mile, he said. The mules were so worn
and tired that the only means by which the *muleros* could keep them

going was to jab them in the sides with sotol stalks. Two Americans were riding ahead of the column on mounts that were fairly fresh; each of them was leading two mules. Quintana hid in the brush but pretty soon he was surprised by two other Americans. From his description they must have been Red Curly and Hughes, for these two had turned off to buy some flour in Murphysville (now Alpine). They asked Quintana if he had seen the pack train. He said that he had. He could not understand English, but he understood that the two men now debated killing him. However, the pair rode off without having lived up to their principle: *Los muertos no hablan*. That is all of Quintana's story.

When Hughes and Red Curly joined the other two Americans, the lead *muleros* were halted until the straggling rear should catch up. Then with Juan Estrada accompanying them, they galloped ahead, leaving their mules to be brought on by some of the Mexicans. Just how they murdered Estrada is not known, but certainly they murdered with dispatch and in silence. As the Mexicans, *"carajoing,"* hissing their mules, and jabbing sotol stalks into their bellies, turned up the blind pass leading to El Muerto Springs, they knew that their long three hundred and ninety mile march was almost over. Indeed, it was to be over sooner than they expected.

In all their unreadiness the Mexicans were met by a deadly fire from the treacherous gringos. Only one escaped. He happened to be on his mule, the freshest of the outfit, and ran away. About ten years ago, so the tale runs, Beau McCutcheon, a well-known ranchman of the Davis Mountains, found two silver bars weighing over a hundred pounds each on his ranch. He will not talk about these bars, but Bill Cole is sure that they were dropped by the escaped Mexican. Furthermore, Bill has talked with a Texan who while down in Mexico heard from the escaped Mexican's own lips the whole story of the raid in Monterrey, of the almost unparalleled flight, and of the massacre of his confederates by the American outlaws.

During the massacre Zwing Hunt was severely wounded by a machete that one of the Mexicans managed to seize before he was killed. Hunt's companions put him in a cave, transplanted some river grass, which they got at the springs, in front of the cave and watered it copiously. Meantime, in a hole twelve feet deep, put down in plain sight of Hunt's cave, they buried their plunder. Then they did a strange thing. If I were making this story up, I should not allow them to do it—but "facts are stubborn things." After providing Hunt with a supply of food and water, they left him alone while they went back farther into the mountains. There with brush and pickets they made a kind of fence across the mouth of a grassy canyon, wherein they turned their jaded mounts loose to eat, drink, and rest. The mules—that is, those that had not been killed in the melee—were released, and some of them eventually drifted back to the hay camp at Lobo. At the end of two weeks Hughes, Red Curly, and Doctor Neal returned to their wounded comrade.

They found him nearly well. He said that eight days after the Estrada gang had been butchered, Mexican cavalry appeared in the valley below his cave. He saw them ride about, take spurs and other equipment off the dead bodies, and then at the end of reatas drag them all to a gully and cover them up with rocks and loose gravel. The cavalry went back towards Mexico. The officer in command, so it was later reported, advised the Mexican government that the bandits had been annihilated by him in a pitched battle, but that the Monterrey loot had been taken over by a fresh force of outlaws and carried on into the interior out of reach.

Jim Hughes and his *compadres* now had little fear of further pursuit. Their cache was safe. They filled their saddle bags and *morrals* with coin and rode to El Paso, where they spent money right and left. After carousing a spell, they drifted on out into New Mexico. At Hachita, a stage stand, Hughes wrote his mother: "We rounded up the stuff and buried it in a twelve-foot hole." Hughes had the reputation of being a very dutiful and affectionate son.

In the spring of 1881 the gang made three separate robberies—apparently not from need of money but for the love of the game. The boldest of these acts was holding up the train near Tombstone. In this holdup they killed a mail clerk, blew open the express safe, and got off with a sum of gold so vast that the express company would never admit the amount.

Next, in the Chiricahua Mountains, east of Tombstone, the outlaws killed a man and his son for nothing more than a wagon and two horses. They put their plunder in the wagon and proceeded on across the parched world to El Muerto Springs. Nothing had been touched during their absence. They now had new riches to add to their storage, and they decided to make a thorough job of burying it.

Not far away from the springs they found four Mexican miners tunneling into a mountain. This tunnel, incidentally, has been "lost." They engaged the Mexican miners to dig a deep hole, through solid

rock, right down beside the twelve-foot hole in which the Monterrey stuff was stored. The Mexicans went down eighty-five feet and then tunneled back under a shelving rock for eighteen feet. In lieu of dynamite they had to use sotol heads, which they heated until the sap exploded in the form of steam. They made buckets out of deer and antelope hides. A log was fixed horizontally above the shaft; then by means of a rope cast over it and tied to the horn of a saddle the loosened rock was hoisted in the hide buckets.

After the great hole was completed, the twenty-five mule loads of Monterrey stuff were taken out of the shallow hole and lowered into it. Then on top of this was let down the wagon load of booty freshly brought from Arizona. In the big hole but somewhat apart from the main storage was carefully placed a tomato can full of precious stones taken from the Monterrey cathedral, among them the jeweled eyes of a priceless image of the Virgin Mary. Of course each of the desperadoes held out all he wished, but these personal reservations hardly made a showing on the main treasure.

When the gold and silver and jewels had all been stowed away, the Mexican miners were ordered to seal the hole so that no prying hand could ever get to it. Surely the bandits must have intended to return at some time and take more of the wealth; yet they now, apparently, locked out themselves as well as all meddlers. There were thousands of antelopes in the country, many of them watering at El Muerto Springs. Blood is stronger than water. The outlaws shot antelopes and brought the carcasses in. The miners took the blood from them, and, mixing it with granite gravel, made a cement as irrefragable as the Pillars of Hercules. In the end Jim Hughes boasted that he could tell the world where the riches were buried and they would still be as secure from pillage as though they were locked within the strongest vault of the Bank of England.

While the Mexican miners toiled, Hughes, Red Curly, Zwing Hunt, and Doctor Neal sat in the shade under a juniper tree growing upon the mountain-side and there played poker by the hour. The juniper is still growing. I have sat under it myself, gazed down upon the holes that Bill Cole has been so many years digging, heard a mocking-bird quarreling in the limbs overhead, and watched a bumblebee at red phlox flourishing in the stony soil. What a peaceful and far away world it is that one realizes under that juniper tree in the boundless pasture lands surrounding El Muerto Springs! But that quiet and restful juniper tree forms a valuable piece of evidence in locating the site of an immense prize mortared down not only with antelope blood but with the blood of one hundred and forty-two men who met their death because of it.

The outlaws spent five months, from April to September, in the Davis Mountains. While they were here a consumptive in quest of fresh air came by. He offered them six hundred dollars—all he had—if they would let him live in their camp. They made him keep his money and took care of him until he died, which was within a few weeks. Then they gave him a decent burial, stowing away with him the six hundred dollars in a boot.

And now, with the great treasure all cemented down, the outlaws had to decide what they should do with the Mexican miners who had done the work. *Los muertos no hablan.* They put the bodies of the four miners down in the original treasure hole and covered them with twelve feet of earth.

Whether they so purposed or not, the Hughes gang were through with El Muerto forever. Loaded with money, they went back into New Mexico. They were on the dodge now. They made camp in the mountains east of Silver City. Here a fifth outlaw by the name of Russian Bill joined them. One day while they were all "celebrating" in Silver City, one of them asked a quiet, rather retiring young stranger to have a drink. He declined.

"You're too damned nice to live in this country," yelped an insulted member of the gang and forthwith shot the young man dead.

This was the straw that broke the camel's back. A heavy reward was out for the train robbers, and it was pretty well known who the train robbers were. A posse organized to round them up. Doctor Neal was caught in camp and mortally wounded. He died leaning against a juniper tree. The other bandits scattered.

Zwing Hunt was shot, captured, and taken to Tombstone, where he escaped from the hospital only, it is thought, to be killed by Apache Indians. Many people, however, claim that he was not killed but that he eluded the Apaches and on his death bed in San Antonio years later gave a map—a rather baffling map—to the Monterrey loot.

Russian Bill and Red Curly (Sandy King) were overtaken by the Law and Order League in Shakespeare, a mining town near Lordsburg, and in the absence of trees were hanged, as the ballad has it, from the rafters of the Pioneer House dining room. As they were about to be strung up, Red Curly begged to be shot instead of hanged. He was refused; then he offered to show his captors a wagon load of gold if they would grant his request. Nobody believed that he could fulfill his promise, and so, with handcuffs on, he and Russian Bill had to swing. This was late in the afternoon; the Pioneer House served supper as usual that night. After the bodies were taken down, Jim Engle, a blacksmith and horseshoer, was called upon to file the handcuffs off the dead men. He later moved to West Texas, where Bill Cole has had much talk with him. True, certain chroniclers of the bad-man tradition have set it down that when Russian Bill and Sandy King were hanged, the only charges against them were that Bill was a horse thief and Sandy "a damned nuisance"—but even granting thus much, "what," in the language of Bill Cole, "has that to do with the Monterrey holdup stuff?" As for Jim Hughes, it seems that after leaving the San Simon valley he ran a saloon in Lordsburg for a while, but the only certain thing about the rest of his career is that he never came back to El Muerto Springs.

About ten years after Doctor Neal died leaning against a juniper tree, a New Mexico goat man named Stevens visited the old outlaw camp east of Silver City. He was looking for evidence concerning the Monterrey loot. The first thing he noticed about the camp was "a mummified deer," with only one quarter gone, hanging in a tree. He began to dig around. He uncovered a rock slab. Under the slab he found a box, and in the box, along with some letters addressed to the affectionate Jim Hughes by his mother, was a map to the El Muerto Springs cache. A handful of flour in the bottom of the box showed that it had been used for holding provisions.

When, after devious negotiations, Stevens turned the map over to Bill Cole, Bill at once recognized it to be true to the El Muerto Springs topography. He located thirteen points called for by the map and then beyond all question—in his own mind—he located the exact spot under which the treasure was cemented down. Among the points he located were the juniper tree that shaded the outlaws while they played poker and overlooked the toiling Mexican miners; the cave in which the wounded Hunt stayed for two weeks; the ruins of some adobe corrals that Quintana, the *pastor*, once penned his goats in; also the remains of an early-day stage stand; the trace of an old Indian irrigation ditch; an Indian grave on a peak west of the treasure hole; and a rock called, from its shape, Woman's Head Rock. In the cave Bill found an old gun with some of Hunt's blood still on it. Any Doubting Thomas who wishes to inspect that blood-stained gun may do so.

After making his location, Cole had dug only a few feet before he was convinced beyond the shadow of a doubt that he was following the shaft sunk by the four Mexican miners. Less than ten feet down he struck that extraordinary cement made of granite gravel mixed in antelope blood. The dried blood was still so strong that it attracted blow flies by the tens of thousands; many a hot day Cole had to stop working, the flies were that thick in the hole. On down he found clots of antelope hair. He found a piece of antelope hide, doubtless from one of the hide buckets. The miners had left various rocks jutting out from the walls of the shaft, and in some of these rocks Cole discovered round holes worn by the rope that carried the buckets up and down. On other rocks he found chisel marks. He found a sliver of steel "from some old Spanish tool." Fifty feet down he found a piece of bark from a juniper tree; then a horn button cut out round like a marble with an eye through it for a buckskin string. All along as he went deeper and deeper he found pieces of surface rock.

But a shaft eighty-five feet straight down and then a tunnel eighteen feet back require an enormous amount of digging and lifting for one man's hands. Cole had no funds. The winter after the first season of digging he undertook to enlist capital. He convinced a doctor that there was a fortune at the bottom of the well. The doctor gave up a few dollars to carry on the work, and then the doctor's wife found out what he was doing and put a stop to such extravagance. Meanwhile the Valentine folk and the ranch people around joked, as they still joke, about "the champion money finder of West Texas."

"Talk about the big fight at Muerto Springs," exclaimed John Z. Means, who came to that country about the time the Apaches left it and who is known as the mildest-mannered gentleman that ever drove a cow, "the only fight that ever occurred there was between two old horned frogs."

But no banter has ever caused Bill Cole to draw a faster breath or swallow a drop of tobacco juice. He went on digging. At last when he was nearly down to the eighty-five foot level and was ready to tunnel back to the booty, he struck water. He could not pump it out. Then he got a well driller, for an interest in the loot, to dig an off-set hole, thinking by it to control the water. It was controlled long enough for Cole, working on the floor of his shaft, to jab his crowbar into solid silver. A bit of the silver stuck to the bar, he says. Then the water rushed in again.

Bill has had other partners, other foilings. He sank a second shaft, but water broke into it. Repeatedly the owner of the land has threatened to run Bill off the premises. But his camp is still out there at El Muerto Springs, and the last letter I had from him expressed the expectation of "lifting the wad out in a couple of weeks now." It also expressed unusual concern over income tax laws.

And this concern brings on a sequel. Without knowing anything of my particular interest in the Monterrey loot, a dentist who lives about six hundred miles away from it apprised me not long ago that he had been out to Valentine and while there had become acquainted with an old blacksmith named Engle—the man who cut the handcuffs off the dead bodies of Red Curly and Russian Bill. Engle was morally outraged and was expressing himself in no ambiguous tones. "A certain ne'er-do-well" of the village had proposed that the blacksmith melt up "some cathedral candlesticks to be excavated in the near future." He had indignantly refused to take part in any such sacrilege. Engle also reported the unnamed ne'er-do-well to be constantly discussing means of getting around the income tax laws and at the same time to be living comfortably without any *visible* means of support.

"All this talk about excavation in the near future," concluded Engle, "is just a blind to cover up what has already been done. I can put two and two together."

The reader can make the same addition.[2]

CHAPTER XI

The Challenge of the Desert

The Paiute Indians who used to live in the Death Valley region called the valley Tomesha—*ground afire.*
BOURKE LEE, Death Valley

The impulse to reproduce the species, the impulse to protect offspring, the impulse to wrest gold from the earth—I know not which of these three can operate the most madly and fiercely. The last, usually operating far removed from the humdrum of family cares, seems most romantic. It is on the other side of the world from merely acquisitive money-grubbing. A man who lived among the early California gold hunters wrote of them thus:[1]

"I felt as though I had been translated to another planet. There was nothing here that I had ever seen or heard of before. The great forests, the deep cañons with rivers of clear water dashing over the boulders, the azure sky with never a cloud were all new to me, and the country swarmed with game, such as elk, deer, and antelope, with occasionally a grizzly bear, and in the valleys were many waterfowls. Tall bearded men were digging up the ground and washing it in long toms and rockers, and on the banks by their sides was a sheet iron pan in which were various amounts of yellow gold. These men had neither tents nor houses. They camped under lofty pine or spreading oak trees, for it never rained there in the summer time. They were strong and healthy and lived a life as free as the air they breathed. . . .

"Where all the gold came from was a much mooted question, and they pondered deeply over it and finally settled down to the belief that it must have been thrown out by volcanoes, as the country bore evidence of ancient volcanic convulsions. In 1851, a report was started (but no one knew who started it) that high up in the Sierra Nevada was a lake, evidently the crater of a large volcano, and that the shores of this lake were covered with gold so plentiful that there was little sand or gravel there. As soon as the miners heard this rumor, they at once said, 'That's just where we thought all this gold came from, and

180

what is the use of us digging here in the mud and water for a few hundred dollars a day when we can go up there and just shovel it up by the ton?' And incredible as it now seems, several hundred of them abandoned rich claims and went up into the mountains and spent all summer looking for the 'gold lake.' When they came back, ragged and foot-sore, they found that all their rich claims had been taken by others. I personally knew two men who, in 1851, were working in Rich Gulch on the West Branch of Feather River, taking out three hundred dollars a day apiece. As soon as they heard of Gold Lake, they at once quit their rich claims and spent months and all the money they had searching for this imaginary lake. [It is often called Lingard's Lake now, for Lingard, somebody said, found it, though he was unable to find his way back to it, and it is still an object of search.] . . .

"I once asked some men who, I knew, had families in the states, 'Why don't you quit drinking and gambling and save your money and go back home to your families?' To which they all answered, 'So I would, but don't you see that at the rate gold is being taken out, by the time I got home with a lot of it, it wouldn't be worth any more than so much copper; therefore, I am going to stay right here and have a hell of a good time while it is worth something.' And so they stayed and had that kind of a time. No such enormous amounts of gold had been found anywhere before, and, as they all believed the supply was inexhaustible, there was some justification for their thinking it would soon lose its value."

NUGGETS IN THE SAND

Nothing in nature is more maddening than a summer sandstorm in the desert. The thermometer mounts to 110, 120, even more degrees in the blazing sun. Then the wind rises and begins shifting the dunes. It moves them fifty feet, five hundred feet. Above the swirling, cutting sand the sun becomes a dim copper disc; then there is no sun. The peaks of arid mountains, generally so clearly defined in the distance, blur out. A man caught in the storm cannot see his own hand. At one place the wind scoops out sand until "bottom" is reached; at another it piles up sand into overwhelming crests. On the grazeable fringes of the desert the sand sometimes plays humorous tricks. It has covered up a windmill. The yarn goes that a cowboy awoke one morning to find his horse standing on top of a mesquite tree instead of under it where he had staked him. But in the deadliest wastes of the desert there are no grazing grounds or windmills. A lizard does well to live there.

Somewhere out in the midst of the desert sands of Arizona—I am unable to give the particular region—is a famed aggregátion of gold nuggets—thousands, millions of them. They have been seen twice at least.

One day a Mexican girl was herding goats in the scraggly brush along the eastern fringe of the desert. Some of the goats had strayed considerably out, and it was getting along towards night when the girl saw that a windstorm was rising. She gave the customary call to start the goats homeward, but the strays refused to come. She hurried out to drive them in, but she could not hurry like the wind.

She had walked less than a hundred yards when she became almost blinded by the driving sand. She lost view of the goats. Then she faced the teeth of the wind to make for the shelter of the little Mexican ranch where she lived. Now the sand was cutting like knives. She tried to bear against it, and veered. She zigzagged. She could not see a foot away. She let the wind carry her as it would. She never knew how many hours she stumbled, crawled, cried. She lost all sense of time, direction, purpose.

Finally, though, she realized that she was being swept away like the sand itself and that she had done much more wisely had she not attempted to walk in it. She knew that she was lost, and then she huddled down against the earth to remain there until the storm was over and she could get her bearings. Sometimes such a storm lasts for days, sometimes only for hours. She found herself in what seemed a kind of depression, and there with back against the storm she waited.

The wind grew stronger, if possible, and she felt the sands being carried away from around her. But she remained where she was, settling as the sand settled. After a time, a very long time, she seemed to be at the "bottom," on solid ground. She could feel little rocks about her. There was a difference in light but not in visibility between night and day; the night and half of a day went by, and then the wind lulled.

The shepherd girl could see. She looked at the mute and unfamiliar horizon about her. She looked at the appalling sky. She looked at the ground beneath her feet. The little rocks she had felt were gold nuggets! Far away across the waste of sand she saw the smoke of a train.

Home was perhaps nearer than the railroad, but the girl did not know where she was. She had lost all sense of direction and could not recognize a single landmark. She knew that if she could reach the railroad, the next train would stop for her.

She gathered into her lap as many nuggets as she could carry and started towards the railroad. Not a mark on the sand was there to go by, only the memory of the faint line of smoke and the smoky sun. She ran, she walked, she fell, she staggered, she crawled. She reached the railroad.

When a train came, it, according to the custom of the desert, stopped, and the trainmen took the shepherd girl on board. The sight of her nuggets drove them wild and assured her careful attention in the nearest town. She was quickly restored; meantime a train crew that had quit their jobs waited for her to guide them.

They need not have waited. All she knew was the direction she had waded from in the sands to reach the track. She was vague as to the time it had taken her to traverse the distance. Perhaps she had not moved in a straight line. There was not a mark on the horizon to go by; there remained not a footprint in the restless sands.

The search was fruitless, and the winds came again, and the sands shifted back and forth in their way, and the Mexican shepherd girl never saw again the golden rocks that lie below the sands.

However, tradition has it that a cowboy who was once trying to cross the desert came accidentally upon the marvelous display of gold. He gathered enough of the nuggets to fill his saddle pockets and he even removed his saddle blanket so that he could roll the gold up in it. He forgot the fearful price one may pay for gold in the desert. Had he taken the right direction, he might have ridden to water. But he forgot or missed directions. His horse at length sank exhausted, and he shot him to drink his blood. Then the cowboy went on. He threw away everything that he had even to the last nugget. At last, as it seemed by the providence of God, he dragged his perishing frame to a water hole and to human aid.

In the desert the hot winds blow and the sands shift and there is never a traveler's track but is blown away. The skeletons out there buried so deep one day and exposed so bare and naked the next tell no stories, write no epilogues. Only be sure of this: what the sands uncover one day they will cover again the next. And, the desert rat says, what they cover they will also uncover—some day.

THE BREYFOGLE MINE

One day in 1862 while racing across Nevada a horse ridden by Pony Bob Haslam of the Pony Express stumbled to his knees. In recovering his feet, the horse kicked loose a chunk of rock that caught the eye of his rider. He took it to Virginia City, where it was pronounced to be silver ore of extraordinary richness. Hell breaking loose in Georgia was nothing compared with the stampede that California made to the Reese River district. The "excitement" centered in and around the present town of Austin, Nevada.

Staying in Los Angeles at the time the news broke were three men who, although without funds or means of conveyance, determined to get to Reese River. Their names were McLeod, O'Bannion, and Breyfogle. The great silver strike was four hundred miles north across the most desolate, forbidding, and inexorable region of mountain and desert on the North American continent. The stage route led nearly four hundred miles northwest of Los Angeles to Sacramento City, still three hundred miles away from the silver, and then cut east. I am giving air line measurements. Either route twisted like a corkscrew. There was no traveled road of any kind across the desert. All people of sound judgment took the stage route. Some of the forty-niners who had tried the shortcut paid their lives to give one spot it traversed a name—Death Valley. Still, if you are going afoot, it makes a difference whether you are to walk, say, six hundred miles or a thousand. Breyfogle and his partners were going to Nevada silver afoot. They decided to cut straight across.

It was about the first of June, summer in the desert, when they set out, carrying some provisions, a blanket apiece, canteens, and rifles with which they hoped to procure jack rabbit meat along the way. At the San Fernando Mission the hospitable padres tried to persuade them to abandon such a perilous undertaking, but they trudged on. They crossed the Mohave Desert, skirted the southern spurs of the Argus Range, crept across the glittering waste known as the Panamint Valley, and at length began ascending the awful Panamint Mountains, from the heights of which can be seen to the east the weird, unearthly basin of horrors called Death Valley and on beyond it the Funeral Range.

On the eastern slope of the Panamints they came, while following a crude Indian trail, to a rock *tinaja* in which they found water. Here they prepared to spend the night. The ground was so rough that they

184

experienced great difficulty in finding smooth places on which to lie down. McLeod and O'Bannion made their pallet together near the water hole; Breyfogle found a bedding place about two hundred yards down the slope. The men, as was their custom, slept with all their clothing on, removing only their shoes.

That unusual separation of himself from his comrades saved Breyfogle's life. He woke in the night to hear shouts and groans and to realize that Indians were murdering the other sleepers. He jumped from his blanket, grabbed his shoes, and with them and nothing else in his hand fled barefooted to the valley below. Only a crazy man of brute toughness could have run barefooted in darkness over rocks and thorn stubble as Breyfogle ran. Breyfogle was very near the brute both physically and mentally, and now he was utterly crazed with fear.

At daylight he found himself down in the bottom of Death Valley. Fearful lest the Indians might still follow him, he secreted himself for several hours in a fold of gravel and sand before attempting to cross to the eastern side, a distance of about ten miles. His feet were so bruised and torn that he was unable to put on his shoes.

The terrific June sun beat upon his bare head. Thirst became stronger than fear. In the afternoon he began traveling. By some mad chance he came at the eastern edge of the valley to a little geyser-like hole of alkali water. He drank it, the first water he had tasted since the previous evening. It made him deathly sick, but he soon recovered, and, filling his shoes with water—they were big shoes and they were stout—limped on. Not after the experience of the night before would he ever again lie down to sleep near a water hole.

After traveling about an hour into the lower foothills of the Funeral Range, he halted, heaped up some rocks in the form of a wall to lie behind, and went to sleep. During the night he drank the contents of one of his shoes. At the break of day he drank the water from the other shoe and then set out to gain the top of the range eight or ten miles ahead of him. He was sick. The alkali water whetted more than it allayed thirst.

About half way up the mountain Breyfogle saw off to the south a green spot that he took to be growth marking a spring. He judged it to be about three miles away. He turned towards it. He had covered about half the distance to the green spot when his attention was arrested by float rock of a soft grayish-white cast with free gold showing plainly all through it.

Fearful as he was of Indians, exhausted and battered as he was from the torture he had endured, mad as he was for a swallow of fresh, cool water, he paused at the sight of the gold ore. He picked up several of the richest pieces and tied them in his bandana. He started on again towards the green spot and had taken but a few steps when he came upon the vein itself from which the float had washed. Here the ore was pinkish feldspar, much richer in gold than the float. Breyfogle discarded his first samples and gathered a bandana of the pink ore.

The time spent gathering ore amounted to only a few minutes. Breyfogle skulked, limped on towards the green spot. It proved to be a low, bushy mesquite tree, very green and full of green beans. The man ate so ravenously of them and was so disappointed in not finding water that he collapsed, and, as he afterwards said, lost his mind.

But he apparently never lost his sense of direction. He recovered, though he could never recollect when. The experiences he endured for days following remained ever afterwards absolutely blank to him. Water of some kind he must have somehow found, but how and where he could not remember. He knew the value of *viznaga* juice. He no doubt ate roots and herbs. The indisputable fact is that he kept walking north, across the Funeral Range, and then across the wide Amargosa Desert. At the clear fresh water of Baxter Springs, fully two hundred and fifty miles—as one must travel—from the point where he had emerged from Death Valley, Breyfogle came to his right mind. After remaining here for two days, drinking water and eating whatever green and edible vegetation he could find, he continued on—bound for the Reese River silver strike. He crossed into Smoky Valley and there saw the first human being he had glimpsed since the murder of his partners.

A man by the name of Wilson was ranching in Smoky Valley. While out one morning cutting for horse tracks, he came upon the prints of a man's bare feet. Astonished at their size and shape, he put spurs to his horse and within a few miles overtook Breyfogle. For many years afterwards his description of the human object before him was a part of a fireside story familiar all over Nevada and eastern California.

Breyfogle, he said, was all but naked. His pants were in shreds, the shreds coming only to his knees, while the tattered remains of a shirt did little more than cover the shoulders. His black hair and beard were long and matted. Breyfogle was a Bavarian and at this time he was about forty years old. He was heavy-boned, thick through the breast, stood all of six feet high, and under normal conditions weighed around two hundred pounds. He was strikingly bow-legged, and, as has already been suggested, had enormous feet. He was naturally of a swarthy complexion. He appeared to Wilson a cadaverous giant parched and seared as if by the fires of hell. He was still carrying his shoes. In one of them was stuffed a bandana tied around some specimens of ore.

The rancher took the wild man of the desert home with him and, aided by his wife, provided him with food and clothing. A few days later he took him to Austin and there turned him over to a mining friend named Jake Gooding, who put Breyfogle to work in a quartz mill.

Breyfogle told Gooding all he could about his mine. The samples of ore he showed told more. Some were almost half gold. The season was too hot for an immediate expedition, but three months later Gooding and Breyfogle, accompanied by five or six other men and well provided with saddle horses, pack mules, water casks, and provisions, set out. Upon reaching the Funeral Range, however, they were met by a war party of Panamint Indians and turned back to Austin for reinforcements.

Meantime authorities in Los Angeles had been notified of the fate of Breyfogle's partners; a search party had gone out and had found the remains of the victims at the place described by the survivor.

During the winter a second expedition made up of about a dozen men set forth to find the gold. They got through the mountains to Death Valley without Indian troubles. Breyfogle led them to the geyser-like hole of alkali water where he had filled his shoes. Without much difficulty, he led them to a low, wall-shaped heap of rocks, where he had spent the night after his partners were murdered. From this he led them on up the Funeral Range a distance; then he turned abruptly south—towards a spot no longer green, though only a few months before so green that it had appeared to mark a spring of water. About three miles from where they started south the party came to a bare, scrubby mesquite tree.

"This," said Breyfogle, "is where I gorged the mesquite beans, fainted, and lost my mind. We ought to have passed the gold on our way here from the north. I picked up the specimens of pink feldspar just over yonder and put them in my bandana."

Of course there were other mesquite shrubs in the country, but Breyfogle was sure of the one. He was sure of the water hole; he was sure of the heap of rocks. But the gold? Breyfogle coursed and re-

coursed away from and back to the mesquite. He saw another mesquite. He wavered. The men with him searched frantically in every direction. Then some of them jeered him; some cursed him for having led them on a wild goose chase; some were sure that if they could remain in the region a reasonable length of time they could find the gold. But a party full of discord will not persist at anything. The gold hunters packed up and returned to Austin. Breyfogle left the country, and thus ended what promised to be but an easy walk to the mine he gave his name to.

Not all the hunters who have gone out since have got back to explain their failure. But desert rats still search. George Hearst, father of the notorious publisher and one of the most successful mining men of his day, secured a piece of Breyfogle's ore and for two winters kept prospectors in the field looking for the lost vein. He believed in it. Many men still believe in it, though most of them think that while Breyfogle was waiting in Austin for cooler weather before returning to claim his gold a cloudburst swept down the slopes of the Funeral Mountains and covered it up. They are hoping that another cloudburst will uncover it.

This is just one of many stories about Breyfogle, some of them very different. But I put particular credence in this, for the original narrator of it, Donald F. MacCarthy, made, thirty years ago, two visits to Jake Gooding, and thus received his information first-hand. Gooding had talked many times with Wilson, rescuer of Breyfogle; he had himself befriended Breyfogle, seen his golden rocks, listened to him tell his story over and over, and then gone with him to refind the gold. Mr. MacCarthy's own hunts for the Breyfogle Mine at least acquainted him with the terrain.[2]

YUMA'S GOLD

Some sixty miles to the northeast of Tucson, Arizona, the sand bed of Arivaipa Creek joins with the sand bed of San Pedro River, both sand beds generally being "as dry as a lime-burner's hat." At this junction was Old Camp Grant—to be distinguished from new Camp Grant— and at the time of which we are to tell, the early seventies, the Arivaipa band of Apaches had their main camp amid the Arivaipa Hills about ten miles distant. The route between Camp Grant and Tucson was marked by piles of loose stones indicating places where Apaches had killed their white enemies, the cairns for Mexican victims usually being distinguished by rude crosses of stalks from the mescal and Spanish dagger plants. Those crosses were unutterably lonely. The Arivaipa Indians wanted to keep their homeland.

The one white man who became intimate with them and wormed from them the secret their harsh land concealed, thus unwittingly acquiring a fame that will probably last as long as that so striven for by "the poet of the Sierras," is remembered only by the name of Yuma. A graduate of West Point, he had seen several years of border service when, still a lieutenant, he came to Fort Yuma on the Colorado River as acting-quartermaster of that post. Ocean steamers in those days brought freight through the Gulf of California to the mouth of the Colorado, where it was transferred to river steamers, which carried it on up to Fort Yuma. Here it was discharged to be hauled by wagons far inland. Thus the acting-quartermaster's position gave him supervision over all supplies not only for his own post but for other posts strung across a vast territory. The tonnage he handled was enormous, payment for supplies usually being made by vouchers on the Quartermaster General's office in San Francisco. Such a volume of business in such an isolated region gave opportunity for peculation. The lieutenant fell under the sway of dishonest army contractors, and when official investigation revealed their practices he was court-martialed and discharged from the army.

A man of gentle breeding and an officer in whom military training had inculcated the highest degree of pride, he felt his disgrace keenly. He became a pariah from his own people and took refuge among the Yuma Indians, who lived about the fort and among whom he had made many friends. The chief of these Indians was Pascual, grave and gaunt, with leathery wrinkled cheeks and a prodigious nose, from which hung an ornament made of white bone embellished by swinging pendants. Few chiefs among American Indians have enjoyed such absolute power as Pascual wielded over the Yumas. His people at this time were living in peace and plenty. Their superior physique struck the eye of every traveler. The women were like noble partridges, and one of these old Pascual gave to the exiled lieutenant, who married her and became an adopted member of the tribe. Thenceforth he was known to white men by no other name than Yuma.

Yuma became an Indian trader. His adopted people were at peace with the various divisions of the Apache tribes, and among these, with his bride as a protective talisman, he was free to travel and traffic.

Taking pack mules loaded with rifle ammunition and other goods desired by the Apaches, Yuma and his wife penetrated where no white trader before him had dared intrude. He seems to have been genuinely in love, and he was loved. The life was congenial; profits were satisfactory; he confessed himself happier than he had ever been before in his life.

About a year after his marriage he found himself among the Arivaipa Apaches, who received him well. From his wife and from other sources he had heard that the Arivaipas possessed a deposit of gold from which they had been known to barter rich specimens. This deposit they, of course, guarded with fierce secrecy. Presuming now on his own reputation for being "a good Indian," which to all intents and purposes he was, he took the friendly chief apart, and, displaying before him a fine rifle, a beaded belt full of ammunition, and some curious silver spangles, offered them in exchange for a glimpse of the coveted spot.

The chief parried and debated with Yuma—and no doubt with himself—a long time. It was his office as it was that of no other Apache to keep the traditional secret of the gold. Still, the fact that Yuma was a member of an allied tribe entitled him to certain rights and privileges. Also, the fine rifle, the beautiful belt, and the gaudy spangles were powerful orators. Finally the chief acquiesced.

"I will show you tomorrow morning," he said.

Shortly after daybreak the next morning he and Yuma, unaccompanied, left camp afoot, ostensibly to hunt deer. Traveling in a northerly direction, they ascended a long ridge, on which they kept for about three miles. Then they came to the crest of a low but asperous range of mountains overlooking the San Pedro valley to the east. Still pursuing a route generally northward, they continued in this rough country for about six miles.

They were picking their way along the side of a gulch, keeping well up from the bottom, when the chief stopped. He stood beside an inconspicuous crater-like depression, perhaps six feet in diameter at its shallow bottom and rimmed with rock.

"Here," he said, scanning the horizon.

Yuma got inside the depression and began digging with his hunting knife and hands. A few inches down he struck ore. It was so compact that he could only with great difficulty break off a handful. But that handful, together with the sight of the marvelous vein from which it had been taken, filled him with such joy that he could scarcely keep

192

from shouting to the hilltops. The ore, wonderfully rich in gold, was a rose quartz. It was very beautiful.

After getting the sample, Yuma, aided by the chief, filled in the hole and carefully smoothed it over. Before leaving, he noted the lay of the ground on every side; he noted that the gulch below him headed only a few hundred yards beyond. The terrain, as he later described it, was so exceedingly broken and rocky that no one who had not seen the spot marking the ore would be likely ever to come upon it. The chief told him that, while he had nothing to fear from himself, if any of his braves ever found him in that vicinity they would kill him on sight.

Now, Yuma knew nothing of mining, but from his description of the place from which he took the ore, it must have been at the top of what is technically known as a chimney. Its position assured it against being obliterated by either cloudburst or landslide. A "chimney" of such ore as Yuma showed samples of might well produce a million dollars in gold in a very short time without much expense.

On the way back to camp Yuma and the chief killed a deer. Then to avoid the suspicion that a hasty departure might breed, the trader remained among the Apaches for several days before leaving for Tucson. There he expected to meet a friend whom he wanted for a partner. He found him.

The man was a young freighter named Crittenden, who had several wagons hauling ore from mining camps about Tucson to Fort Yuma for loading on river steamers. He was from Kentucky, a worthy kinsman of the brilliant statesman, John J. Crittenden.

Keeping the secret of the great find to themselves, Yuma and Crittenden prepared to explore the mine at once, it being arranged that the young Indian wife should stay with Mrs. Crittenden.

Leaving Tucson late one afternoon, the two men rode on horseback all night and early next morning reached Camp Grant. Here they rested until evening and then, without committing themselves, struck northward down the San Pedro. After they had ridden some ten miles, Yuma said that they were about opposite the mine; accordingly, they unsaddled, picketed their horses, and lay down to await daylight. They did not sleep much.

At daylight they began climbing the range to the west. It was so steep and rough that they were obliged to lead their horses most of the time. Hours of climbing brought them to the gulch up which the Arivaipa chief had led Yuma. They had a pick and shovel. They worked two hours, took out about thirty pounds only of the richest

193

ore, and then, after covering the hole over and burying the pick and shovel, they set out for Tucson. Instead of returning to the valley of the San Pedro and going by way of Old Fort Grant, they coursed down the western slope of the mountains and then crossed a trackless basin. They traveled all night and arrived in Tucson about daylight.

Immediately they had the ore crushed—all but a few lumps to be preserved as specimens—and the gold panned out. From less than thirty pounds of ore they recovered $1200 worth of gold. The operation could not well be kept secret; the whole town went wild.

Yuma and Crittenden now decided that it would be wise to allow excitement to subside before attempting development. So Crittenden continued with his freighting business, and Yuma, once more accompanied by his wife, struck out on a trading expedition among the Papago Indians on the Papago Desert, a hundred miles west of Tucson. Never before had this idyllic couple traveled so gleefully, in such gay spirits, with prospects so bright. It was their last journey.

The Papagos were ever a gentle people towards the whites. It was the Papagos who under Father Kino built the mission of San Xavier del Bac on the Santa Cruz, nine miles above Tucson, pronounced by competent critics to be the most beautiful example of mission architecture in America. But gentle as they were towards *cristianos*, towards the Apaches the Papagos were as fierce and relentless as "the tigers of the desert" themselves, and they regarded the Yuma Indians as Apache allies.

Why Yuma should have taken his wife among them or why she allowed herself to go among them will never be known. She was immediately recognized as belonging to a hostile tribe. The older Indians were consternated. They believed the traders to be spies sent by Apaches to forerun a raid. No details of the fate of the young couple ever reached the outside world, but in Tucson and elsewhere it came to be the general opinion that they had been lured into the fastness of the desert and there destroyed.

Crittenden knew where his partner had gone. He waited long weeks for his return. Finally he gave up hope and prepared to set out alone for the mine in the Arivaipa country, so that he might there post notice of his discovery and thus legally complete his title. As he and Yuma had traveled before, he now rode to Old Camp Grant. He remained there for two days, and this time he seems to have made no secret of his mission. He rode a particularly fine horse, which the soldiers much admired. Telling them that he would return that evening, he left the camp early one morning.

Crittenden did not come back. Three days later some soldiers who scouted out on his trail found his horse entangled in a picket rope and almost starved for water. He had been picketed on the west side of the San Pedro sand bed about ten miles below (north of) the army post and near the foot of a broken range of mountains. Near by were saddle and bridle untouched. The best trailers in camp scoured the surrounding country for days; they found where Crittenden had climbed the mountain afoot. That was all. He must have taken his rifle with him, but the probability is that he had no chance to use it. Quite likely he was near the mine when the bullet from an ambushed Apache put an end to his life.

It may easily be surmised that Apaches had come upon the sign of horses in their hills and had seen where the forbidden earth had been

disturbed. Ever alert, they had then awaited the return of prospectors.

Soon after the disappearance of Crittenden a band of about a hundred Papagos, led by a few Americans and aided by some Mexicans, surprised the Arivaipa Apaches, who were at the time in a condition unwontedly docile, and literally butchered man, woman, and child. This horror is known in history as the Camp Grant Massacre, 1871. It assured perpetual muteness to most of the band's secrets.

As to Yuma's Mine, it is still out there in the Arivaipa hills untouched. The million dollars in gold are still to be taken from its "chimney" formation. The beautiful rose quartz that Yuma uncovered and then covered up again is still hidden by the loose shale of the mountain side. And though "the tigers of the desert" no longer guard it, it is guarded by something fiercer and more relentless than all the tigers of the world. It is guarded by the desert itself.

CHAPTER XII

In the Sunshine of the Pecos

For them still
Somewhere on the sunny hill,
Or along the winding stream,
Through the willows, flits a dream;
Flits, but shows a smiling face,
Flees, but with so quaint a grace,
None can choose to stay at home,
All must follow, all must roam.
ROBERT LOUIS STEVENSON

And nowhere are the tales of Coronado's children quite so bright and fresh as along the upper Pecos. That must be because of the sunshine, in which all day long the children sing:

Tu eres Lupita divina
Como los rayos del sol.

Pecos village, seven thousand feet up in the mountains of New Mexico and thirty miles southeast of antique Santa Fe, was a pueblo of Indians centuries before Columbus dreamed of a sail. On his long march in search of the Gran Quivira, Coronado camped at the village, then called Cicuye; it was at that time the largest and strongest of the pueblos. By 1620 the Spaniards had erected a church at the place, and in the great Pueblo revolt of 1680 the priest of this church was assassinated while fleeing the village. The Pecos Mexicans point to the red earth along the high mesa southwest of the Arroyo Pecos and say that the priest's blood stained it. The Santa Fe Trail from Missouri twisted by Pecos village. In the quadrangle against the Pecos church the fated Texans of the Santa Fe expedition were, in 1841, herded as prisoners before setting out on their two-thousand mile Journey of Death to the prisons of Mexico City. Meanwhile the Pecos Indians had declined until the remnant, only seventeen souls, "abandoned the crumbling ruins of the dwellings that had housed their ancestors for so many centuries" and went to Jemez eighty miles away, leaving the relics for legend to mystify and archaeology to excavate.[1]

The modern Pecos village is down under the hill from the ancient pueblo. Here lives José Vaca. I shall never forget him. First of all, he took me to inspect the deep cave that for four years he had been boring into the crooked seam of a mountain. After we had explored it, we climbed high above, whence we could see the Pecos River winding and shining in the sun and land after land of mountains beyond. Then, high up there in the sunshine, José told me the history of his cave and many another tale out of his inexhaustible supply. I say inexhaustible, for his father and grandfather sought all their lives and he has sought all his life to find the golden treasure that for each succeeding generation shines brighter and more alluring.

With many apologies to José—and to the sunshine on the Pecos—I set down some of the stories that he told, only omitting the most joyous profanity that I have ever heard. Picture him cross-eyed, his mouth twisted into an extraordinary slant, and his whole body gesturing with Latin energy while he talks and talks. Think of him, too, as very honest, for he knows how to say "I do not know." And remember, as you listen to the tales, that New Mexico is a land of dead cities and that the Indian of today is as chary of his secrets as are the Indian skeletons that have lain drying in those dead cities hundreds of years.

BEWITCHED SAND

"My grandfather live in Pecos down there to be more than a hundred years old," said José Vaca. "When I was young before he die, I hear him say many things, but I was not careful then to listen. He knew Indians that lived here in this Pecos pueblo and he bought a piece of land from one of them. After he pay for the land, and the Indian was leaving to go far away, the Indian he say: 'You have here now more wealth than is in the world elsewhere.'

" 'How?' ask my grandfather. 'Show me.'

"Then the Indian take him and a burro to where was some sand in the creek. They put some sand in sacks and bring it on the burro, and they get twenty-five dollars worth of gold out of that one load of sand.

"That night the Indian disappear, and the next day my grandfather he go with two burros and load both with the sand. He bring it up, and from it he do not get one thing. Nothing, I tell you. That old In-

198

dian is gone, but he has his eyes on the sand. Maybe he was *un brujo* [a wizard]. Maybe the sand was *embrujada* [bewitched]. I do not know. I know when the Indian is here the sand has gold. I know when the Indian is gone the gold is all gone too."

EL MACHO

"El Macho is little way up the river from Pecos. A long time ago one Mexican living there named Epimeño bought a boy from the Indians and raise him to be *pastor*. This boy used to go out with the sheep and stay all day. He was very wise. He was strong wrestler too. Now, this Epimeño has a son named Licencio. One day while Licencio is wrestling with the Indian, he feel something hard against his own chest.

" 'What is that?' Licencio ask.

"But the Indian boy will not tell. The Licencio t'rew him down and found a piece of pure silver, as big as hen egg, tied to a buckskin string around the Indian's neck.

"The Mexican boy tole his father, and then old Epimeño commence to follow the Indian everywhere. 'Tell me where you find that silver,' he say. 'If you do not tell me I will kill you.'

"The Indian he took Epimeño first to one hill, then to another, but he never show him the silver. Old Epimeño beat him and starve him and crawl behind him in the pasture like a coyote. After a while the Indian boy tole Licencio that he is going to run away and find his own people. 'I cannot stand such hard master,' he say.

" 'You been brought all this trouble on me,' he say to Licencio, 'but you are kind. I remember always the food you steal for me. I will tell you where the silver is. It is on the mountain just west of Epimeño's house. Go there and you will see an old shoe hanging from a tree. By that shoe is enough silver to make you rich forever.'

"The Indian left. Licencio was scared to tell his father how the Indian came to trust him. Maybe he did not believe the story about the silver. He was too lazy to climb the mountain to hunt the old shoe. But one day he tole a friend named Parrilla.

" 'Let's go,' say Parrilla.

"They go. Sure enough they found the old shoe. But they cannot find the silver.

"Perhaps the Indians were watching them."

199

LA MINA PERDIDA

The big mine of the Pecos country is somewhere far up towards the head of the canyon. It was worked centuries ago by the Spanish, and much of the wealth buried by them down the river, while they were trying to reach Mexico with their precious cargoes, came from it. The mine may have been either gold or silver, but the consensus of opinion is that it was gold. It is called simply La Mina Perdida—The Lost Mine.[2]

"One time," said José, "my father-in-law and I were hunting deer up in that country. Oh, it is far, far from here! We had a deer loaded on one horse when it began to rain. We got under some trees, and while we waited what do you think we found there? We found an ole flume and an anvil. The anvil was more big than any anvil I ever see before. Very certainly some big work was done there at one time. Well, it kept raining and we stay there for two hours, and I look and look at the mountains all about and the trees and at everything so that I can know the place when I come back.

"There was a canyon close by with very pretty water in it, and I want to stay and try for fish, but my father-in-law he keep saying, 'Let's go, let's go.' I know very well there are fine trout in that canyon, but I must wait for another time to catch them. Then we left while it was still raining.

"We come back here to Pecos, and I tole ole Martín Salazar about that flume and anvil, and he say: 'Very surely you have found The Lost Mine.' Ole Man Hughes he say the same thing, and Francisco Ortejo, and many other ole mens also. Those ole mens been live a long time and surely they know some things, but all are dead now.

"I tole my father-in-law if he can go back to the flume and anvil, and he say of course he can. So when the time is come to hunt we go. But, son-of-a-gun, if we can find that place. I never even see that canyon with nice water in it where I know very well the trout are waiting. By holy saints, but to hunt for lost mine and lost money is hard work, very hard. Always something, always something, look like, is against the man. The Indians they watch that lost mine too."

THAT OLE MAN DEVIL

José's most fatalistic experience, however, is connected not with gold or silver but with what he calls a mica mine. It is above the headwa-

ters of the Pecos. Like La Mina Perdida, it was found by him while he was hunting in company with his father-in-law.

"We come on a whole mountain side of the mica," said José. "The mica was clear to see like that shining water down there in the *acequia*. We stay there a long time and get a lot of the mica and pack it on the burro. The slabs be so big I have to break them up. Oh, there was a quarter, maybe a half mile, of the mica all clear, right there on the ground, uncovered. It was joy to see it.

"After I load the burro, I feel a nail in my shoe, and I take the shoe off and hammer down the nail with a rock. While I am working, a piece of the heel come off and I leave that ole heel there on the ground —right where I get the mica to load on the burro. Then we all feel fine and come back to Pecos.

"Soon afterwards I was working on the new road up the river. Mr. McCarch he was boss, and I have plenty of time to talk to him. It is my business to shoot the dynamite, and often I have to wait long times for the other men to get ready for me. While I wait and talk, I tell Mr. McCarch about this mica mine. He get very excite and ask me to show him samples. I bring him a piece; he send it off, and after he hear from Denver—or maybe it was some other place—he get more excite. I never see a man so eager like that.

" 'We will have to work no longer,' he say. 'There is plenty mica for you and all your children and grandchildren and all your *parientes* and all the children of your *parientes*. Plenty too for me. I will be pardners with you, and we will work the mine.'

"Then we make pardnership and go before a judge and sign paper. I was one; Mr. McCarch was one; my father-in-law he make three, and Francisco he make four. Francisco is brother-in-law. He want to bring another American, but we will not let that, and we talk too much. Then we get ready to go up for the mica. It was the right time of year, in July, when it is not too cold. But Mr. McCarch he cannot leave his work. So he sent a man was named Iglehart in his place.

"It takes us three days to go from the Pecos River into those mountains. And then high, high up we make camp close to the mica mine. When we stop, Mr. Iglehart and Francisco begin to sleep, and I never see such men for sleepy. I do not know what is the matter with that man Iglehart. He sleep till eleven o'clock next day; then he eat some breakfast and dinner and go back to sleep. He sleep all that day and all that night. The second day I say to him if he has come to hunt mica mine or to sleep. 'Oh, I am so sleepy,' he say, and he sleep all that day.

"When third day was come, I say to him, 'Let's go find that mine. What for you come up here? You never going quit sleep?'

"Then he look round and say, 'Oh, see that cloud. Rain coming this day. I do not like to go out.'

"Then he sleep all that day.

"I do not know what to do. I look and I look and I know very well we are in the right place, but there is no mica. I tell you I find that heel of my old shoe which I leave there when I was loading mica on the burro. But there is no mica now. My father-in-law he look too and he say that sure we are in the right place of the mountains. Francisco at last was looking also, but that man Iglehart will do nothing.

" 'I cannot walk,' he say. 'It looks like rain,' he say.

"Nobody lives in that mountains—nobody. After while I go down into a canyon, and there I meet an ole Mexican man. He is looking at the ground and has no gun.

" 'What you doing here?' I ask him.

" 'I hunt bear,' he answer.

" 'You hunt bear here all alone and so ole and have no gun!' I say.

" 'Huh,' he say, 'what you do here? You hunt mica mine. You no can find it. No use for you to hunt mica mine. You never put cross up when you see it first time.'

"I do not know who that ole man is. Maybe he is devil. I never see such looking man before. But I want to be friends with him. He knows something about these mountains, I think. Perhaps he has been here long time. I want to treat him nice so he will tell me something.

" 'Come to camp,' I say. 'We have plenty to eat. Come and eat with us.'

" 'Oh, I have lots to eat,' he answer. 'I eat up there.' And he point to the sky. I cannot understand what it is.

"Then I go back to camp and tell my father-in-law and Francisco what I have seen. Francisco laughs at me and thinks I am liar. Then next morning over in another canyon, there he see that same ole man, and the ole man talk to him just like he been talk to me. Then Francisco knows I am speaking truth.

"It is no use to hunt for mica any longer, I see very well. When I say, 'All right, let us go back to Pecos,' that man Iglehart jump up.

" 'Oh, I am feeling fine,' he says. 'I can walk. I do not know what has been the matter with me. It is not going to rain now, sure.'

"Son-of-a-gun, damn! I know that he has bad heart, and I was wishing many times on that trip that he was not with us. That Francisco, too, had some bad heart.

"We come back and Mr. McCarch was very sorrowful. 'You and I go all alone sometime,' he say. 'We will not take the others, but we will be honest and give them their part when we have found the mine.'

"We make plan to go the next summer, but when summer is come Mr. McCarch is having trouble with his wife. She is getting divorce from him. He cannot go. I do not know what has become of that man. That was eight, ten year ago. I wish he write me and say, 'Let's go.'

"Sandoval—he lives here in Pecos—has seen that mica too. It is there. If we had it we could live always in pleasure. I never see anything like that mica. I thought I could go to it with my eyes shut; I went with them open and I could not see. What you think about that ole man devil had talk with me?"

THE MONTEZUMA OF THE PECOS

All over northern Mexico and the southwestern part of the United States the fable of Montezuma is believed and told. The word *montezumas* has among Mexicans become a synonym for *ruins*. At Del Rio, four hundred miles down the Rio Grande from the *montezumas* of El Paso, Sugar Loaf Hill hides the fabulous riches of Montezuma secreted there to prevent their falling into the hands of the Spaniards. The famous ruins of Casas Grandes, Chihuahua, are but "the old houses of Montezuma." At the head of an inaccessible canyon in Sonora, Apaches today are guarding Montezuma's millions. Out in Arizona a gigantic sink into which legend has cast Montezuma's wealth goes by the name of Montezuma's Well, and in the same region some ancient cliff-dwellings bear the name of Montezuma's Castle.[3]

Various localities of New Mexico claim to be the birthplace of Montezuma and to be now the repository of his hidden treasures; but the claim of Pecos village is most insistent, most famous. Somewhere in the mountains about Pecos, according to belief among both Indians and Mexicans, a fire is kept constantly burning in a cave awaiting the return of Montezuma from the south, though a giant serpent sometimes devours the pious tenders of the fire. Some of the Pecos Mexicans say that Montezuma wore golden shoes and that he walked in them to Mexico City, where the Spaniards confiscated them—so that he could not walk back. According to other *pecoseños*, Montezuma never left their village at all.[4]

Be all this as it may, a young Pueblo Indian a good many years ago was put in jail at Las Vegas on the rare charge of raping a girl of his tribe. Now the tribal punishment for rape, so José say, is to strip the guilty man naked, stake him down in an ant bed, and leave him there until the ants have left nothing but the bleached bones. The Indian in Las Vegas jail was less afraid of the courts than of tribal punishment; he knew that even if he were sent to the penitentiary, he would be watched by his tribesmen and put to their terrible punishment the day he was released. But I shall let José tell the story.

"The Indian tole his fear to Don Salamón. He was sheriff to watch the jail. This Salamón has a very kind heart, and he told the Indian he will let him run away in the night time so he can go far, far from his people and not have to die in ant bed. So he let the Indian loose, and that Indian is so happy and so grateful that he tole Don Salamón the great secret of all the Indians of the Pecos country. Now the Indian could surely never come back, for it was death to tell this secret.

" 'You go,' the Indian say to Don Salamón, 'to the ole church at Pecos pueblo and find the Spanish road to Santa Fe. Right on that hill where the pueblo is, not more than the length of a *cabrestro* [hair rope] from the road, you will find a white rock with an old cross on it. The cross is made of wood; it is very little, and is planted down in the rock so that it will not fall. Right next to that white rock is a black rock. The black rock is to hide a cave. But do not go into the cave. Dig under the white rock. You will not have to dig deep. A very little work will do the business. As soon as the white rock with the cross on it is pulled up, you will find the *patrón*; then only seven feet under the *patrón* you will find the gold.'

"You know," José reminded me, "what *patrón* is. It is the dead man who guards the treasure. All these peoples long time ago who hide great treasure been careful to have *patrón*. The Indian tole Don Salamón this *patrón* was Montezuma. Montezuma was half Spanish and half Indian, but he love his Indian people more, for he grow up with them and is a great chief. And Montezuma have gold—more than any man today can count—and he knows if the Spanish find this gold is among Indian people, it be worse with them than if they keep poor.

"So when Montezuma was dying, he ordered that all his gold be put in one great hole close to his pueblo. When he see the gold all down in the ground, he order that they fill up the hole but leave room for him at top. Then he make his people put him in the hole so he can sit with his back against the wall. All his people are around him. 'Swear,' say he to them, 'that you will never take the gold away from this place until the Spanish are gone from Indians' land.' And they all swear. Then Montezuma he die in the hole and they leave him there for *patrón* to guard the gold, and over him they place big white rock with cross.

" 'All these centuries,' the Indian tole Don Salamón, 'my people been keep the order of Montezuma, and it is the law with us if any man tell the secret he will die more hard than in the ant bed. But you save my life. I have gratitude. I leave now my people forever. I tell you the secret to thank you, for I have nothing else. Let me tell you when you go to dig, you must go in the night, you must dig quick. Work like lightning, for eyes will be on you. It will be danger to stay there after you dig. Have big car ready to take you away as soon as you get the gold. The *patrón* watches also. You must guard your life.'

"After the Indian tole these things he left, and then Don Salamón he come up here to see me, for I know the country. I do not know where the white rock with the cross is, but I know all ole Spanish roads. Don Salamón say he can find the rock if I show him the right road.

"Then we get axes and spades and picks and everything in his car ready to go. Don Salamón's wife was there and she begin to cry out that her husband do not go. 'You will get killed, you will die,' she cried. She put her arms around his neck and there she cry until Don Salamón is ashamed to go. He must stay home.

"Since that time I have been looking for that white rock with cross on it next to the black rock. I have not found it. Perhaps the cross is gone now, but I know very well no man has got Montezuma's gold. I cannot understand this *patrón*. I am strong man. He is dead, but he keep me off. I wish I know when he sleep."

JOSÉ VACA'S CAVE

All of José Vaca's other labors in search for lost treasure dwindle into insignificance when compared with his *magnum opus*. For years now he has been tunneling into one of the Tecolote Mountains overlooking the Pecos River just below the village of Pecos. During the summer he works for wages, saving what he can; during the fall and winter he follows the business of excavation with an unflagging abandonment that only genius can realize. "I used to have many guns, plenty of horses; now I have nothing. All is spent on the cave," José says, "and I am not through yet. I wish some rich man with interest in this work might come along to help me finish."

José's own "interest" began with his finding in the cave a conch with an Indian design on it—a "spoon," as he calls it. His initial hope and expectation was to uncover a rich hoard of antique Indian pottery. But he had not worked long at clearing out the cave before the sole object of search became Spanish treasure. The fame of his digging brought from every quarter other treasure hunters with their *historias* and *derroteros*. A local woman became interested and ventured a hundred dollars in the enterprise. In the cave today may be seen picks, cans, ropes, spades, lanterns, wheelbarrows, wooden supports, all the paraphernalia of a mighty work uncompleted. Tons and tons of earth substance have been carried out and dumped down the mountain side.

During his years of work José has had various partners. One partner, a man well along in years, came from Mexico, worked a while, and went on. He was to return, but word came that he died in Canada. He was an Englishman, and he was significant for the kind of instrument that he used in locating treasure. It was a *cartucho* (a kind of metal cartridge shell) filled with opium, poison, black rock finely powdered, and a varied assortment of other elements. Leaning over, the man swung the *cartucho* from his forehead and followed the direction in which it oscillated most strongly. When over the treasure, the instrument was supposed to cease its oscillations.

Another man, a Mexican who had made "a big find" at Albuquerque and who had the reputation of being extraordinarily successful as a treasure hunter, came seeking to join in the Pecos Cave venture. But one of José's party was against him, and so the greatest opportunity of all to enlist a man of means and also of "interest" was let pass. This Albuquerque Mexican had an *horqueta* (fork) fashioned from the flat scapula of some animal.[5] It was shaped thus:

207

The upright branch fitted into a glass knob, on top of which was a hole with threads. An assortment of hollow screws fitted into these threads. One of the screws was filled with gold dust, another with powdered silver, another with lead, another with copper, and so on. The owner used the screw filled with whatever metal he was looking for. To make the *horqueta* work, he grasped the lower prongs in his two hands, thumbs out and palms turned up, and then followed the "pull" if there was any—and there generally was. The *horqueta* would twist and strain in the direction of the sought-for mineral as if drawn by some powerful magnet, and then, when over it, would point straight down in the manner of "switches" that "turn" to water.

In testing out José's cave the owner of this remarkable instrument used both gold and silver screws, and he declared that his *horqueta* had never "pulled" so hard in any other place. He went into the cave

and remained there alone for half a day. According to José, he was transported into a kind of ecstasy, lying on his back and holding the instrument over his head so that he might sense the "pullings" more delicately. It certainly is a pity that such a meticulous artist should have been excluded from the treasure hunt.

Once José went to Santa Fe for a famous *brujo* (wizard) and fortune teller named Nicolás. Nicolás declared absolutely that treasure is stored in the cave. "Go on," he said to José. "The treasure is hard to find, but if you work long enough you will get it out." Indeed, Nicolás was himself going to join in the undertaking, but a short time afterwards he located a great treasure in a certain old *gachupín* house at Santa Fe, and as a result he at once bought a fine automobile and left the country.

The most remarkable of all the men who came to José, however,

seems to have been Charlie Rose. Rose knew about every lost mine and buried treasure from Mexico to Alaska. He is dead now, but the *derrotero* that he brought from Las Vegas has been the basis for practically all of the work so far done in the cave.

This *derrotero* called for a rock cemented into the ground somewhere down the slope from the cave entrance. On this rock was to be found a small wooden cross. Beside an ancient wood road that led down from the mountain, José and Charlie Rose found a rock that seemed to be cemented into the ground. The cross was gone, as naturally it would be after so many centuries, but they detected a hole where it had been and some "cement." José showed me the rock. It weighs several hundred pounds and is flat on one side and convex on the other, resembling in shape those old Mexican cart-wheels hewn out of solid tree trunks. I was unable to detect any cement.

The *derrotero* called next for a marked rock at the entrance of the cave. This rock should have certain letters, figures, words on it. It was not hard to find a rock at the mouth of the cave. The one settled on as *the* rock weighed several tons. The treasure hunters believed that they saw signs and figures on one of the exposed surfaces, but they could not make out any particular letter or figure. They dynamited the rock so as to ascertain what might be inside or under it.

The legend on which the *derrotero* is based is that the early Spanish were bringing an immense cargo of pure ore from La Mina Perdida up the Pecos, when they were attacked by Indians. The Spanish retreated with their bullion to the cave, stored it, and cemented some rocks over the entrance in such a way that they should seem left thus by nature. Then followed a battle in which all the Spaniards were killed.

Certainly the rocks of the cave now have the appearance of having been placed there by nature. Some of them weigh thousands of tons and cover acres of ground, and there are gigantic seams that extend probably for miles. Far back in one of these seams José and one of his ill-starred partners have sunk a well thirty feet deep. While they were digging rock out of this well, a violent explosion of stinking gas occurred. This explosion is the most encouraging thing that has ever happened, for, according to all gold hunters, buried gold gives off a gas that is deathly sickening and highly explosive. The problem now is to get at the source of the explosion.

Meantime, the silent watchers of all things in the Pecos country, the Indians, have not been blind. No one has seen them near, but the track of their moccasins has more than once been found by the cave. Sometimes, too, the whole side of the mountain has been enveloped in a vague light rising and falling, the portent of which José and his partners—these modern inheritors of the wisdom and hope of Coronado —are in no doubt of.

JOSÉ'S ONE LUCKY FIND

The last partner to appear in the strange procession that has dreamed and delved through José's cave called himself a Frenchman. "I never been lucky only one time in my life," went on José as he told of the Frenchman. "That was right here in Pecos. A man got scared to live in his ole house. He was hearing strange noises and seeing lights. So he move into another house, but he can still see lights in the adobe he left.

"One day he come to my pardner, the Frenchman, and say he think there must be some treasure in that house. He will go with the Frenchman and help get it, he say. But when they are ready to go one night, they see strange lights burning and the ole man is afraid to go. So he give the key to the Frenchman and tole him to look.

"Well, the Frenchman he say for me to go with him. When we come to the house, that Frenchman say for me to stay outside. He go in and I can hear him talking. I do not know who he is talking to. I do not know what language he speak in. It is not Spanish; it is not English; it is not French. Then after while the Frenchman come out. 'All right,' he say, 'we come back tomorrow night at this hour and take out the money.'

"When we got back the next night, the Frenchman unlock the door. We step inside, and while he is holding the lantern, he gives me the pick. 'Hit into the wall over the door,' he say. I do not want to dig into that wall, but he keep saying, 'Go on, go on.' So I take the pick and give just one hit into the adobe where he say, and out come money rolled up in an old paper. There is one hundred and twenty-five dollars. The Frenchman say it is not necessary to give any to the man who was coward. So he take half and I take half.

"It is not much money for so many years of trying."

CHAPTER XIII

The Pecos Barricade

On the rocky banks of the Pecos
We laid him down to rest,
With his saddle for a pillow
And his gun acrost his breast.
Cowboy Ballad

The waters, fresh and crystal, of the upper Pecos River, springing out into sunshine that blesses rather than blisters, are not the waters that hurl themselves bitter and murky into the Río Bravo. The Pecos is a long river, a strange river, a thousand miles of twisting canyon from the pine-clad mountains of New Mexico to the gray, bleak bluffs of the Rio Grande on the Texas border. The traveler from the East upon reaching the drainage of the Pecos can yet say, "I have arrived in the West." And until environment and occupation cease to operate upon the character of men, the sparse ranchers of the Pecos will still be Westerners. The mountainous breaks, the alkali flats, the vast stretches of shifting sands, the treeless plains rolling out to far away hills—the Pecos world, despite narrow strips of irrigated land, will not be plowed up or, save around isolated oil fields, transformed by the structures of population into standardized mediocrity.

Far south of the Santa Fe Trail, three other transcontinental routes crossed the Pecos, converging west of it: the Butterfield (also called the Southern Overland and the Emigrant) Trail running from Saint Louis to California, the Chihuahua Trail from New Orleans and San Antonio west, and between these two the San Antonio–El Paso stage road. Of the three principal crossings, the Fort Lancaster, the Pontoon, and the Horsehead, Horsehead Crossing was the most famous by far. No stranger ever reached it from either side of the Pecos without having yearned for many hours and without being surprised at the sudden appearance, at his very feet, of the timberless banks; but no traveler was ever tempted to stop and settle at Horsehead Crossing. Early Spaniards, so tradition says, marked it with the bleached skulls of mustangs; hence the name. Bones of cattle used to line the waterless

Goodnight-Loving Trail that stretched for ninety-six miles between the head of the Concho River and Horsehead Crossing. Bones and graves of human beings likewise marked the routes traversing the Pecos lands. Indians, thirst, and "bad men" were all responsible for these desolate remainders.

Here history is so stark, so real, so dramatic that no fiction can surpass it in picturesque qualities. "Sunday, July 2," runs an entry in the diary of J. M. Bell, who was helping trail a herd of cattle from San Antonio to California in 1854. "The bones of a man were found [at Comanche Springs west of the Pecos]; on the knee-cap and foot the muscles still remain, although it has been 3 years since he was killed. Some of the clothing is laying about him." At Howard's Well, a spring between Beaver Lake and Fort Lancaster, travelers used to see the charred remains of six wagons, the occupants of which had to the last man been killed by Indians. Such a sight was characteristic of the Chihuahua Trail—and the Pecos. "From El Paso to San Antonio," recorded Edward F. Beale in 1857, while conducting what was probably the strangest train that ever traversed the route—the train of United States Army camels—"is but one long battle ground—a surprise here, robbery of animals there. Every spring and watering place has its history or anecdote connected with Indian violence and bloodshed."[1]

The great trains of wagons passing between Chihuahua City and San Antonio were sometimes veritable argosies of treasure. In five years' time the enterprising August Santleben[2] alone transported over a million dollars in freshly minted Mexican silver, one of his caravans in 1876 carrying 350,000 pesos. "In 1853 and 1854," says Theophilus Noel in his strange autobiography, "the ore from all the mines of North Mexico was hauled to San Antonio, much of it on wooden-wheeled carts, where it was taken by Texas teamsters to Port Lavaca and thence to England for refinement."

Out of such a background legend was inevitable. Legend says that not all the silver and gold that braved the routes crossing the Pecos got through. Some of it is still at Castle Gap.

MAXIMILIAN'S GOLD

In 1867 the Rio Grande was the refuge line for two distinct classes of vanquished men. From the north various bands of Confederate soldiers, distrustful of their fate at the hands of Union carpet-baggers and too proud to submit to dominion of a foe, were crossing the Great River to make their fortunes in Mexico and other Latin countries. They were generally desperate men, indeed. To the south Emperor Maximilian, a puppet placed on the throne of Mexico by Napoleon III, had been overthrown, and various adherents of his were fleeing for the safety that lay beyond the Río Bravo.

How Maximilian took refuge in Querétaro; how here, after months of miserable indecision and squalid existence, he was captured; and how he was then at the orders of a savage but patriotic Indian, Benito Juárez, shot to death—all this is familiar history. As he stood before the wall waiting for the "lucky bullet," he gave each of the soldiers a piece of gold and told them to aim true. He had brought with him to Mexico a large private fortune, including rich services of plate. Whether those gold coins handed to his executioners were all that remained of the fortune, history can hardly say. Maximilian and the mad, forlorn Empress Carlotta became the object of pity and the theme of story from Yaqui huts in the canyons of Sonora to the court of Austria. One of the stories long current in Texas deals with Maximilian's fortune.[3]

Among the ex-Confederate soldiers who, after a brief trial of carpet-bag rule, swore they would no longer live under the flag of the United States was a band of six Missourians. Their names are unknown. They came to Texas and rode west over the Chihuahua Trail to Presidio del Norte on the Rio Grande. There they met a caravan of wagons coming out of Mexico.

The teams of this train appeared to have been driven very hard. The man in charge of it was an Austrian, but he spoke English. He was exceedingly anxious for information concerning road conditions to San Antonio. The ex-Confederates told him that the route was infested with Indians and lawless characters. At this the foreigner volunteered the information that he had a valuable cargo of flour, and he offered good pay to the exiles if they would turn back with him and act as guard. Time meant nothing to them; they were ready to accept what fortune offered; they turned back.

The travelers with the wagons numbered fifteen, being made up of Austrians, Mexican peons, and a beautiful young girl who appeared to be the daughter of the leader. During the day, as the newly hired guards came to observe, the drivers were constantly in their seats, and at night some one slept in each wagon. The wagons were tightly covered and no opportunity for looking inside was allowed.

Such caution aroused first the curiosity and then the suspicion of the daring men who had engaged to accompany the train. After consultation they selected one of their number to make a close investigation. His report was astounding. The wagons were loaded with gold —heaps of it—Spanish, Austrian, and American coins, all sorts of vessels of gold and silver, bullion too—a fortune fabulous in value. The guards at once began planning to kill their charges and seize the cargo.

By now the caravan was approaching the Pecos River. The ground seemed clear for action.

At Castle Gap, fifteen miles east of Horsehead Crossing, about midnight, the crime was committed. As the six desperadoes themselves constituted the watch, and as all the Austrians and Mexicans were asleep, the surprise was complete. Not even the girl was spared. The bodies were burned in a fire made of wagons, harness, and other properties. Papers taken from a chest revealed that the leader of the dead band was one of Maximilian's followers entrusted with carrying the royal fortune out of Mexico to Galveston. From Galveston it was to be shipped to Austria, where the Empress Carlotta had already gone and whither at the time the instructions were written Maximilian intended to flee.

The robbers were not prepared to take such a tell-tale store of valuables into the settlements. They agreed to take only enough coin to satisfy their immediate desires and then, when they should have made arrangements for a quiet disposition of the vast fortune, to return for it. Consequently they buried it, noted well the landscape of rock, sands, and lake, and rode on east.

The wasted condition of their horses delayed them in crossing the parched land between Castle Gap and the Concho and they suffered greatly. One of them became so ill that he was forced to stop at Fort Concho. It was well for him that he remained behind, for a day's ride on ahead his five confederates were attacked by Indians and all killed. The lone survivor, having recovered, set out for San Antonio, where a rendezvous had been appointed. He knew nothing of the massacre of the men who had preceded him, but on his way he saw their mutilated bodies. He was now sole owner of Maximilian's fortune. He decided to go to Missouri and there secure the help of the James boys in disposing of it.

Near Denton, on his way north, he camped one night, merely by chance, with a party of three or four men who turned out to be horse thieves. A sheriff's posse surrounded the camp about daylight and took every man in it prisoner, the Missourian included. Horse thieves were frequently hanged without delay, but these were not. In the Denton jail the malady that had forced the Missourian to halt at Fort Concho renewed itself. He was now a very sick man. A certain Doctor Black, a resident of Denton, gave him no hope of recovery unless he could secure his freedom. He sent for a lawyer named O'Connor. Before O'Connor could do anything, however, his client was in a dying condition. Realizing his fate, he turned over to Black and O'Connor a plat to the fortune buried at Castle Gap, told them all the circumstances connected with it, and then gave up the ghost.

When Black and O'Connor got out to Castle Gap—a far journey then that required time and preparation—the lake was dry, and the terrific sandstorms common to the region had shifted the landscape. Hence marks called for by the plat could not be identified. All that

was found were some wagon irons marked by fire. Sphinx-like in its muteness amid the deep and silent sands, Castle Gap still guards Maximilian's gold.

RATTLESNAKE CAVE ON THE PECOS

Away to the southeast of Castle Gap, out of the sand country, the Chihuahua Trail followed up Devil's River, left it at Beaver Lake, ran alongside Dry Draw, and then crossed over the Divide to the Pecos. Somewhere along Dry Draw *was*—for it is not now—a cave known as Rattlesnake Cave. I have never heard how much gold ore was stored in this cave or how it came to be there. Maybe some of it was native to the place. Maybe it was the "gold blocks," stuffed hurriedly into hid-

ing by Spaniards, that early-day cowboys used to look for in every cave they glimpsed between the Concho River and Fort Stockton. One of the J M riders years ago discovered just east of the old Pontoon Crossing on the Pecos what he thought was the right cave, but upon exploring it found only stacks—enormous stacks—of buffalo hides. They were all rotten.

One day while a sixteen-year-old Mexican *pastor* was herding sheep out from his camp at Beaver Lake, he discovered a cave. The entrance was just about the size of a barrel, but he wriggled through it. This was along in the spring, and if he thought anything at all about rattlesnakes, he must have thought that they were out, for rattlesnakes do not "lay up" much in caves except in the winter time or when the weather is blazing hot.

The *pastor* found the inside of the cave as dark as a stack of black cats, but he lit a sotol stalk, an excellent torch, and went on. Then all of a sudden he heard a rattle, and right in front of him he made out "the biggest rattler raring up that ever he'd dreamed of." From the way he described it, it must have been reared a yard high, and was "as thick through as a man's leg." Its tail was singing like a buzz-saw, and then a thousand other snakes set up a rattling in every direction.

The Mexican was scared almost into a state of lunacy, but he had sense enough to begin backing towards the mouth of the cave, the big snake following him. About the time he reached daylight, his foot kicked against some rocks. He reached down and picked up a couple and threw one, either killing or stunning the snake.

Then he was out and thirty steps away before he realized that he was still carrying the other rock in his hand. As he was about to cast it away, he noticed how heavy it was. He looked at it. He hurriedly concealed it in his *jato.*

Three or four days later the *vaciero*—the man who supplies and oversees the various camps on a big sheep range—came along in his buckboard to leave some "grub" at the Beaver Lake camp. When he got there, he found the *pastor* all hunkered up, "*muy malo,*" he said, and wanting to go to town for some *medicina.* The Mexican laborer generally gets sick when he wants to quit or lay off. There was nothing for the *vaciero* to do but leave a substitute with the sheep and take the *pastor* to Ozona.

Well, the first thing the Mexican did when he got to town was to go to the bank. The rock he presented proved to be a crude block of gold and silver, mixed. It weighed three pounds and seven ounces. The banker was considerably excited. But not a word of explanation could he get out of the Mexican. The boy simply would not talk. Then the banker sent out and got the ranchman for whom the boy worked and also the leading merchant. Meanwhile he held the Mexican.

All three of the white men could "talk Mexican," and they had no trouble making the boy understand what they wanted. He was naturally a little scared of his boss. The upshot of the interview was that he promised to take the men to the place where he had found the "rock." He told all about how he discovered it, but he did not describe a single landmark. All they knew was that it was within herding distance of the camp at Beaver Lake. That meant that it could not be more than six or seven miles at most in any direction and was probably much closer in.

The boy said that before he left town he wanted to see his mother. That was all right with the white men. Naturally, when he got to his mother's house he told her all about the cave, the snakes, the gold, and his promise to the gringos.

"Oh, my son," the old woman cried, "do not show them that place. Is that your gold to give away? Did you put it there? Don't you understand that the snakes are spirits to guard it? You will be cursed forever if you tell the secret. Go now and tell the *padre* and he will tell you the same."

Then the boy went to the *padre* and told him the whole story. It was just as his mother had said. The *padre* became even more excited than the old woman had been.

"Do not show the cave to anybody," he said. "That gold belongs to the Spanish and the church. The great rattlesnake and all the other snakes in the cave are there to guard it. They are spirits, and if you tell their secret, you will pay with your life and your soul will end in hell."

The boy had been scared all along and this kind of talk decided him. So he hung around Mexican town and kept out of sight as long as he could. Then his *amo* came after him, and it wasn't any use trying to hold out longer. The white men tanked him up on whiskey, and finally headed him towards the ranch. He and the ranchman rode horseback, the banker and the merchant following in a buggy.

What happened after the outfit left town nobody knows. They made camp somewhere on Johnson's Run. The next day the Mexican was brought back to Ozona with a bullet through him, and he died with-

219

out having told his secret. Some of the circumstances got out, and soon the Mexican consul at San Antonio took the matter up with the governor. The governor ordered Ranger Neal Russell to investigate.

The white men swore that the Mexican killed himself. But the wound was made with a high-powered gun, and the only weapon the Mexican had to shoot with was an old .44 Winchester. The bullet had entered the thigh from the rear and come out at the groin, and men do not shoot themselves in the thigh when they want to quit living.

Neal Russell always held that after the Mexican sobered up he tried to run away and that one of the white men shot at him to scare him and shot too far up. Nothing ever came of the matter in the courts. The men camped for a few days at Beaver Lake and hunted out from it for the cave, but, failing to find it, soon lost interest in the treasure.

In working up the evidence, Russell found that between the time the Mexican entered the cave and the time he went to town, one man had seen him and talked with him. The Mexican told this man a few more details than he had told the banker. They were not too definite at that. From the facts gathered Neal Russell made the best way-bill he could and gave it to Wes Burton. The rest of the story can best be told in Burton's own words.

"I kept the information close for a good while, but just before we got into the war with Germany, I took Preacher Crumley in with me—Neal had died meanwhile—and we started out on an exploring trip.

"When we got into the country Neal had described, we found so many places for caves that I'll confess I didn't have much hope of locating one with an opening no bigger than a man's body.

"Well, while Crumley and I were jogging along up Dry Draw, about thirty miles below Ozona, a mesquite thorn stuck into the front casing. Crumley said he'd patch the tube, and for me to scout around a bit.

"I knew all along that we were close to the old Chihuahua Trail, but I didn't realize how close till I walked right into the gully that marks where it used to run. I follered the gully up a ways until it kinder played out and then I could actually see ruts those old Mexican cart wheels had worn. Then, bang, I came to where it looked as if an explosion of some kind had blowed the whole earth out, and I never seen the like of rattlesnake rattles and bones in my life as was laying all about. I picked up eighteen rattles and put 'em in my pocket to show Crumley.

"By the time I got back to the car I'd killed two rattlesnakes myself, and durned if my pardner hadn't killed another. We were ready to go on, but seeing a man loping over a hill towards us, we waited.

" 'Well, stranger,' says I, 'this seems to be a purty good country for rattlesnakes. I wonder if you know anything of a cave that sometimes goes by the name of Rattlesnake Cave?'

"The feller introduced himself as named Cox, and I could see by his reply that he had us sized up for suckers of some kind.

" 'I guess it is a good country for rattlesnakes,' he says. 'Durned if it don't look like they growed around here on bushes. Look at them bones scattered abouts. They're cattle that died of snake bites. Right up yonder last winter,' and he jerked his arm up the way I'd been, 'we threwed a stick of dynamite into a hole and blowed out a wagon load of the stinking devils. You ought to go up there and see that place. I never heard of it going by any name, but for all I know it might be

the Rattlesnake Cave you're looking for. Ain't much of it left now, I guess. It shore was one cave of rattlesnakes.'

"There wasn't much more passed between us. I didn't let on as to why I was interested in the cave, and d'reckly Cox rode on off.

"Well, Crumley and me concluded right there that we were as good as inside the hole. It seemed as if for once luck was just naturally with us, and I don't know as I ever felt better in my life. We were short on grub, though, and had to have a new spade. So we pulled right on in to Ozona.

"When we got there we found the hardware store sold clean out of spades. It was all the same anyhow, for a letter was waiting for Crumley saying his baby was bad sick and for him to come back home.

"No railroad in that country, you know. So all we could do was to come back east in the car. The baby died, and one thing and another kept us tied up for a year. We figgered that nothing wasn't going to bother our cave while we were gone, anyhow.

"At the end of the year, we were back in Ozona. First thing we learned was how a man named Cox had bought a 50,000 acre ranch down Howard's Draw, stocked it, and had money in the bank. Twelve months before and he'd been nothing but an ordinary cowboy. Now he was swaller-forking all over seven counties. There didn't seem to be any secret about him having picked his fortune out of a cave.

"Of course there wasn't any use for us to go further. We never even went down to see what Rattlesnake Cave looked like after it had been cleaned out.

"Looks like something's always coming up that way. If it hadn't been for my blabbing to that man Cox, and if old man Crumley's baby hadn't took sick and died, I'd have a fortune now the size of Major Littlefield's."

THE FATEFUL OPALS

No form of ancient folklore has survived more persistently than superstitions about precious stones. People in general, as any jeweler will testify, still believe in birth stones and buy them. The imperial jewels of the Romanoffs, which made Lenin's regime cry, "Take the accursed things out of Russia"; the famous stone of the Sultan of Succadana, which in old times brought wars and untold calamities upon that country; the fabulous emerald of the Archipelago, which the Dutch government during the last century officially inquired after and which Joseph Conrad brought into his story of *Lord Jim*; the Sultana Diamond, the presence of which in Morocco herdsmen and fortune-tellers have for centuries regarded as necessary to prevent disaster; the curse laid on the possessors of stolen gems so exemplified in the fate of seven persons who a few years ago stole the Schoellkopf jewels at Buffalo, New York—these are stones and stories of the present as well as of the past.

The opal—symbol of hope—a cure for bad eyes—a stimulant to the heart—a chameleon-hued indicator of the health of its wearer—is, or was, the birth stone for October. During comparatively recent times, however, it has come to be considered a baneful stone, though, according to ancient tradition, the sons and daughter of October escape its malignancy.

> *October's child is born for woe,*
> *And life's vicissitudes must know;*
> *But lay an opal on her breast*
> *And hope will lull the woes to rest.*

So fearful of the opal nowadays are many folk in quest of October birth stones that organized jewelers have arbitrarily substituted the tourmaline.

From the Kremlin of Moscow or from the Sultan's guarded palace in El Ksar El Kebir to the rocky banks of the Pecos near its mouth in one of the loneliest and bleakest reaches of the Rio Grande is a far cry. But the Pecos, too, hides fateful jewels.

Rena Decker was a native of Brockton, Massachusetts, beautiful and adventuresome. In the spring of 1876 she quit her job as waitress in one of the Brockton hotels and went to Jacksonville, Florida. There she made the acquaintance of an exceedingly attractive Cuban grisette by the name of Montez Veronica Rodríguez. In a short time these two young women decided to seek their fortune—by whatever route it could be most speedily gained—in San Antonio.

San Antonio in 1876 was a place for fortune seekers. The dust raised by thousands of longhorn cattle on their way up the trail to Kansas sifted over the town, and cowboys and cowmen jingled their spurs in the streets, eager to surrender their coin to attractive women. The Jack Harris saloon and variety theatre, where the bad Ben Thompson and the brazen King Fisher were later killed, was probably the most noted resort of its kind between the Gulf of Mexico and

Cheyenne. Hard by in the ample gambling emporium over the White Elephant saloon enough gold and silver were stacked on the tables nightly to run a bank. Indian fighters with "vouchers," as they called scalps dangling from their belts, paraded the streets. Great trains of Chihuahua wagons drawn by sixteen mules each and freighted with flour or silver clattered across Main Plaza. Samuel Bell the jeweler was making fine bowie knives. Wild turkeys at fifteen cents a pound were a drug on the market. Dried buffalo, "fresh from the plains," was for sale alongside the turkeys. The military telegraph had just been strung. The Sunset railroad was coming. The big pot was in the little one; the goose was hanging high; the skillet was a-frying. San Antonio was lusty, free, booming, with the sky the limit and the lid thrown away.

Among the sporting gentry were two men known as Pronto Green and Dirk Pacer. They had plenty of money and they were free with it. That does not mean they were not shrewd. For business reasons as well as *par amour*, they formed an alliance with Rena Decker and Montez Rodríguez. From the arrival of the young women until February, 1877, the two couples were the most conspicuous figures about the amusement places of San Antonio. Then they went to Mexico City.

Here they opened what they denominated The Open Palace—a combination of saloon, café, gambling hall, and extensive suites of "private" bedrooms. For some time The Open Palace paid well, but so much trouble arose among the patrons that the owners saw they would before long be forced to close. They decided to try next the city of Durango. While they were preparing to make this change, Pronto Green by methods very dubious managed to acquire from a Chinese trader then in Mexico City a golden idol with eyes, necklace, and other adornments of rare opals. The opals were removed and two of them—harlequins—were set into rings for Rena and Montez, and the idol itself was melted into common bullion. Rena, however, had such a superstition against opals that she refused to wear her ring, whereupon Montez added it to her own jewelry. Meantime Green, as banker for the company, invested a considerable amount of their funds in other opals, for, at this time, Mexico had only one competitor, Hungary, in the production of opals, and Mexican opals were so cheap as to offer a promising investment.

In Durango the company opened a resort similar to The Open Palace and for a while prospered. Then one night a general row broke out in which a man was killed and several other men were wounded.

224

The adventurers were again forced to close. Now they began roving from city to city, often taking in remote mining camps. They continued to make money, but at the same time they became more debauched and less desirable to keepers of the law.

At length Rena Decker grew so disgusted with the life she was living that she determined to quit it. Therefore she asked for her share of the gains, refusing to take any part of the precious stones, and set out for the Texas border. Her comrades saw her across the Rio Grande, whence she journeyed to Brockton, Massachusetts, and passed from the story.

The remaining three adventurers stayed on in northern Mexico until March, 1881, at which time, prompted by a difficulty that arose at a *fandango*, they considered it wise to quit the country. Procuring pack horses and saddle mounts, they set out for Del Rio, but when about opposite that place they learned that certain Mexican *empleados* were designing to arrest them, and so they turned up the river. At the mouth of the Pecos, unwatched, they crossed with their goods into Texas.

Montez Rodríguez had contracted a fever and as soon as she was on Texas soil became too ill to travel farther. Dirk Pacer and Pronto Green nursed her for a few days as best they could, but despite their attentions she died. With tools borrowed from a sheep camp they dug a grave and buried her with the two opal rings still on her hand. A Mexican *pastor* made the sign of the cross over her grave, and a stone with the initials M. V. R. cut on it was placed at her head. The grave was on the east side of the Pecos only a short distance from its mouth.

Green and Pacer now decided to make their way back to the east, taking care to avoid San Antonio and other places in Texas where they were too well known. In order that they might be free to scout, they considered it prudent to leave the major part of their fortune behind until they were ready to dispose of it. This fortune consisted mostly of cumbersome silver. So, taking an ample supply of gold, they secreted the silver to the amount of $37,500 and with it a bag of Mexican opals.

Upon reaching the Kiamichi Mountains, on the line between the Indian Territory and Arkansas, Dirk Pacer became too ill to proceed; years of dissipation had made him a physical wreck. Pronto Green arranged with a generous-natured mountaineer to care for the sick man and pressed on into Kansas. There he was killed in a railroad wreck. A short time afterwards Pacer himself breathed his last breath—but

not before he had learned of his partner's death and imparted to his host both the history that has just been told and the location of the $37,500 in silver secreted with the bag of opals.

The cache, as he described it, is in one of the side canyons of the Pecos not far above the rock on which are carved the initials of Montez Veronica Rodríguez. Several years ago, L. D. Bertillion, a rover in far places, collector of horns, grower of strange plants, teller of strange tales—as witness this, which he told to me—started out with a man from Mississippi to hunt this treasure. At Piedras Negras, across from Eagle Pass, the Mississippian bought some opals, at a bargain, and then the two followed the Rio Grande up to the Pecos. They should have outfitted with packs and water kegs, but they did not. On the hunt, mostly afoot, that followed, the Easterner became crazed with thirst, let his suitcase containing the opals, ammunition, and other goods fall into an inaccessible gulch, and had to be half carried back to the railroad by Bertillion. So far as is known, this is the only hunt that has ever been made for the gamblers' opals on the Pecos, though some *pastor* or range rider must have seen the desolate rock marked M. V. R.

CHAPTER XIV

The Secret of the Guadalupes

He ne'er would sleep within a tent,
No comforts would he know,
But like a brave old Texian
A-ranging he would go.
Mustang Gray, *frontier ballad*

The tradition of gold in the Guadalupes runs back a long, long way.[1]
While governor of New Mexico, General Lew Wallace—at least so he
claimed in a written article[2]—dug out of the basement of the Palace
at Santa Fe an ancient document reciting how a converted Indian of
Tabira conducted Captain de Gavilán and thirty other Spaniards to a
wonderfully rich gold deposit on the eastern spurs of the Guadalupe
Mountains. The Spaniards named the place, on account of volcanic
evidences, Sierra de Cenizas—Ashes Mountains—and left loaded
down with nuggets and ore in the form of both "wires" and "masses."
Then came the great uprising of 1680, in which the Pueblos killed
every Spaniard who did not flee from New Mexico. About the same
time Tabira, the home of the guide to Sierra de Cenizas, was wiped
out. Sierra de Cenizas has for centuries been a lost spot in geography
as well as a lost mine.

Since the advent of English-speaking prospectors it has been the
Apaches who knew the whereabouts of gold in the Guadalupes. Indians have "the best eyes in the world." The wilder they are, the better they can see. Excepting the Yaquis, who still have most of the gold
of Sonora under surveillance, the Apaches were the wildest Indians on
the North American continent. Their most famous leader, hard, un-
tamable old Geronimo, used to say that the richest gold mines in the
western world lay hidden in the Guadalupes.

The setting is worthy of its traditions. Guadalupe Peak, the highest
point in Texas, rises 8751 feet above sea level, just below the New
Mexico line. It is a beacon from all sides. The long, narrow chain of
mountains above which it towers, extends, with gaps, southward clear
to the Rio Grande and northward for nearly a hundred miles. Here in

the Guadalupes the only mountain sheep left in Texas and a majority of those left in New Mexico are, under the protection of the law, making their last stand, eagles and panthers molesting them more than man, their haunts so wild, rough, and waterless that only occasionally does a human being intrude thither. Here the Apaches made final retreat, and on the Mescalero Apache Indian Reservation hardly a day's horseback ride from the northwestern spurs of the Guadalupe chain, remnants of that fierce, secretive, and outraged people yet live, their tribal name an inseparable element in the traditions of the whole Southwestern world.

Of all the seekers for the gold of the Guadalupes "Old Ben" Sublett —William Colum Sublett being his correct name—was the most picturesque and has become most famous. Like the much besung Joe Bowers he went west from Missouri—"yes, all the way from Pike"— to prospect in the Rocky Mountains. He saw other men grow rich from virgin gold, but the pay streak never opened under his pick. He went in rags; at times his wife and children went hungry. Life for them must have been fearfully hard. It killed his wife. Then Sublett with two little girls and an infant son turned southeast and, crossing the Guadalupes, made for "civilization."

Civilization was the new Texas and Pacific railroad tracks—a double line of steel that glittered across hundreds of miles of West Texas land too waterless at that date even for the scant population of ranches. Sublett put up a tent beside a section house where the town of Monahans now stands and where a well had been dug. He got odd jobs from the railroad. Other men were coming in; they contributed to the support of "the children in the tent."

In fact, strangers were so charitable that one day Ben Sublett drove away alone in his rickety old buckboard, pulled by a pair of bony horses and carrying a meager supply of frijoles, flour, and coffee. He did not need much. He could, as the saying goes, live on what a hungry coyote would leave. He again took to prospecting—in the nearest mountains of any size, the Guadalupes. This was long before an oil well was dreamed of in West Texas; it was before the Mescalero Apaches had been securely rounded up. Men who packed lead under their skins and could show the scars of arrow wounds warned Sublett that he had better stay away from the Guadalupes and the Apaches. He laughed at them. Trip after trip he made into the mountains, returning only to work long enough to buy a fresh store of supplies and contribute a little to the direst needs of his children.

He moved them over to Odessa, where there were a few saloons but no churches, where women were scarce, and where the click of six-shooters synchronized with the click of spurs. There the oldest child of the family, a girl, made something by taking in washing. The father was freer than ever to prospect. He knew what he was about. Every time he came in, his return was a surprise to the people of the town; they scoffed at his crazy mode of life. Occasionally he brought in a nugget hardly of enough value to keep him in shoe leather. In vain his children begged him to quit the mountains and settle down to some steady-paying job. He was stubborn; he would take advice from no one. He had a "hunch" that he would some day find the gold in the Guadalupes.

Sometimes he tinkered on the ranch windmills that were dotting the country. Other times he trapped quail and killed antelopes to ship to Chicago. A catch he made of ninety-seven quail together in a net is still remembered. One while, it seems, he trapped in the White Mountains of Arizona. This must have been before he came to Texas. After he had been prospecting for years, he admitted that an Apache whom he met in the White Mountains had told him a story of gold in the Guadalupes.

"Old Ben, the crazy prospector," became the jest of the country. Then one day, after having been gone for an unusually long time, he drove his rickety rig up to the Mollie Williams saloon in Odessa, strode—despite his habitual limp, caused by an old bullet wound—boldly to the bar, in a hearty voice invited everybody present to join him, and called for drinks all around. The bar-keeper hesitated, the men sniggered. But when Old Ben threw a buckskin pouch full of nuggets on the bar, the crowd went wild.

"Boys," he said, "I have been poor, but I ain't poor no longer. I can buy out this town and have plenty left. Drink."

They drank. They cheered. They drank again. Then between drinks Old Ben went out to his buckboard and brought in a small canvas sack filled with gold "so pure that a jeweler could have hammered it out."

"My friends," urged the crazy prospector, "drink all you want. Drink all you can hold. I have at last found the richest gold mine in the world. I can build a palace of California marble and buy up the whole state of Texas as a back yard for my children to play in. Let's celebrate."

Old Ben never built the palace, it seems, or encumbered himself with leagues of land. In reality he had no desire for estates or cushioned halls. His wants were few and elemental. He was not greedy for riches. The golden secret that he bore in his breast—like the hidden light of the "Lantern Bearers"—and the notoriety that the secret brought meant more to him than any amount of taxable properties. He had a kind of hunger for fame. Human chicanery and the mad grasping for property perplexed him, and thus he came to distrust all "prosperity friends." After he struck it rich, he was never known to work at all. Every few months he would slip out to the mountains alone, "and he generally brung back around a thousand dollars' worth of gold." The chief pleasure he derived from it seemed to be in displaying it.

As may be imagined, many men tried to get Sublett to show them the location of his gold. "If anybody wants my mine," he would say, "let him go out and hunt for it like I did. People have laughed at me and called me a fool. The plains of the Pecos and the peaks of the Guadalupes have been my only friends. They are my home. When I die, I want to be buried with the Guadalupes in sight of my grave on one side and the Pecos on the other. I am going to carry this secret with me so that for years and years after I am gone people will remember me and talk about 'the rich gold mine old man Sublett found.' I will leave something behind me to talk about."

Sublett was trailed, spied upon, "laid for," but no lobo wolf was ever more wily in avoiding traps than was Sublett in avoiding detection. His habit was to leave town at some unexpected time, camp on the Pecos a day or two, and then strike out from camp during the night. He might be gone only a few days; he might be gone for months. It is said that he at one time kept his money in W. E. Connell's bank at Midland, which is about thirty miles east of Odessa. Where Sublett turned his raw gold into cash nobody has explained, but the banker came to observe that when the mysterious old prospector's deposit ran low he invariably made a trip and not long after returning invariably banked "hard money." Of course, there are people who say that Sublett never owned a check book in his life; some people will talk. Anyhow, as the best of the talkers tell it, banker Connell and a cowman by the name of George Gray offered Sublett ten thousand dollars if he would show them the source of his cash.

Sublett just laughed at them. "Why," he replied, "I could go out and dig up that much in less than a week's time."

After this conversation Gray and Connell engaged Jim Flannigan to follow Sublett on the next trip. Sublett's funds in the bank were running low and he was due to "pull out" any hour. For two weeks Lee Driver, who was then keeping a livery stable in Midland, fed a horse for Flannigan. Then one day word came that Sublett had left Odessa in a hack pulled by two burros. Flannigan followed his tracks through the sand for fifty miles west along the railroad to Pecos on the Pecos River, and then for twenty-five miles on up the river. There the trail played out—stopped—quit—just disappeared. How any West Texan could lose the plain trail of a hack in soft soil uncut by other tracks is almost inconceivable, but lose the trail Flannigan did. He was not the first or the last man to lose it.

He was still riding around trying to pick it up when he happened to meet a man who had just seen Sublett traveling down the river towards Pecos. He turned back, but before he reached Odessa the cunning old prospector had already arrived. He had been gone from town "only four days," and had in that time traveled at least a hundred and fifty miles. Very good traveling for a pair of burros pulling a hack through sand dunes! Evidently Sublett had not got even into the foothills of the Guadalupes on this trip. He must have had a cache on the Pecos, for, as usual, he brought in a sack of gold.

But, despite his secretive ways, Sublett occasionally relented, and before he died took several people more or less into his confidence. Once when he was coming out of the Guadalupes he met an old crony named Mike Wilson; he must have been feeling almost insanely generous, for he gave his friend such minute directions for reaching the mine that Wilson actually got to it. There he emptied provisions out of a tow-sack and crammed into it as much ore as he could carry home. The trip wore him out, and as soon as he reached town he went on a spree that lasted for three weeks. When he sobered up and tried to go to the mine a second time, he found himself utterly bewildered. Old Sublett just laughed at him and refused to direct him again. "If anybody wants that mine," he said, "let him go out and hunt for it like I did." Years ago Mike Wilson died in a hut within sight of the Guadalupes, trying vainly until the end to recall the way to Sublett's lost gold.

Another time, some men at Pecos finally, after much persuasion, "ribbed up" Sublett to show them the mine. They felt so gay and prosperous that they loaded a big assortment of fancy canned goods into their chuck wagon to supplement the regular camp supplies. The first night out a tin of pineapple gave Sublett a case of ptomaine poisoning.

He was probably already sick from having promised to give away his secret. At any rate, he claimed that someone had tried to poison him, became as stubborn as a government mule, and refused to go a step farther.

Perhaps, though, unknown to Sublett, there was an independent sharer of his secret. Or maybe Sublett discovered the sharer and acted as his jealousy might have prompted him to act out in the wild loneliness of the Guadalupes. Every man is entitled to his own conclusion from the testimony offered by F. H. Hardesty, who used to ranch in El Paso County.

One evening along in the eighties a fellow by the name of Lucius Arthur, known better as Frenchy, rode up to Hardesty's ranch, watered, and accepted the invitation to unsaddle and stay all night. While the two men were talking after supper, Frenchy confided to his host that he was trailing two Mexicans who had left Ysleta, on the Rio Grande, the preceding night. He said that he had started to follow them once before but that his grub and water had played out. He knew that they were bound for a gold mine somewhere in the Guadalupes to the east.

Frenchy had been keeping his eye on these Mexicans for a long time. One of them, according to him, belonged to a wealthy old family of rancheros down in Mexico. Perhaps, as he suggested, some Mexican had found out about the gold back in the days when *gente* from below the Rio Grande used to come up and get salt from the great beds west of the Guadalupe Mountains. A gringo's attempt to control this salt resulted in what is still referred to as the Salt War. Anyway, a member of the rancher's family made a trip to the Guadalupe gold mine each year and brought out a supply of ore. The Mexican now after it had come to Ysleta to meet his brother-in-law and together they had left that place in the dead of night.

"After hearing all this," Hardesty related, "I told Frenchy he ought to go better equipped. I told him he might have to stay out for weeks trailing the Mexicans and waiting for them to clear out from the gold mine before he could get into it. Then I offered to stake him with everything he needed. Well, we went in pardners, and when he left my place he had as good an outfit as any man could want and was carrying enough supplies to last two months. Six weeks later he was back. He had gold quartz to show.

"According to his story, he had trailed the Mexicans and from a place of concealment had watched them climb a rope ladder into a chasm. He saw them haul up sacks of ore and water for their horses, which were staked on the rim. But he himself had to depend on water so far away that he couldn't keep regular watch. After he had hung around several days, the Mexicans left and then he made a closer inspection. The chasm, from the way he described it, must have varied in width from forty to a hundred feet and was all of sixty feet deep. Down at the bottom he could see the entrance to a cave with freshly broken rock in front of it. He claimed that he didn't go down into the chasm because he was short on rope for a ladder. I thought he might have been a little more resourceful, but I said nothing. The chunks of quartz he brought in had been dropped by the Mexicans, so he said.

"Frenchy rested up a few days, took a fresh pack of supplies, including enough rope to picket out a whole *caballada,* and left again for the Guadalupes. He never came back. I have never heard of him since. That's all I know about the gold of the Guadalupes."

As we shall see presently, Frenchy's description of the Mexican mine jibes perfectly with that which has come down of the place where Sublett resorted. Let us get back to Sublett.

About 1895 a jack-leg carpenter by the name of Stewart was roofing a house for Judge J. J. Walker, of Barstow. He had been a guide over the Butterfield route to California; he could many a tale unfold, and one very hot day while he rested in the shade he unfolded this one to his employer.

Along in the late eighties several officials of the Texas and Pacific Railroad engaged Stewart to guide them into the Pecos country on a hunt. Camp was made in some trackless hills east of the river. A rumor racing over the range had it that the Apaches had broken out and were back on their old stamping grounds. Stewart was naturally uneasy lest they foray down from the mountains and either kill some of his party or drive off their horses. He had his son, a mere child, with him.

One evening about sundown he saw a wagon coming towards camp. It was a light spring wagon drawn by a single horse—a very large horse. When it reached camp, the driver alighted. He was Ben Sublett and he was alone. Stewart had known him for years. Of course he was invited to stay all night, and he unhitched. After the hunters and Stewart's boy had settled to sleep, Sublett told Stewart that he was going to his gold mine *at the point of the Guadalupes.* He said that while riding along that day he had realized as never before how old he was and that he had decided positively never to make

another trip after gold. "I have always declared that the secret would die with me," he said, "but now that I have met up with you out here I somehow want to take you with me and show you the mine."

Stewart replied that he would not think of leaving the men who were depending on him for guidance in that wild country and that even if he were willing to leave them he would never take his own child on into Apache range. In reply to this argument Sublett remarked that no man accompanying him would ever be in danger from Indians. Nevertheless, Stewart did not go.

When Sublett set out next morning, however, Stewart did accompany him "as far as the top of a blue mound towards the west." Here Sublett halted and, while Stewart looked through a long spy glass, tried to show him where the mine was located, asserting at the same time that such long-range directions would never be of any use. He said that he would be back in three days.

The third day, just after dark, he drove into camp. As soon as supper was over and the hunters had bedded down, Stewart asked, "What luck did you have?"

For answer Sublett picked up a dried deer hide and put it, flesh side up, on the ground where the low fire cast a light over it and also where some boxes of provisions hid it from the eyes of any man who might be awake on his pallet. Then he poured on it a Bull Durham tobacco sack, of the fifteen cent size, as full of gold nuggets as it would hold. Stewart ran his hand through them and scattered them over the hide.

"You do not seem to have any small nuggets," he observed.

"What," Sublett rejoined, "would be the use of picking up a small nugget when with one more rake in the gravel I could bring up a big one?"

In the morning Sublett left. He had gathered his last nuggets. The next that Stewart heard of him he was dead. Stewart soon afterwards attempted to find the mine—but failed. What has become of him or what "point of the Guadalupes" he gazed at through the long spy glass while from an unidentified "blue mound" Sublett pointed towards the gold, are unknown. It turned out as Sublett had predicted.

"Come with me and I will show you the gold," he had said, "but if you go alone, even after I have pointed out its general location, you will never be able to find it."

So far as is known, Sublett never wavered again in his determination to hold fast the secret. When he was dying, his son-in-law, Sid

Pitts, of Roswell, New Mexico, tried to persuade him to hand over the golden key he had clutched so long. Apparently the old man—he was eighty—started to tell him how to go to the mine. "First," he began, "you cross the Pecos at . . ." Then he broke off with, "Hell, it ain't no use. They'd beat you out of it even if you found it." Evidently it was not the philanthropic desire to save his kin from the worries of wealth but his tenacious determination to keep "the damned human race" from sharing it and from learning what he had spent so many happily contrary years in withholding that caused old Sublett to keep silent to the end.

Sublett's death occurred in 1892. He was buried in Odessa, a little too far away from the Guadalupes to realize his wish for a grave within sight of them. Certainly, however, he left behind him "something to talk about." In the wide, wide lands of the Pecos, from its mouth far down on the Rio Grande to old Fort Sumner in New Mexico, there is hardly a town, a squatter's cabin, or a rancher's home in which the story of Sublett's Mine has not been told. Prospectors by the score have looked for it, and prospectors as well as many men who are not prospectors are still looking for it.

Among the most constant seekers has been Sublett's son Ross. In fact, Ross has been as constant as grubstakings from strangers would allow him to be; he has even on occasions grubstaked himself. This constancy is logical, for Ross Sublett probably knows more concerning the whereabouts of the mine than any other living man. When he was a little past his ninth birthday his father took him to it. That was the only time he saw it, but see it he did. Five years later when the secretive old prospector lay on his death-bed, Ross, of sufficient age by that time to feel responsibility, tried to get him to describe the way to the gold. The dying man—a little gentler to him than he was to the son-in-law—merely mumbled: "It's too late. Any description would be useless. You'll just have to go out and hunt it down like I did."

An accommodating disposition on the part of Ross Sublett to recount his childhood memories has not dimmed them. Like the annular rings of a tree, his memories increase in both number and compass. He lives at Carlsbad, New Mexico, is easy of access, and should you interview him, he would respond in this wise: "Yes, I have a distinct recollection of how the mine looked. The last stage to it, going west from the Pecos, was always made on horseback or with pack burros. It was down in a crevice, and the only way to get to it was by a rope ladder that my father always removed as soon as he came up with the gold. I played around while he got the ore out of a kind of cave. I seem to remember, too, that pieces of ore were in plain sight right in front of the cave. I am confident the mine is within six miles of a spring in the Rustler Hills."

The Rustler Hills[3] are a good forty miles east of Guadalupe Peak, but more than one tradition has made them the site of Sublett's gold. Not long after Sublett died, a New Mexico sheriff familiarly known as Cicero, while prospecting in these hills, met a cowboy called Grizzly Bill.

"You'd as well pull in your horns, Cicero," bawled out Grizzly as soon as the two men, both on horseback, came within hailing distance of each other. "I've done found Sublett's gold and I'm on my way to spend it."

Grizzly went on to Pecos, Texas. He rode into town shooting his six-shooter at the sky and yelling, "Hide out, little ones, yer daddy's come home." He got on a high lonesome, displayed his gold, and, while trying to "show off" on a wild horse, was thrown in such a way as to have his neck broken. Nobody who knows anything about the matter, however, has ever supposed that Grizzly Bill found the Lost Sublett Mine. In fact, all he found was a nugget near a spring—where more than likely Sublett had camped and lost it.

CHAPTER XV

Not Only Gold and Silver

He had bought a large map representing the sea,
Without the least vestige of land:
And the crew were much pleased when they found it to be
A map they could all understand.
LEWIS CARROLL, The Hunting of the Snark

THE FOXES HAVE HOLES

"Gold is where you find it." So is lead, so is zinc, so are quicksilver and copper.[1] The story of mineral wealth is the story of accident. In 1545 an Indian hunter named Diego Hualca was chasing a goat up one of the most formidable mountains of Bolivia. In order to pull himself over a ledge he caught hold of a bush. The bush came out by the roots. Clinging to them and strewing the torn ground, masses of silver glittered in the eyes of the hunter. Thus were discovered what for centuries have been the world-famous silver mines of Potosí.

The badger, the prairie dog, and the gopher are the mascots of the mining West. Coyotes and burros seem to have directed more prospectors to "pay" than all the practical geologists combined. In 1859 "Pancake" Comstock, a half-witted prospector, saw "some queer-looking stuff" in a gopher hole. He ran his hand down and scooped out dirt sprinkled with gold and silver. The great Comstock lode was located.

In the fall of 1857 a mob of army teamsters, freshly discharged by General Albert Sidney Johnston, struck out from Fort Bridger, Wyoming, for somewhere. In the vicinity of what is now Denver they noticed fresh signs of another party of white men. They followed the tracks, and pretty soon came upon two newly made graves. Something about the graves, however, appeared suspicious. In those days traders cached their goods in the ground. The Fort Bridger men investigated the mounds and without much trouble dug up two casks of Kentucky whiskey. In no time they were hilariously drunk and had matched a horse race. The course across the prairie was indented with

prairie dog holes; that made no difference to the frolicsome riders. A
fellow by the name of Nathaniel Ax, called Than for short, led the
race, but just before he reached the line his horse plunged into one
of the holes, throwing Than so that his head was rammed up to the
shoulders in another hole. The lick slightly sobered him, and as he
extricated himself he took note of the gravel into which he had bur-
rowed.

"Boys," he yelled, "this looks like Hang Town grit."

Hang Town was the most famous mining camp in California. Pick
and pan were soon out; sluice boxes were hollowed from cottonwood
logs. Within six months the hills and mountains around the prairie
dog town were alive with gold diggers.[2]

About 1880 ten postal clerks in Washington put up a hundred dollars apiece and sent the money to Alexander Topence at Bellevue,
Idaho, to stake a prospector. When Topence received the money, he
went out on the street and spied Dan Scribner.

"Dan," he asked, "what are you doing now?"

"Nothing."

"How would you like to do a little prospecting?"

"Fine."

Dan outfitted, struck for Wood River, and pitched his camp in a
shady place near water and grass. He hobbled one horse, put a bell
on the other, and turned them loose. The next morning he could
neither see nor hear anything of his horses. The often quoted saying
of an old prospector comes to mind. "How long have you been prospecting in these mountains?" somebody asked him. "Nigh unto forty
years," he answered. Then he caught himself. "I haven't exactly been
prospecting all that time, though. About thirty of them years I've been
looking for burros; just ten were left for actual prospecting."

Dan Scribner began climbing a hill so that he could get a view of
the country and thus perhaps locate his horses. Halfway up he saw a
badger hole and stopped to look at the rock that the badger had
thrown out. He found a fine piece of galena. He went back to his tent
and got a pick. Before noon he had uncovered three feet of almost
solid galena ore running high in silver. He let the horses hunt him up.
What became of the badger is not told. The mine was named the
"Minnie Moore" and it sold for half a million.[3]

At Tonopah, Nevada, Jim Butler's mule kicked off a shallow cap of
rock that hid one of the richest bodies of ore discovered in recent
times. In 1927 a desert rat by the name of Horton chanced upon a

badger hole out in the malpais north of Tonopah; the dirt from it assayed thousands of dollars per ton—and the Weepah stampede was on.

That ground squirrel on the Sabinal River in Texas did not burrow deep enough maybe to establish a mining camp, but it exposed enough quicksilver to start a story that has already lasted longer than most mines last. Along about 1870 a company of rangers were camped four miles above Sabinal town. They often practiced shooting at prickly pear leaves and ground squirrels. Then suddenly, in accordance with ranger custom, these protectors of the frontier were ordered to some other place.

After thirty years or more had passed, one of the veteran rangers appeared in Sabinal and went up the river. He was gone a day or two, took no one into his confidence, and quietly left the country. Within a few weeks he returned with another member of his all but forgotten company. They secured the help of some of the oldest settlers and definitely located the site of the ranger camp. Next, the former rangers drew up with the owner of the land a contract allowing them to mine quicksilver. Then they told their story.

According to it, while they were camped on the Sabinal a generation back, one of the rangers shot a ground squirrel on the edge of its hole. In stooping over to pick up the dead creature, he happened to glance into the hole. The sun was shining at just the right angle to throw light down it, and there the ranger glimpsed some free globules of quicksilver. He got a can, dipped up some of it, and passed it around for his comrades to examine. Some of them rubbed their guns with it. None of them knew anything about minerals, although they knew that quicksilver was worth something. It was a day or two after this episode that they were ordered on.

The two veterans who, after so long a time, returned to the site, set up camp and began work. They dug many trenches, but there was no friendly ground squirrel to direct them now, and, to be brief, they were unable to find even a trace of what they were after. The ground where they dug is near a great fault that has exposed millions of tons of igneous rock. Quicksilver, it is said, sometimes occurs under just such conditions; but to this day the elusive mineral once glimpsed by the Texas rangers—down in the hole of a ground squirrel—has not been found, and their story has passed into the tradition of the Sabinal country.[4]

PRECIOUS LEAD

No story of the frontiers is more common than that about savages extravagantly shooting bullets of silver. Felix Aubry, who, among other exploits, rode eight hundred miles from Santa Fe, New Mexico, to Independence, Missouri, in five days and sixteen hours, claimed to have found Indians on the Gila River who were actually shooting gold bullets. But, after all, lead moulds better into bullets than either silver or gold. A ball of lead was often worth more to a frontiersman than all the gold and silver in the world. Lead for bullets meant life; lack of it meant death. The pioneers melted bulk lead and moulded their own balls. A bullet mould was as necessary as a rifle. It is not strange that even in territory lacking almost altogether in evidences of mineralization, stories of hidden lead mines should have grown up.

Caddo Indians, so the story is told all along the upper Louisiana-Texas line,[5] used to bring lead to Shreve's Landing (now Shreveport) to trade. They would never tell where they got it, nor would they allow any white man to accompany them to the source of supply. Secret spying on their movements, however, led some woodsmen to conclude that the lead mines must be in what is now Cass County, Texas. Years later a fox hunter while following his hounds one morning up John's Creek, a tributary to Caddo Lake, noticed as he broke with difficulty through a strange mixture of debris at the mouth of a crude shaft some pieces of galena lead and broken timbers. He was just then too much interested in getting a fox to care about galena ore, and after the hunt was over he was too busy to investigate it, but eventually he became thoroughly convinced that he had seen the lost lead mine of the Caddos.

The resourceful pioneers had more lead mines, now lost, scattered over the country than Indians ever had. James Goacher, so history relates,[6] came to Texas from Alabama in 1835 and settled on Rabb's Creek, near the present town of Giddings, in Lee County. On the way up from Austin's coastal settlement to his wilderness home he blazed a way that was long known as Goacher's Trace, but his name is kept alive now by his supposed connection with a deposit of lead, which he not only used but sold and traded to others.

When settlers came to Goacher's home to buy lead, so legend remembers, he would, if he did not have a sufficient supply on hand, insist upon their staying at the house while he went for some. He always reappeared in a quarter different from that in which he had gone out. Sometimes he would be gone for hours; again, only a short while. He guarded the secret of his leaden ore as jealously as though it had been a trove of precious gems. Only three souls shared with him knowledge of the whereabouts of the mine; they were his two sons and a son-in-law named Crawford. One day about two years after the family had settled on Rabb's Creek, all four of the men met death while rushing to the house, unarmed, to repel a horde of savages. Those savages, so it is claimed, knew the whereabouts of the lead, knew the fatal worth of lead bullets, and in annihilating the Goacher men and carrying off the women and children they did not kill, were but following a plan to render the colonists less formidable. Perhaps, after the massacre, they covered up all trace of the lead mine; so remote was the Goacher homestead that other settlers knew nothing of the havoc until several days later. Certainly the mine has never been found, though more than one sign pointing to it has been glimpsed, always, however, in such a manner as to foil arrival at the goal.

One fine spring morning thirty-five years ago Doctor John M. Johnson and his newly wedded wife drove out of Giddings in their buggy to spend the day on Rabb's Creek. They stopped at Two-Mile Crossing, fished until noon, and ate lunch. Then, gun in hand, the doctor struck afoot down the creek after squirrels, leaving Mrs. Johnson to drive the horse. There was no hurry, the road was rocky, Mrs. Johnson had a fancy for pretty rocks, and several times she stopped to pick some up and put them in the buggy. At Five-Mile Crossing the couple met and drove back home.

A few days later the young housewife arranged the rocks to border a flower bed—all but one. She thought that it would be suitable for a door stop; so she took it inside to use for that purpose, and for many years it kept doors from slamming. Then the Johnson family—there were children now—moved to a new home. A few days later Mrs. Johnson found that her old door stop had been lost in the move; she was regretful, but as it was only a rock, no particular search was made for it and it was soon forgotten.

More years passed. Then one morning Doctor Johnson was called in to see the town jeweler. The jeweler and his family were living in the house formerly occupied by the Johnsons. After prescribing and talking for a while, the doctor picked up his case and was leaving the room when his glance fell on a rock beside the door.

"Why," he exclaimed, a tone of friendly pleasure in his voice, "there is Mrs. Johnson's long-lost door stop."

The sick man, failing to grasp the meaning of the remark, asked: "What door stop?"

The doctor pointed to the rock by the door and said: "Mrs. Johnson and I began married life in this house, and she used that rock for a door stop just as your wife is using it." Then he went to his office.

He had scarcely arrived when again he was summoned to the jeweler's home. Fearing that his patient had suffered a sudden attack, he hurried into the sick room without knocking.

"Where," the jeweler eagerly greeted him, "did that chunk of lead come from?"

"What chunk of lead?"

"That door stop you called a rock. After you left just now I cut into it and found it to be pure lead. Here, see for yourself."

The doctor looked. The familiar door stop was indeed lead ore, almost pure.

But the doctor had forgotten where it had come from. He took it home to his wife. Of course she recalled instantly how she and her lover had brought it in from a honeymoon excursion to Rabb's Creek so many years back. The couple drove again to Two-Mile Crossing and then slowly, examining many rocks, on down to Five-Mile Crossing. But Mrs. Johnson could not recall at what particular place she had picked up the heavy rock, and no other rock resembling it could be found. This is just one of the stories that hinge on Goacher's lead mine.[7]

Along in the fifties an old Dutchman by the name of Frank Vanlitsen, who lived near Wallace Bridge on the Lavaca River down towards the Texas coast, began supplying his neighbors with lead in a pure form. No one knew where he got it; certainly he did not receive it off ships that then regularly put into Lavaca and Matagorda bays. As may be imagined, the source of his supply became a subject for conjecture and imaginative play.[8] But he never told. In fact, he seldom told anything, and no one ever heard him refer to his past. A great part of the country along Lavaca River was, as it is today, heavily timbered and sparsely settled; the goings and comings of Vanlitsen could not well be spied upon. About three years after he had begun selling lead he was found dead in his cabin with a bullet hole through

his head and a pistol clutched in his hand. When discovered, he had been dead for several days, and his neighbors, judging that he had committed suicide, buried him without making any particular investigation. The Civil War came on, the country was disrupted, the demand for lead was stronger than ever. The "Dutchman's lead mine" was not forgotten.

About 1867 a noted character of the Lavaca country, nameless here, for it is necessary to say that he bears the reputation of being an extraordinary liar—also, he has killed several men—noised it about that he had at last discovered Vanlitsen's lead. One afternoon while riding after cattle in the Lavaca bottom he became so tired, he said, that he dismounted and threw himself down on a well-shaded sand bed in the bottom of a gully and went to sleep. When he awoke, his eye fell on some chunks of lead sticking out through sandstone that the gully had cut through. He broke some of it off, tied it on his saddle, and rode home. Darkness was coming on when he left the gully; he made no mark to guide him back to the place; he had no reason to doubt his ability as a woodsman to return and open up the mine. That night a heavy rain fell, washing out all signs of his tracks. As soon as the water had run off the country, he set out with pick and sacks to gather more of the lead. He could not find it. He tried many times to relocate it, always in vain. To prove the veracity of his claim, he used to offer for inspection about half a bucket of poorly smelted lead. Many men have looked for the lead-bearing gully, but no one has ever found it.

But there is no doubt that solitary old Frank Vanlitsen had plenty of lead and that for three years he sold lead to settlers of the region. Geologists have declared that the country shows absolutely no indications of lead or associated minerals. Where did the Dutchman get his supply? Some people—for it is human nature to demand explanations—claim that Spanish pack trains following the old Atascosita Road, which traversed the Lavaca country, used to carry bullion, generally silver, from Mexican mines to New Orleans. They tell how one of these trains was robbed near Chicolete Creek and opine that Vanlitsen, who came to the country very early, helped rob it, found that the bullion was lead, took his share of it, years later began selling it, and then was murdered by a confederate, who arranged that the deed should appear suicidal. Anyway, the Dutchman had lead.

Yet another early-day provider of lead from a secret mine was a rancher by the name of Hoffman who lived north of Sabinal.⁹ He had come from California—and so knew all about minerals. Scattering settlers used to go to his cabin to buy lead. One day while Will and High Thompson, brothers, were helping Hoffman brand calves at his ranch pens, they said something about needing lead for bullets. Hoffman replied that if they would keep on working he would get them all the lead they could use. He had plenty of it, he said. The Thompson boys kept on branding; Hoffman rode away, and in about two hours returned with the lead. He said that he had got it out of his mine and that as soon as he could sell his cattle he was going to work the mine on an extensive basis. Within a short time he sold out his stock of cattle, but almost immediately thereafter he was killed by Indians.

The Thompson brothers then began to hunt for the mine. One day while they were searching for sign of it, High called out to Will to come and see "this great big blue cow chip." The cow chip proved to be lead. They were at the mine—and didn't know it. A very short time after this Will, who was always leader, was killed either by Indians or by bandits. The mine was now forgotten, or neglected, for a period of years, and meanwhile the land on which it is supposed to be located passed into the hands of a man who would not allow any but his own kin to prospect on it.

Finally a brother-in-law of the land-owner resumed the search and got High Thompson to help him. They sank several shafts near the place where High, as he remembered, had seen the "big blue cow chip," but they never found any lead. The mine is still a lost mine, talked about by many and even today searched for by more than a few.

In 1887 Thomas Longest and Luke Callaway, who kept a stable at Dalton, Georgia, came to Texas to buy horses. They bought five carloads on the upper Brazos, and while Callaway went back to Georgia with the shipment Longest remained to look over the country.

One day while riding with a cowboy near the intersection of the Salt Fork and Double Mountain Fork of the Brazos, Longest saw a steer with such wide-spreading horns that he expressed a desire to have the animal killed. He wanted to send the horns to a friend in New York, his former home. The cowboy, however, declared that the horns on this steer were short compared with the horns on a certain brand of steers ranging a day's ride to the northwest. Longest promptly set out to find the horns, the cowboy going with him only far enough to show him a crossing on the Salt Fork free from quicksands and telling him the general direction of trails to Croton Creek.

After Longest had ridden for several hours, a storm forced him to take shelter under a canyon bluff in a very rough and desolate-looking country. Here, while waiting for the weather to clear, he noticed on the ground a rusty piece of iron. Upon closer examination, he found it to be an old pick. With it he poked around in the dirt and uncovered the remains of a shovel. He kept on investigating and presently discovered a ledge of ore. From it he broke off a piece weighing four or five pounds. He was sure that it was silver. He lost all interest in cow horns and at once returned to Georgia, where he dispatched the ore to an assayer in New York. To his great disappointment, it was pronounced lead, but seventy per cent pure—a valuable find.

Longest now set about trying to interest a mining company, and by the spring of 1888 arranged to show its representative the mine. However, during the trip to Texas the year before he had contracted a severe cold and cough, which developed into tuberculosis. Hoping to get better, he put off the trip, and affairs were at this stage when L. D. Bertillion—the man who knows where the Mexican opals are buried on the Pecos—met Longest in Georgia.

"In a few months," says Bertillion,[10] "Longest was dead. I don't think that he ever made a way-bill to the mine. Somebody had evidently worked it before Longest saw it. Thus for a second time became lost what is perhaps one of the richest lead veins in America. From the description of the country given by Longest, I judge that the ore is located in either Stonewall or King County, more likely in the latter."

COPPER ON THE BRAZOS

The tradition of copper worked by the Spanish up the Brazos River—high up where the water runs clear and where cliffy eagle perches look down upon it—goes far back. And along with the tales of copper that used to stir settlers plowing in the flat muddy bottoms many hundreds of miles downstream were tales too of "inexhaustible" mines of gold and silver, "a mountain of iron," and a monstrous "lump of platina" that Indians worshiped and fashioned arrow spikes from.[11] As frontiersmen pushed west and north into the Cross Timbers along the Brazos they came to fix the location of the Spanish copper workings somewhere near the junction of the Salt and Double Mountain forks and within sighting distance of Kiowa Peak—the region in which Thomas Longest of Georgia found such a fine specimen of lead.

One very pretentious expedition to find the Brazos copper was organized in Washington by a group of men who called themselves "the Washington and Texas Land and Copper Company."[12] The personnel of this expedition when it set out from Fort Richardson, at Jacksboro, Texas, in 1872, consisted of about sixty men, among them a Virginia congressman of ante-bellum dignity, an orientalist, an "official artist," a chemist, the "sometime State Geologist of Texas" named Roessler, and various other "characters." They did little but travel leisurely and "locate" ten or twelve sections of land about Kiowa Peak.

Yet let no one scoff at the idea of copper in Texas, and let not the prospectors who follow legend lag in their sanguine pursuit. Geologists have actually conceded the presence of copper on Los Brazos de Dios.[13] The most extraordinary hunt into these copper realms, however, seems to have been chiefly concerned with gold. Mr. R. E. Sherrill has supplied an account of it. His narrative follows.[14]

"About 1908 a large old gentleman, whose name I cannot now recall, suddenly appeared in the sleepy little town of Haskell from somewhere on the Mexican border and began inquiring about the topography of the country and the tradition of Spanish treasure. Having learned what he could, he took into his confidence a few select men and explained to them that he had gathered from reliable Mexicans definite information regarding a gold storage on the Brazos and that he proposed to search for 'the key' to this hidden wealth.

"Adding his own information to what he heard from the natives, the stranger gradually let out a tale that ran somewhat as follows. At an early date, when Spanish miners were gathering great quantities of gold in Mexico, a company of them in search of further treasure wandered far to the northwest, taking along, for some reason, a large store of the precious metal. Directed by an Indian or by their own keen instinct for such things, they located the copper mines on the Brazos and proceeded to work them. Here they aroused the hostility of the native Indians and were in danger of massacre. So they hastily hid their treasure, made a plat of the country, and fled. The Indians continued so hostile that they never dared return to take away their gold. Amidst the turmoil and dangers of Mexico at that time, the plat was delivered for safe-keeping to a faithful mestizo who was attached to the Spanish party. It remained in his hands until the old man, approaching death; delivered it to a member of his family. Thus the plat passed along for two or three generations until Texas fell into the hands of the hated gringos and it became certain that no poor Mexican could ever get possession of the treasure. Finally, for some small favors and a little money, a Mexican turned the plat over to the portly American who had now come with it and its tale to Haskell County.

"The company he organized to assist him in digging up the treasure kept the plat a secret, though it and the oral directions pertaining to it were so complicated that not even the wisest of them pretended not to be confused. The map covered a large territory, including the two branches of the Brazos, Kiowa Peak, and numerous minor features of the vicinity. It called for many specified rocks and many marked trees. The rocks had been covered with soil or the markings on them had been weathered away. Most of the trees had perished in fires long years past. An explanation was given to some of the signs, but the meaning of more had to be guessed at.

"The search was thorough and long continued, and a deal of money was spent in digging. Most of the prospecting was along the river, and a Mexican who was herding sheep in the neighborhood began to enter into counsels of the treasure hunters. To use his information, they made him a partner. He announced that if they could produce a rock bearing certain letters and symbols, the picture of which he drew, he could find the gold. Only a few days after this, the party did uncover, about eight or ten inches under the surface of the soil, a rock that they called the 'Spider Rock.'

"The rock had many curious markings on it, among them the letter H, in old Spanish chirography, as the Mexican had called for. Presuming to interpret the markings, he said that the little hill on which the Spider Rock was found was underlaid with the 'base rock'; that underneath the 'base rock' were buried a great many bodies; and that buried nineteen steps west of the skeletons would be found a large bone of some prehistoric animal. He said that, in excavating, the diggers would find a kind of wall, as if a trench had been dug and then filled in with a much harder substance.

"Fired with hope, the treasure hunters set to digging for the 'base rock.' They came against a wall-like wedge of very firm substance, wider at the top and narrower at the base, as if a trench had been filled in with it. When they had got down some fifteen feet, they were met by such a stench that they could hardly work. They found a great many decayed bodies and many relics of various kinds. Furthermore, at the specified distance, they found the bone of a prehistoric animal. It was of about the thickness of a man's body and very porous.

"The Mexican now directed that the diggers go to the bluff a little farther to the west. He said that there they would uncover a great bone like the first and other things buried by the Spaniards. The bone was found, and with it were an old-fashioned sword, some copper ornaments thought to be epaulets, some silver ornaments also, forty-two gold buttons, and a great number of beads.

"But here ended the findings. A majority of the relics were placed in Doctor Terrell's drug store at Haskell, where they remained until a fire, about 1909, destroyed them. After turning up more than an acre of ground, the depth of the excavations varying from a few inches to twenty feet, the diggers dispersed to their farms, the large man from the border left, and the Mexican disappeared. Many men think he knew more than he would tell. Not long after he vanished, a skeleton was found several miles to the east across the river, in the opposite direction from that in which the Mexican had led the Americans. Near the skeleton were two small, heavy copper pots, one shaped somewhat in the form of a canoe, the other round and of the capacity of a gallon and a half, built much stronger than any vessel now made for commerce and capable of holding molten metal. The popular conclusion is that the Mexican took from these copper vessels at least a part of the vast Spanish treasure.

"Nearly every man of that searching party was a friend of mine. I wish to give an illustration of their sanguine nature. At one time the party believed that they were within a foot or two of their treasure, but they feared to uncover it before they had made arrangements to take care of it. They were afraid, so one of them confided to me, to put much of the money in local banks, lest the banks be robbed, but wished to entrust it to our private vault, where no one would suspect its presence. I agreed to take care of the money and was to be notified a little after midnight. The amount to be deposited was $60,000 in gold. I was never called to open the vault."

CHAPTER XVI

Sartin for Sure

I cannot say how the truth may be;
I say the tale as 'twas told to me.
SCOTT, Lay of the Last Minstrel

MORO'S GOLD

About a hundred years ago some daring young *caballeros* who lived south of the Rio Grande in the state of Tamaulipas organized for protection against Indians and desperadoes. As a badge of office they rode garbed in the picturesque robes of the Moors and were for that reason called Moros. One of them, Ramón Berrera by name, owned a ranch in Texas, and on a certain occasion when he was returning home with money for which he had sold a herd of cattle, he was murdered and robbed by his servant. The fellow Moros of the dead man spurred far and long in search of the servant but could never capture him. However, years later some of them heard that he was in a distant part of Texas living under the name of Moro and was a very rich man.

What connection, if any, may exist between this tradition and another that has for more than three generations been famous all over southern Texas, the reader must conclude for himself. Fannie Ratchford, a descendant of the chief participant—other than Moro himself—has thus told the story.[1]

"Before the Civil War, my grandfather, Preston R. Rose, lived on a large plantation, called Buena Vista, lying along the Guadalupe River, seven miles from Victoria. Late one afternoon in the summer of 1859 he was sitting on the porch reading, when my mother, then a little girl, called his attention to the unusual sight of a stranger coming across the field from the direction of the river. The stranger was of small stature and dark complexion, evidently a Spaniard. When he reached the porch, he addressed my grandfather in the easy, courteous manner of a gentleman and an equal, and requested hospitality for the night, explaining that his pack mule had gotten away from him and that he had exhausted himself in a fruitless search.

"His request was granted without question, and Moro took up his residence at Buena Vista, which on one pretext or another lasted for several months, in spite of the suspicious and disquieting circumstances that soon arose. The first of these was a report brought in by the negroes the next morning after Moro's arrival, that a mule, with a pistol shot through his head, had been found partly buried in the river bottom. Another was the fact that Moro was never seen without a glove on his right hand, not even at meal time. The negro boy who waited on him in his room reported that he once saw him without the glove when he was washing his hand, and described a strange device on his wrist that was probably a tattooed figure. But the most disturbing circumstance connected with Moro was his eagerness to get rid of money. He distributed gold coins (of what coinage, I never heard) among the household servants like copper pennies, until Grandfather rather sharply requested him to stop.

"Though there was not much to be bought in Victoria, Moro never came back from a trip to the little town without the most expensive presents that could be bought for all the family in spite of the fact that they were invariably refused. My mother seems to have been particularly impressed by a large oil painting which he once bought from a local artist at an exorbitant price, as a present for my grandmother. When she refused to accept it, he asked permission to hang it in the library, and there it hung as long as the house was in possession of the family.

"Frequently Moro proposed the most extravagant things. Once he urged Grandfather to allow him to build a stone mansion of feudal magnificence to replace the colonial frame house in which he lived. Again he proposed that he take the entire family to Europe at his expense and leave the girls there to receive an elaborate education.

"One day as Moro was walking about the plantation with Grandfather, the question of plantation debts came up, and Moro remarked in a significant tone that Grandfather was at that minute standing within fifty feet of enough gold to enable him to pay all the debts of the plantation and still be a rich man, even if he did not own an acre of land or a negro slave. Grandfather's prideful indignation prevented his continuing the disclosure that he was evidently eager to make. The only landmark of any kind near was a large fig tree fifty feet away.

"In the meantime the negroes had caught the idea of buried treasures, and many were the tales they told of seeing Moro digging about the place at night.

"A guest staying in the house one night reported that he had been drawn to the door of his room by an unusual noise, and had seen Moro painfully heaving a small chest up the stairway, step at a time.

"My grandfather was a man in whom the spirit of adventure was strong. He had left his plantation to the direction of his wife while he went adventuring into the California gold fields in '49. Consequently Moro was able to catch his interest by the story of buried treasures down on the Rio Grande, and Grandfather consented to go if he were allowed to make up his own party. The party as finally organized consisted of friends and neighbors, most of whom were well-to-do planters, but one man included was somewhat out of the social class of the others, though well known and trusted throughout the neighborhood. To this man Moro objected strenuously, saying that he would either prevent their finding the treasure or, if it were found, would murder them all to get the whole for himself. Grandfather insisted, and the man went.

"Moro was nervous and sulky from the start, and so aroused the suspicions of the party that by the time they reached the Rio Grande, he was not allowed out of sight. But despite the close watch kept upon him, he finally made his escape by diving from one of the boats in which the party were crossing the Rio Grande to the point where he said the treasure was to be found. The man whom Moro feared would have shot him as he rose above the surface of the water if Grandfather had not intervened.

"There was nothing left for the party to do but return home, for Moro had given them no map or directions that would enable them to make an independent search. But before setting out on the return, Grandfather foolishly accepted a dare to swim the river in a very wide place, and in doing so caught a severe cold that developed into 'galloping consumption,' from which he died a few months later.

"The rest of the story, so far as there is any, is confused and contradictory. A few weeks before Grandfather's death, some of the negroes on the place came to the house, begging for relief from Moro's ghost, which was seen almost nightly digging at various spots on the plantation, but most often near the big fig tree in the field.

"Grandfather was too ill to make any investigation for himself, but he questioned the negroes closely, and came to the conclusion that all the stories had grown out of one real incident—that Moro had prob-ably come back to recover money he had buried on the place.

"The man whom Moro feared went to Mexico to escape service in the Confederate Army, and his sudden rise to fortune, coupled with a wild story he told on his return of having met with Moro below the Rio Grande, convinced my grandmother that he had in some way come into possession of the treasure.

"The legend of buried money still lingers around the old plantation of Buena Vista. About ten years after the Civil War, my father bought the part of the estate on which the home was situated, and during the years that he lived there was much annoyed by treasure seekers who begged permission to dig for 'Moro's gold,' or who came at night and dug without permission. One day as he was showing a 'free negro' how to run a straight furrow in the field not far from the old fig tree, the horse stumbled and his right foreleg sank in the ground up to the shoulder. Moro's gold seems not to have entered my father's thoughts at the time, but later he remembered it and was convinced that if there had ever been any money buried on the plantation it was in that spot."

THE MYSTERY OF THE PALO DURO

Lighthouse Canyon is a tributary of that strange and wonderful cleft across the Panhandle Plains of Texas known variously as Prairie Dog Creek, Red River, and the Palo Duro. Coronado doubtless wandered over the region while in quest of the chimerical Gran Quivira. Long after him the *comancheros*—Spaniards and Mexicans who traded with the Comanches—were familiar with it.

In Lighthouse Canyon itself was born in the year 1850 Jesús Ramón Grachias. He became a man of marked intelligence, fair education, and wide experience. At the age of seventy-six he happened one day while hunting burros to enter the camp of a college professor who was taking his vacation in New Mexico, and there he related one of his experiences.[2]

"I lived in Lighthouse Canyon until my father died in 1854, and then my mother brought me away. My remembrances of those four years are very dim. More than thirty years later I was working on the Fort Worth and Denver Railroad then building into Amarillo. As I was thus again on Palo Duro Canyon and as I had some money saved up, I decided to visit the place where I was born and where my father was buried. I put my wife, baby, and camp things into a wagon and started west.

"We traveled slow. The country was still wide—ranches, ranches, ranches. I did not know if there was a road into Lighthouse Canyon. I only knew that it was west. After two weeks I came upon a Mexican who was trapping lobos for the J A Ranch. He guided me to within ten miles of the place I wanted to go and then, after telling me how to take the wagon, turned back.

"Many times my mother had described the place to me: the great pillar projecting up from the center of the canyon almost to the level of the plains like a lighthouse; the strange markings on the walls of rock; the fine spring of water; the shaggy old cedars around whose gnarled roots I used to play; the herds of buffaloes and antelopes that came into the breaks for winter; the owls and panthers and lobos that made their cries in the night. Remembrance of all these things helped me locate the spot where my father had built his *jacal* nearly forty years before. The place was still wild and there was not one sign of former habitation, but when I unloaded the wagon and put up a tent, I knew I would sleep that night on the spot where I was born.

"Many times I had promised my mother that some day I would come back here and put a cross over my father's grave. I found two flat stones lying near each other on the ground. When I turned one of them over, I saw the letters J. R. G. They were roughly cut. They stood for my father's name, my name also, Jesús Ramón Grachias. The stones had marked his grave and had very likely been pushed over by cattle or buffaloes. Also, my mother had told me that the grave was fifty feet east of an old cedar. I found only the burned stump of a cedar, fifty feet away in the right direction. Accordingly, I heaped up a hill of earth between the stones, set them in place again, and made a cross.

"The night after I had accomplished this I had a dream. I saw in this dream someone digging near the stump of the burned cedar. As I had myself dug there to get earth to put on the grave, and as I had, moreover, dug in several other places to find fishing worms, I did not regard the dream as very unusual. But the next night the dream came again, and this time I heard very distinctly these words: '*Dig fifteen feet east of old cedar tree.*'

"All the next day I was disturbed, thinking that my mother had perhaps said the grave was fifteen feet east of the cedar instead of fifty feet east and that I had maybe marked the wrong spot. I was much troubled, for now that I was on the ground I could not bear to leave the exact spot of my father's remains unmarked. Then I determined to make another mound fifteen feet east of the cedar tree and put a cross on it also. I measured off the distance and began to work. But the voice of the dream kept ringing in my ears: '*Dig fifteen feet east of the old cedar tree.*' '*Dig,*' it said. '*Dig.*'

"If I dig, I thought, I can tell if the earth has ever been disturbed. So I began digging. At first the ground seemed no softer than any other ground. Then very soon my spade struck something hard, something of iron. Quickly I uncovered it. It was the lid of a chest, about eighteen inches wide and thirty inches long. More quickly yet I uncovered one end and prized it up. The chest was about eighteen inches deep. With the help of my wife I now got it out of the ground. We

were very excited. I had to break the clasps of the lid. We opened it. It was full of coins. They were all Spanish and were all dated before 1821, the year of Mexico's independence.

"The grave of my father was after all properly marked. We could now leave. I backed my wagon up to the chest and dug little trenches for the hind wheels so that the rear end of the bed would be low. Thus I managed to load the chest. I drove up the canyon to its head and topped out upon the plains. I had no desire to go back east. I made for Santa Fe. It took us ten days to arrive. The banker there was a friend to the family of my mother. He counted the coins and gave me credit for $7600.

"I do not know which was bigger in me, the joy or the mystery. My mother was still alive and I at once traveled to her to tell her all things and to take her money. She could not understand the meaning

any more than I could. We talked and talked. She told me much about my father that I had never known or had forgotten. You will see if what I learned explained anything.

"When the Texans whipped Santa Anna, a great many Mexicans living in that state left. My father was among them. He and four other Mexicans set out for Santa Fe over a country they did not know even by report. There were no roads. Winter overtook them on the plains. They camped in a deep canyon—Lighthouse Canyon—well protected. They made friends with the Comanches; game was everywhere. Early in the spring all their horses but two got away with the mustangs. On these horses two men left for Santa Fe to secure aid. Those messengers never returned. My father and his companions stayed, hunting and living on the country. I think they were happy.

"In the late summer of 1841 a body of Texas traders and soldiers—the Santa Fe Expedition—came among them, lost. The Mexicans joined them as guides. It is well known how the Texans were made prisoners and sent to Mexico City. My father was made prisoner also. He was kept for four years. Then he was released and came back to Santa Fe.

"There he married my mother. She was thirty-five years old; this was in 1849. He was twenty years older. As soon almost as they were married, he loaded a wagon with goods and set out for the plains of Texas. He told her that he was going to hunt buffaloes, but she said he seemed to hunt nothing but canyons. At last they came to the place he had been looking for. It was Lighthouse Canyon. 'I once lived here,' he said. 'I will live here again.' He died there, as I have already told you, in 1854.

"For a day before he died he seemed out of his head. He kept talking wildly to my mother of fights, of gold coin, of escapes, of enemies, of friends—of many things that she did not understand, for he explained nothing. He had never explained anything to her. The last hour of his life was calm. She was holding me over him to see if he would take notice when she heard, 'Buried fifty feet east of old cedar tree.' I recall only being lifted up and looking at him.

"So my mother with her own hands dug a grave fifty feet east of the big cedar tree, just as she supposed my father had directed. Then alone she got the horses, which were hobbled in the canyon, hitched them to our wagon, and drove with me to Santa Fe, leaving forever the lonely Palo Duro."

It has been said that the narrator—this finder who was not a searcher—was a fairly well educated man. The activities of the sub-conscious mind have long interested many people who make no claims to education. Jesús Ramón Grachias was quite averse to being regarded as superstitious.

"I do not believe in spirits," he said. "I do not believe in voices of the dead. Now listen. My mother was even when she married slightly deaf. What my dying father said to her was probably this: 'Dig fifteen feet east of the old cedar tree. It is buried fifteen feet east of old cedar tree.' My mother, failing to catch the first word of his command, thought he was talking of his grave and heard 'fifteen' as 'fifty.' At the same time, although I was too young to attach any meaning to the words or to store them away in my memory, my subconscious mind registered the sounds. More than thirty years later when I returned to Lighthouse Canyon and rested in the shade of the cedars around which I had played as a child and drank from the spring that my little mother as a bride used to dip from and stepped on the soil where my father's feet had worn a trail and where he had died—then old associations stirred the subconscious mind to activity. My nerves were all active, my imagination was alive. It was natural for me to dream a dream in which the subconscious mind brought to the surface those words stored away so long ago: 'Dig fifteen feet east of the old cedar tree.'

"The real mystery to me is how the money came to be there. Was my father at some time a robber—some time before 1821, for no coins were dated later than that year? Why did he live for years beside the money without using it, without telling his wife of it? Was he awaiting the return of some confederate? I do not know. I only wish that all the money were not spent now."

CHAPTER XVII

The Treasure of the Wichitas

The metropolis of the Wichita Mountains, in southern Oklahoma, is Lawton. One time while I was traveling thither by train I met a young lieutenant who had been assigned to duty at Fort Sill, which is adjacent to Lawton. He was eager to learn all about "the old Indian country" and to explore the Wichita National Forest. As he did not have to report for duty for several days, he intended spending some of his free time in scouting around.

"Well," said I, "I'm going down into the Wichitas myself to learn something about the country, and I'll tell you what I'll do. I'll bet you a pair of shopmade officers' boots against the best Stetson hat in Lawton that within two hours' time after we register at the hotel I can get you up a hunt for one of the biggest lost treasures in America."

I needed a new hat and the lieutenant did not, apparently, need any more boots.

"Did you ever hunt for it?" he asked.

"No, I have never been in this section before."

"Do you know anybody there?"

"Not a soul, so far as I am aware."

"Have you a hunt planned out?"

"Oh, no, not at all."

"Then what makes you think you can get one up in two hours' time?"

"I've lived in the Southwest a good while. I have read some history. I know that in the seventeenth century Spanish priests came into the Wichitas to convert Indians and that Spanish prospectors tried to mine. When they left, they left a tradition.[1] There's bound to be Spanish gold buried back in the hills and there are bound to be all sorts of lost mines."

The lieutenant was simply wild to get out into the hills and look for Spanish gold. He took up my bet and was afraid he would win.

Twelve minutes after we registered at the hotel we were at the court house. A stenographer told us that she thought the county surveyor was at his home, three or four blocks away. We found him; he made us comfortable on some logs under a shade tree on his grassy lawn. His name is Sam Joyner and he is a most affable gentleman. Within twenty-five minutes after we registered at the hotel we were down to business.

IN A CHICKEN'S CRAW

"Well," Joyner said, "you've certainly come to the right place for information. I guess there is more stuff hidden right here in the Wichitas than anywhere else in America and I guess I've had more calls for running lines than any other surveyor in Oklahoma.

"For instance, about 1905 an old duffer from up in Kansas dropped into this country with a map. At first he was mighty cautious about letting anybody have a look at it. He began by asking if I knew where a group of seven springs might be. I had to confess that I did not, 'but,' says I, 'if you'll give me your other locations, I might be able to work out the site you're looking for.'

"Finally he showed me the map. The words on it were in English, but the lettering seemed to be German. It called for exactly nine cart loads of gold and silver buried near Seven Springs thirty miles northwest of Duncan's Store on the old road to Fort Sill and between Cache and Big Beaver creeks.

"The spot called for put us at some springs I was familiar with on Charlie Thomas' place. There were only four of them, but it was easy to figure that time and the tramping of cattle had covered up the other three. We located a mark on a very old cottonwood near the springs and dug around considerably. Then the old duffer got tired and went back to Kansas.

"Years passed and another character floated into the country. He kept hanging around Charlie Thomas' place and harping on what a good piece of land that was by the springs to raise truck on. Finally Charlie told him he'd fence off a field and rent it on shares.

265

"He put in a crop and worked it fairly well, but every now and then Charlie or one of his boys would catch him punching down into the ground with a steel rod. They never let him know they were watching. He seemed to be making a systematic probing of the whole valley. This went on three or four seasons.

"Then one spring, just as his truck was ready to market, he disappeared without a word, leaving his crop, his wagon, everything belonging to his shack, and a team of horses behind. From that day to this he has not been heard of. Undoubtedly that steel rod of his finally plunked the right spot, though Charlie Thomas was unable to locate the hole. That old fellow was clever enough to cover it up, I guess.

"Now, whatever the Spaniards concealed in the ground they took out of the ground. They had mines somewhere. Yet it is a fact that although I myself have surveyed hundreds of mineral claims in the Wichita Mountains, not a single mine in this country has to my personal knowledge paid. That does not mean a paying mine won't some day be opened.

"Before I came here a prospector who had a dugout on Deep Red found nuggets galore. One time when I was in that vicinity trying to locate the abandoned dugout, a farmer came to me and said he had something he wanted examined. It was a gold nugget polished as slick as a greased pinto bean.

" 'Why, good gracious,' I said, 'where did you get this?'

"Well, his wife had accidently found it in the craw of a chicken she was cleaning.

" 'But where did the chicken get it?' I wanted to know.

" 'I wish I could tell,' the farmer answered me. 'The chicken must have picked it up in a sand bed. The only sand about is some I hauled up for the children to play in. I hauled it from two different creeks and they have both been up since then, so that I don't know exactly where I took it out.'

"Now, down here on Cache Creek . . ."

"Hold on, Mr. Joyner," I cried. "Wait a minute." Then I turned to my companion.

"Lieutenant," I said, "we have been in Lawton over an hour. If we go on listening to Mr. Joyner you'll win your boots and miss the hunt and I'll be out both money and a Stetson hat. The decision is yours to make. Shall we attend to business or get more tales?"

"Then," replied the lieutenant—and I tip my Stetson hat, which I am wearing this minute for an eyeshade, to his gameness—"we'll do both. Mr. Joyner is going to take me to the farm where that chicken swallowed the nugget and we're going to pan sand in both those creeks. You are invited to come along."

I could not go along, for I had business with Pete Givers.

Pete Givers is what Trader Horn would pronounce "convivial." A little, dark, wiry man with a kind of foreign accent to his speech, he combines in himself the ease that characterizes lovers of good tales and the intensity that great dreamers habitually evince. By trade he is a tailor, but his thoughts habitually dwell as far above stitches and ironing boards as the mind of the tinker who wrote *Pilgrim's Progress* dwelt above pots and solder.

"Yes, sir," Pete Givers announced soon after he got launched on his subject, "I studied Hindu philosophy under that great teacher Lorentz. I can take an astral body out of its spiritual relation. That is something! Yet my science is helpless to recover the Spanish treasure in the Wichitas. This is why.

"Clairvoyancy is simply opening up the subconscious mind. The subconscious mind, though, can open up only while the conscious mind is closed. That is why the subject must be put to sleep. To the sleeper space is nothing. If there is anywhere in the world a mind that consciously or subconsciously knows the fact sought for, a good subject can realize it. In Wisconsin, for instance, a man once came to me to locate some money that had been stolen from him. I procured the services of an excellent subject, put her to sleep, and she revealed the money as being hidden in a barn. Within twenty-four hours we had secured it. A living person, the thief, knew where that money was.

"On the other hand, not for a hundred years perhaps has a human being lived who knew the hiding place of the Spanish treasures here in the Wichitas. Concerning that stuff no mind exists for a subject to work upon. However, one treasure hereabouts does have a chance of being revealed. It is modern enough that some human being may know subconsciously where it is buried. That is the James' loot."

THE JAMES BOYS' LOOT

The best book about any American outlaw that has been written, *The Rise and Fall of Jesse James* by Robertus Love, has a great deal in it about Frank James, but it has not one word about the two million dollar loot he helped bury in the Wichitas and then could not find. To get that incident in the history of the famous Missouri brothers one must go to Pete Givers.

Just how and where the James gang came by the $2,000,000 is not quite clear. Some say they took it from a Mexican transport crossing Oklahoma on the way to Saint Louis; others say that it was an accumulation from various bank and train robberies. The James gang robbed not to live; they lived to rob, and they robbed on a magnificent scale. Anyway, they stored $2,000,000 in the earth somewhere along the old road between Fort Sill and the Keeche Hills to the northeast, intending to leave it there until peaceful days should come in which to spend it.

The peaceful days never came. After having been hunted for nearly twenty years, "poor Jesse" was laid in his grave, as the ballad runs, by a "dirty little coward" named Bob Ford. All his companions but Frank were in their graves too or behind bars. Frank was still on the dodge. But Frank "came in," gave himself up, was tried, and acquitted.

Thereupon, as the Wichitas have the history, he set out to recover the long-buried loot. He had left the region a hunting ground for Indians; he found it homesteaded, fenced, plowed. He could not locate the spot. He knew that it was alongside the old Western Cattle Trail leading to Dodge City; he knew in a general way where it was; but despite his tenacious memory and his falcon eye, the bit of earth concealing $2,000,000 looked no different from ten thousand other bits of earth.

Frank James bought a little farm so that he might have a strategic base from which to search. He would ride daily from his farm to Cache Creek over the piece of trail he once traversed at the head of the most daring band of robbers known to American history. He always covered the distance in a flying gallop, hoping that when he got to the scene of the secreted treasure the doors of memory would flash open. But daily the doors of memory remained locked. Riding thus, he wore out six horses before he galloped away from the Wichitas forever.

Thus the treasures of the Wichitas unfold themselves in legend. There is the great government treasure lost to view in the sands of Cache Creek. There is the treasure of Cut Throat Gap—a name that was not bestowed without reason. And always there are characters and characters.

DEVIL'S CANYON

For tradition and digging the cynosure of the Wichitas is Devil's Canyon. It seems to be a fact that one of the homesteaders of the region, in plowing a rocky patch of soil, turned up nearly as many human bones as boulders. Here at first was a mystery, but soon it became known that those bones belonged to treasure-bearing Spaniards who had been overwhelmed by Indians.

"Well, it was this way," began "Old Man" Sloan after I had ribbed him up to tell his story. "When that Wichita country was opened for settlement, I took up a squat that enclosed a good part of Twin Mountains, seven or eight miles from Devil's Canyon. A few years later an old Indian woman came in there with some of her people and began poking around. She claimed to be one hundred and five years old and she looked every day of it.

"According to her story, when she was a girl her people had a big fight with some Spaniards bringing a pack train out of Devil's Canyon and killed off the whole band. After the battle, she and two warriors captured three of the Spanish burros. They were loaded with gold ore. They buried it at the foot of Twin Mountains. As the old woman had been gone eighty years or so, it wasn't any wonder she couldn't find it now.

"She got me interested. I knew about that field of Spanish bones, but these were the first definite details I had learned. I began to investigate.

"There was a young woman fortune teller in Snyder named Dolly who'd been successful in finding a good many things, and I took the matter up with her. She looked down at the ground a while with her eyes shet, like she always done when she was a-studying, and then she says, 'Yes, the gold is there.'

"Dolly wasn't very definite, though, and she seemed afraid all along that somebody would prosecute her for telling fortunes. She asked me if there wasn't three hardwood trees close to my fence. I told her yes. Next, she asked if there wasn't a big flat rock near by. I told her yes. Then to test her, I asked if there was anything on the rock.

"She kept her eyes shet a long time. 'Yes,' she finally replied, 'there's some letters on it, but I can't make out what they are.'

"That satisfied me, for there were letters on the rock which I'd put there myself in white paint—N O H U N T I N G A L L O W E D—and they'd been weathered off.

"She ended up by saying that if I expected to find anything, I'd have to keep the search absolutely secret and not reveal her part in it. I told her I just had to have somebody help me dig.

" 'Well,' says she, 'Fay can help you, can't he?'

"Fay's my son, you know, and I said, 'That's exactly who I was figgering on getting to help me.'

"I was so anxious about the matter that I couldn't think about anything else. I let out and told Fay even before I'd settled on a place to dig. About this time a nephew came out to visit us. Before I knowed it, Fay had told him and both boys were deviling me to start the search.

"Well, I went back to Dolly to get more specific directions. As soon as I saw her, I knowed something had happened. The first thing she said was: 'Certain people has been told what you're doing.'

"I couldn't deny it.

" 'Mr. Sloan,' says she, 'I can't tell you another thing.'

"I argued, but it didn't do no good.

"Of course, I dug. I dug a plenty—and never found a thing. Nevertheless, the gold's there all right, I guess. There's certainly been plenty of proof as to Dolly's power in finding things.

"For instance, one time a merchant there in Snyder was busy with a customer when a man came in in a big hurry to buy something. I forget now what it was. He helped himself, laid a silver dollar down on the counter, and rushed out. The merchant was occupied for a few minutes. Then when he went to get the dollar it had disappeared. That night he went to consult Dolly.

" 'Dolly,' says he, 'I've suffered a business loss, and I wish you'd help me. I want to know who it was took my dollar.'

"Dolly looked down in her way for a little while. 'I know who it is,' she says. 'Go to your store in the morning and the third man that comes in, look him square in the eye and say to him, I guess you've carried my dollar about long enough.'

"Sure enough, the next morning when the third man came into the store, the merchant looks him in the eye and says, 'I guess you've carried my dollar about long enough.'

"The man pulled out a dollar and laughed and said he'd took it off just for fun.

"I could go on with other instances. You see what sort of vision this woman has. If it hadn't been for my blabbing when Dolly told me not to, that gold might be doing somebody some good right now instead of laying out there rusting to dust."

THE POTHOLE OF NUGGETS

One time in the early days a band of men who were going across the plains to trade in New Mexico were attacked by Indians somewhere south of the Wichitas, in Texas. They made a corral of their wagons and fought off the Indians as long as they could, but when night came they were so thinned in numbers and the Indians were so strong that the survivors decided to break for their lives. They broke, and all but one man were speedily overtaken, killed, and scalped.

He saved his life by falling into a pothole that lay concealed down a ravine. He found it big enough for him to move around in and remained in it. When daylight came, he detected amid the rounded pebbles and sand at the bottom of the hole something that made him glad he was a prisoner. He was in a hole of gold nuggets. He began sorting them from the gravel, and while digging down with his bare hands found a little water. Thus hiding, living on water, and growing rich, he remained all day. He said afterwards that there must have been a barrel of the nuggets.

Finally, feeling satisfied that the Indians had left and having collected as much gold as he could carry, he set out for a distant fort. The Indians had burned all the supplies with the wagons. A shot at game might mean betrayal and death. Soon he began to realize how weak hunger can make the strongest man—even a man loaded with gold. He left his gun in a wild plum thicket loaded with green fruit that mocked him. His fear of being discovered led him to pursue a very twisting course. The precious gold made him exceedingly cautious. At length he grew so weak that he put a part of his burden in a gopher hole, tamping dirt down on top of it. He grew weaker; he began dropping the gold. When at last, only three specimen nuggets left in his pocket, he staggered into the army walls, he was hardly conscious of his loss.

As his strength and health recovered, the one subject that engrossed his mind day and night was the pothole of nuggets. He knew that he could never retrace his path. He knew that when he and his companions were attacked they were in a pathless region, traveling only by

the sun and watershed. But the hills around the besieged wagons and the ravine down which he stumbled into the pothole were pictured indelibly in his memory. The irons of the burned wagons would verify the exact spot. He began the quest alone. The riches belonged to him; he had bought them fair.

For years and years he wandered. He entered the region from the north; he entered it from the east, from the south, and from the west. But no hill or ravine corresponding to the picture so clear in his brain ever revealed itself. As the country settled up, he, vainly hoping to receive intelligence of the burned wagon irons, told his story to the settlers. It became, one might say, an element of the soil. Years ago he died in Wichita Falls, leaving to descendants three specimen nuggets that yet bear testimony to the truth of his often told tale.

CHAPTER XVIII

Laffite and Pirate Booty

Or if thou hast uphoarded in thy life
Extorted treasure in the womb of earth,
For which, they say, you spirits oft walk in death,
Speak of it.

. . . . . .

It faded on the crowing of the cock.
Hamlet

THE MAN OF MYSTERY

For more than a hundred years Laffite's treasure has been the El Dorado of the Gulf coast. The search for it today is as fresh as it was when Jackson fought the British at New Orleans. Probably a majority of the people in New Orleans could give a more extensive account of Jean Laffite than of Andrew Jackson. In Galveston schoolboys cherish a bit of what is purported to have been Laffite's jacket, and a fine new hotel—perhaps with unintended irony—bears his name. A recent dispatch from Yucatán said that his seal had there been dug up. His strange career, his fabled hoard, and his uneasy ghost will not let his name die. Yet, despite a considerable body of undisputed facts about Laffite's political machinations, the man himself remains veiled, enigmatical.

Various popular historians have glorified him as patriot; others have denounced him as pirate; hardly one who has written of Louisiana or Texas has neglected him. Regardless of all this interest, however, only one scholar, Mr. Stanley Faye, has studied him with any thoroughness, and Mr. Faye's extraordinary revelations remain yet to be published.[1] Enough novels and pulp paper stories to fill a deep five-foot shelf have made Laffite their theme. Folk whose only knowledge of history consists of inherited tradition tell of his daring adventures and look for his legendary millions all the way from the Keys of Florida to Point Isabel at the mouth of the Rio Grande. They call him "the Pirate of the Gulf."

Maybe he was not a pirate. Maybe, as he always claimed, he was a gentleman smuggler and privateer. His birthplace has been variously fixed as St. Malo, as a village on the Garonne, as Bayonne, as Marseilles. Mr. Stanley Faye, relying on documentary evidence not wholly satisfying, thinks he was born in Orduña, a valley in the Basque provinces of Spain. He could pass for either Spaniard or Frenchman. A Spanish agent in New Orleans reported that his friendship for Spaniards was equaled only by his detestation of English and Americans; indisputably he spent good part of his life preying on Spain. Biographers with imaginary gift have said that his family were Bourbon aristocrats; also, that they were mere peasants. His very name has been in dispute; he signed it—two or three times at least—as Laffite, but traditionally it has been spelled Lafitte.

His whole life was a series of contradictions. In New Orleans he owned a blacksmith shop; and he lived in the manner of a cavalier, winning the sobriquet of "Gentleman" Laffite. Defying American law, he pitted his own cannon and cruisers against the American Navy; then at the battle of New Orleans, he, by fighting with Jackson against the British, won pardon for all past offenses and glamour for future memorialization. The government placed a price on his head; then the government placed batteries of defense under his hand. He was gallant to women, but whether he was ever in love is doubtful. Legend says that he married more than once; it also says that he had a low caste Creole mistress in Louisiana who gave birth to a son. At Galveston he was accompanied by a luscious quadroon. A journalist who saw this quadroon and asked Laffite for "the story of his life," received—so he reported—the following account. At the opening of the nineteenth century Laffite was a rich merchant in San Domingo, where he married a rich and beautiful wife. Soon after marrying, he sold out his business with the intention of going to Europe to live. He bought a ship and loaded it with goods and specie. At sea he was captured by a Spanish man-of-war. "They took everything—goods, specie, even his wife's jewels." Then they landed the Laffites on a barren sand key with just enough provisions to keep them alive a few days. An American schooner rescued them and took them to New Orleans, where the wife contracted fever and died.

It is asserted that from boyhood Laffite "loved to play with old ocean's locks" and that once he recklessly dared a West Indian hurricane by driving his fleet straight across water-covered Galveston Island. On the other hand, it is asserted that he was so subject to seasickness that he seldom boarded a vessel and that he "did not know enough of the art of navigation to manage a jolly boat." In truth, he was not so much a seaman as he was a boss of seamen. He was a brilliant conversationalist, but in conversing he was careful to avoid the secrets and duplicities that characterized nearly his whole existence. It seems safe to assert that he died quietly in a bed in Yucatán, in 1826; nevertheless, the story has come down that he died in a dare-devil engagement with a British war-sloop, his buccaneers cheering around him, his locks "matted with blood," the dagger in his swarthy hand streaming red.

Patriotic in one act, yet not a patriot; piratical through a lifetime of activities, yet not a pirate, he was—he is—Legend, Paradox, Mystery. His whole life, as Montaigne defined death, was *un grand Peutêtre*— a great Perhaps. He must have been a puzzle to himself. Truth is precious; so is an interesting story, even though the facts therein be overshadowed by fable. Legend, ever contemptuous of history, is still expanding and spinning the story of Laffite. I tell it as I have gleaned it from sources dubious as well as authentic.

There may have been three Laffite brothers, but only two, Jean and Pierre, enter the story. One tradition has it that Jean was an adopted brother. Whether brothers by blood or adoption, never were two men more devoted to each other than Jean and Pierre. They appeared in New Orleans about the time of the Louisiana Purchase (1803). New Orleans in those days was French to the backbone, and— despite any Spanish blood that may have flowed in their veins—the Laffites found themselves among their own kind. What they did upon arrival we know not. They apparently had money. Ere long they were the proprietors of a mighty blacksmith shop between Bourbon and Dauphine streets. It seems, however, that they never worked at the smithy themselves but had the work done by a corps of efficient slaves. Their real business was over on Barataria. Some old maps mark Barataria as "Smugglers Retreat."

From New Orleans the Mississippi River sprangles out into the Gulf through a maze of bayous and interlocking lakes. To the west the great Bayou La Fourche sprawls gulfward through another maze of marsh and sluggish, twisting currents. Between the two is Barataria Bay. Curtaining off Barataria Bay from the Gulf is a sliver of an island called Grand Terre, sometimes Barataria. From Grand Terre to the coast the Bay is sprinkled with islands. A pass from the Gulf into the Bay gives entrance to a fine harbor on the main island.

Even today, says Albert Phelps, historian of Louisiana, this land of delta and island is "a desolate waste of salt marsh, jungle, and forests of cypress and water oak. A sad land with a sombre beauty of its own, these wide acres are still the haunt of wild things, untraversed for the most part save by the pirogue of the pot-hunter or the negro moss-gatherer. The waters of the almost currentless bayous are alive with garfish; turtles, snakes, and alligators bask on many a log, and herons, cranes, flamingoes, kingfishers, and pelicans hold a monopoly of the fisheries. More dense, more intricately water threaded than all is the district lying about Barataria Bay."

The men who plied their piratical trade in this region, the Baratarians, as they were called, were a motley crew—Portuguese, French, Italian, Malay, adventurers from every nation. For a full and vivid picture of these highly interesting people there is only one place to go, though there are many places where one might go—a chapter upon them in *New Orleans, the Place and the People,* by Miss Grace King, who has, I think, blended literature and history more effectively than any other writer of the land where Laffite's memory dwells. The Baratarians were not exactly pirates in the manner of the ship-scuttling and throat-slitting Blackbeard, Morgan, and L'Olonoise crews who more than a hundred years before had given to the Mexican waters their tradition of piracy. The days of the great pirates had waned. British warships had chased their successors into marshy holes of refuge. The Baratarians were privateers—licensed pirates.

The times were propitious to privateers. South America, Central America, Mexico were all seething with the yeast of revolt against Spain. The republic of Cartagena, a mere seaport of Colombia, was glad to issue letters of marque against Spanish shipping. France and, for a time, the United States were authorizing privateers to prey on English commerce. England, embroiled in the Napoleonic wars, had only limited forces to police the western seas. The naval power of America was a farce. Armed with their letters of marque and also with brass cannon and steel cutlasses, the Baratarians could sally forth from their snug refuge and thrive off Spanish merchantmen, with now and then a prize of some other nationality thrown in for lagniappe.

But the Baratarians needed a market for their plunder. Next door to them was New Orleans. Perhaps thirty thousand consuming human beings made up its population; it was the gateway to the commerce of the Mississippi valley. Most of the goods that the Baratarians had for sale could not be declared. It was not their manner to pay duty anyhow, and they sold cheap, as buyers from Memphis and Saint Louis as well as from New Orleans soon learned. The marshes and bayous afforded approaches that no revenue officer could ever follow. The citizens, almost without exception, were as friendly to the smugglers as was the secret land.

With plunder in hand and a market at their door, the Baratarians required an agent and banker. Jean Laffite became that agent. He was an energetic and efficient business man. He spoke English, French, Spanish, and Italian fluently, if not correctly. He had a gift for making phrases. He had a conscience as elastic as any politician could wish for. Nature seemed to have designed him for agent to the Baratarians.

From agent to chieftain is only a step. Laffite insisted upon two things: strict obedience and that word "privateer." He avoided the term "pirate" as a "mortician" avoids "undertaker." Once, according to an old story, a certain Grambo, who had known rougher days, hooted at the name, boldly declaring himself a pirate and calling upon his comrades to put down this genteel privateer who had come to rule over them. Laffite pulled his pistol and shot Grambo through the heart. Thereafter his rule and his choice of diction were undisputed.

Early in 1813 certain American merchants and bankers of New Orleans became so alarmed over the loss of their legitimate business to the smugglers that they called on the naval authorities for help. The naval authorities sent out two minor expeditions that were successively put to flight. Then the merchants and bankers called on the state legislature. The legislature debated and declared that they had no funds. It was clear that Laffite had friends. While the legislature was debating, he held at Barataria one public auction of 450 negroes.

Meantime Governor Claiborne of Louisiana had proclaimed the Laffite brothers to be "banditti and pirates," and had offered a reward of $500 for the arrest and delivery of Jean. Jean retaliated by offering a reward of $15,000 for the arrest and delivery of Claiborne to him! He continued to visit New Orleans when he pleased. He even dallied on the streets, laughing and chatting with his friends while he leaned on a wall that placarded the governor's proclamation.

One day Claiborne's men captured Pierre and clapped him into jail. He soon escaped, but the federal grand jury brought an indictment. To fight the case Jean engaged the two best lawyers in Louisiana at a stipulated fee of $20,000 each. One of the lawyers was the district attorney, John R. Grymes, who resigned his office to enter Laffite's services. After the trial, which amounted to nothing, he was invited out to the "Pirates' Lair" to receive his fee. He stayed a week amid feast and revelry, and then "in a superb yawl laden with boxes of Spanish gold and silver" was returned to the mainland. "What a cruel misnomer it is," he declared upon returning, "to call the most honest and polished gentlemen the world ever produced bandits and pirates!" Only on the stage he had elected, at the time nature had destined him, could Laffite have gestured so magnificently.

In 1812 the United States declared war on England. The British prepared to lay siege to New Orleans. In September, 1814, two English officers landed on Grand Terre and offered Jean Laffite $30,000 in cash, a captaincy in the British navy, and a chance at enlistment for all his men provided he would aid in the proposed capture of New Orleans.

The British did not know Laffite. He played for time. Then he informed the United States officials of what was brewing and offered his services in defense of the city. "Though proscribed by my adopted country," he wrote, "I never let slip any occasion of serving her or of proving that she has never ceased to be dear to me."

As a reply to such friendly advances Commodore Patterson of the United States Navy made an attack on the privateer stronghold and captured a large quantity of booty. Laffite himself was away at the time; most of his men escaped and fortified themselves on Last Island.

Hickory-tough old Andrew Jackson was at Mobile when he heard of the British proposal and of Laffite's offer. Forthwith he issued a thundering proclamation to the Louisianians in which he bitterly denounced the British for attempting to form an alliance with "hellish banditti." "The undersigned," he concluded with a flourish, "calls not upon pirates and robbers to join him in the glorious cause."

When he reached New Orleans, however, and saw the desperate need for more men, he came down off his high horse. These Baratarians were men of his own mettle. He placed Laffite and his "hellish banditti" in charge of two important batteries. The battle was won, and in a general army order Old Hickory praised Laffite and his captains as "gentlemen of courage and fidelity." President Madison issued a full pardon to all Baratarians who had taken part in the battle.

What Laffite next did legend has been profuse in explaining. One story has him going to Washington and squandering $60,000 in gaudy living. A persistent story has him returning to Europe and in his own ship carrying Napoleon from Elba to France—and the Hundred Days' War that ended with Waterloo. The story goes on that Laffite had even made arrangements to bring Napoleon to America and that he did bring a vast treasure belonging to the fallen emperor, which, of course, he properly buried. Impossible fictions!

Laffite had become associated with Toledo, Herrera, Gutiérrez, Peter Ellis Bean, Perry, and other adventurers who were seeking to overthrow Spanish rule in Mexico and establish an independent state in Texas. He now secretly engaged with Spanish agents to act as spy upon such filibusters and insurgents. Such an engagement, however, in nowise checked his privateering upon Spanish shipping. The record of his double-dealings from the time he landed on Galveston Island until he was driven away from it would make a steel windmill giddy.

It was along in 1816 when he began making a new Barataria at Galveston and, with Pierre to aid, resumed the old business of distributing "purchases"—goods and negroes—to Louisiana buyers. To his American audience he announced that he had selected Galveston as headquarters, first, in order to be near the United States should that dear country again need his services; second, in order to further the cause of liberty in Mexico. To his Spanish masters he announced that he was going to collect in one place—Galveston—all the privateers infesting the Gulf so that they could be captured at one fell swoop. He seems to have collected them all right.

Galveston Island already had a history. At the time Laffite arrived, Louis Aury, a Mexican "republican" soon to vacate, was using it as a base for smuggling slaves and pilfering ships. Here with a thousand men of mongrel breed under him, making and unmaking captains, Laffite lived in his Maison Rouge like a lord in feudal splendor. An old French legend has it that the devil built Maison Rouge in a single night. In contracting with the devil for its erection, Laffite agreed to give him the life and soul of the first creature he cast his eyes upon in the morning. Laffite then contrived to have a dog pitched into his tent about daylight; so all the devil got out of the deal was a dog.

They called him "the Lord of Galveston Island." He was at this time about forty years old, and is described as being exceedingly handsome, even noble in appearance. He had magnetism, charm, suavity, every quality necessary for one who would run innocently with the hare and at the same time bay lustily with the hounds. He seldom smiled, but he cultivated in a rare manner the art of being agreeable. He set an orderly table with abundance of plate, linen, and choice wines. Generally he went unarmed, but, with a nose that sniffed the lightest wind of adversity, he could be depended upon to appear at the right moment provided with a brace of pistols and a "boarding sword." When aroused, he was a desperate man indeed, and he was both an expert swordsman and an unerring shot.

On his lonely island, a wilderness of wild land behind it, a world of silent waters before it, "the Pirate of the Gulf" played host to a train of strange characters. Here—if report be true—came Peter Ellis Bean, who mustanged in Texas with the filibuster Nolan, who had for six years somehow existed in a solitary cell of a Spanish prison, his only companion a pet lizard, and who had then secured his liberty in time to fight beside Laffite at New Orleans. Here came "Old Ben" Milam, "war-born," who had also fought at New Orleans, who was to help Mexico throw off the Spanish yoke, and who was to meet his death leading the Texans into San Antonio. Doctor Long, who at the head of three hundred men had declared Texas a republic—this was years before Austin settled Texas with Americans—came also, seeking Laffite's aid in his enterprise. Laffite was generous in giving "good wishes"—and at the same time reported him to Spanish authorities. Here, too, came half a thousand French refugees seeking an asylum, and Laffite sent them up the Trinity River, where they established the short-lived and tragic Champ d'Asile—happily ignorant of their benefactor's plot to annihilate them. The savage Carankawas came to wonder and barter. Their visit ended in blood.

"Spanish doubloons," said a frontiersman whom Maison Rouge entertained, "were as plentiful as biscuits." Jim Campbell, one of Laffite's lieutenants, who remained on to become a citizen of the Republic of Texas after his master had sailed away, used to tell how Galveston Bay, preceding any dangerous expedition, "was covered with boats seeking select places to bury treasures." Once from a rich haul, so the story goes, Laffite took for his own share—though he usually received a "royal fifth"—only a delicate gold chain and seal that had been removed from the neck of a Spanish bishop on his way to Rome. He gave the chain to Rezin Bowie, brother of the famous James Bowie. The Bowies must have been visitors more than once, for we hear of their buying negroes from Laffite at a dollar a pound to smuggle into Louisiana. Another man who was to win a name in Texas, L. D. Lafferty, in his old age recalled clearly how in urging him to enlist as a buccaneer Laffite "frankly confessed that he had enough silver and gold on the island to freight a ship."

Of all Laffite's men at Galveston, Jim Campbell was the most famous. There was much that he never told, but he told plenty. That

fellow had seen service, and he was not niggardly in telling about it. He had been with the notorious Captain Rapp on the *Hotspur*, privateer, when two Spanish ships engaged her. The fight lasted from dawn till dusk. In the end the *Hotspur* got away with most of her crew dead and only fourteen unwounded. One of the Spaniards was so shot up that she could not pursue; the deck of the other, the *Consalada*, at last sight "was literally covered with the dead—they had to walk on the bodies." Then Campbell had served with Aury and Mina. On one cruise of six weeks under Laffite he had captured five prizes with cargoes valued at $200,000; another time he "took a Guinea-man" with 308 slaves.

In time an American warship put in to call on the Lord of Galveston. His letters of marque, furnished now by Mexican revolutionists, authorized him to prey, as usual, upon Spanish shipping; but his men frequently made no distinction in flags. To show his sentiment and patriotism, Laffite had an offending pirate hanged on the seashore, and the warship departed. But the offense against American traders was soon repeated. Lieutenant Kearney, in command of a United States man-of-war, appeared one day in 1820 with polite orders that Laffite abandon Galveston. Laffite left forever. The rest is legend— mostly about pirate treasure.

THE LEGENDS

Just before he sailed away, so one oft-told tale runs, some of Kearney's men saw him walking to and fro, apparently in great distress, and heard him muttering words about "my treasure" and "the three trees." The three trees were a well-known location on Galveston Island. The eavesdroppers stole thither and began digging in ground that had evidently been disturbed only a short time before. The earth was loose. They made fast time. Soon they struck a box. They dug it up. They tore it open. It contained the body of a beautiful girl, Laffite's bride—his "treasure." Henry Ford was not the first man to regard history as "bunk."

For a thousand miles along the Gulf coast every inlet and island has its Laffite treasure. Somebody is always searching for this treasure, and nearly always there is a legend of great detail and realistic circumstance to back up the search. Once or twice a year—of recent years more frequently perhaps than in the past—a newspaper item from some town in Texas or Louisiana reports a hunt for Laffite treasure; but the most ardent hunts are made in secret and the best tales never get into print. Sometimes, of course, sheer pertinacity will betray the golden dream of a secret hunter.

Newell, a New Orleans printer, was one of these solitary and silent seekers. For twenty years he lived with and for his aureate vision. Along about the middle of the last century Newell's father befriended a battered old sea-faring derelict who was soon to make the final voyage. The derelict was grateful and bequeathed to the elder Newell a chart to a vast treasure purporting to have been buried by Laffite's men on a little island in Lake Borgne. The father turned the chart over to his son, the printer.

Printer Newell had all confidence in the chart and at once began hoarding his wages to fit out an expedition. He bought an old smack, a camping outfit, and tools, and disappeared from the printing establishment. For many weeks he cruised among the islands along the coast line, sometimes digging for days in a barren sand bar. The winds and tides were so constantly shifting these islands that he could never be sure which one his chart called for. Yet as he searched he was all the more certain the great swag of doubloons was there—if he could only find it. His supply of food ran out, his clothes wore out, and he returned to set type a while longer and save another stake.

He lived apart from the other printers, seldom speaking, never treating, his mind in another world. He became a marked man. It must have been a great relief to him when he could escape for another expedition. These expeditions went on at irregular intervals for years. Finally Newell took in a partner; but increasing eagerness and intentness made him suspicious of the partner and again he wandered alone.

Years and years passed—five, ten, fifteen, twenty of them, the golden dream more luminous with each lustrum. Among the unnumbered islands outside the Rigolets, Newell spaded up thousands of tons of sand. Sometimes he dug holes so deep that "you could have buried a fishing smack in one of them." His persistence was sheer genius. Youth turned to middle age, and Newell's hair was white. In the summer of 1871 some coast men saw him scudding out to sea in the teeth of a fearful hurricane. The next day a lumber vessel limped into Pearl River harbor towing a little boat that was recognized as Newell's. Then his body was found washed up on a drift. Presumably the storm had swept him off the deck of his smack and he had drowned.

As uncertain as the island in search of which Newell spent and lost his life was the Spanish dagger (or yucca plant) on Padre Island west of Corpus Christi, Texas, that a band of adventurers came looking for a generation ago. They engaged old Charlie Blutcher, surveyor of Nueces County, to run lines for them, and all went to Padre. Their orienting points were to be one Spanish dagger and three brass spikes. They found hundreds of daggers but not one brass spike. So far as anybody knows, the Spanish ship with its hold full of plate still rests against Padre Island, where Laffite's men lost it during a storm and where the welling sands covered it up.

When Laffite was run away from Galveston Island, so more than one legend avers, he did not leave the Texas coast as he was supposed to do. He released three of his four vessels to shift for themselves, but first he picked from his followers a crew to sail his own craft, the *Pride*. Then he slipped down to the mouth of Lavaca River, to hide when necessary and to sally out and privateer when opportunity offered.

Port Lavaca consisted of treacherous sand bars through which meandered a narrow channel known only to Laffite's men. The channel twisted its way up the river to a landing well out of view of any ships that might pass on the sea.

One day while cruising for a prize, Laffite came in view of a United States revenue cutter. He fled for the Lavaca refuge, getting inside the sand bars just in time to keep from being overhauled. The captain of the cruiser was as sly as Laffite. He sailed away as if he had given up the chase, but as soon as he was out of sight he put into a cove to await the reappearance of his quarry. In a few days Laffite slipped out. Again the cutter bore down upon him, and again he headed for his hole. But the cutter was so near him this time that it could follow his path through the bars, at the same time raking his ship with shell. Laffite was bottled up.

He ran as far as he could up the river, then nosed the *Pride*, already sinking, into the bank. In the few minutes that were left to him he divided a vast treasure among his men and told them to scatter and make out the best they could. Two men only remained with him.

When they went ashore with Laffite, they carried a chest containing a million dollars' worth of gold and jewels. It was very heavy. They could not lug it far. So when they had gone about a quarter of a mile east from the Lavaca River and were well hidden in a salt grass flat, they buried it, at Laffite's orders.

After the chest was in the ground and covered up, the pirate captain took a Jacob's staff—a brass rod used by surveyors instead of tripod—which he had brought along, and set it up immediately over the chest. Then he fixed his compass in the socket on top of the Jacob's staff and took bearings on two mottes of trees within sight. These mottes are well known today as the Kentucky Motte and the Mauldin Motte. What the readings were only Laffite knew; his men observed that he did not make notes on paper. Finally he drove the Jacob's staff down in the ground until the socket on the end of it stuck out only a foot or so.

After leaving the chest, Laffite and his two companions traveled for three days without food. It was winter time, and they were cold and almost starved when they came to the cabin of a settler. There they were fed and cared for; Laffite arranged for three horses, though no saddles were to be procured, and when he got ready to leave, he gave his hosts a thousand dollars. He now told the two men, whom he had retained thus far, that he was going among the Indians north of Red River and that they had better go to New Orleans, their old home, and live honest lives. He said that if they or their representatives came back at any time after the expiration of three years and found the chest unremoved, they might have it. He rode off towards the north, and that was the last his trusted mates ever heard of him.

A few months later one of these men, while dying in a New Orleans saloon, confided his secret to an Irish bartender. The other married, had two sons, and when they were mature told them facts that corroborated the bartender's story. Many years ago the two sons came into the Lavaca country searching for Laffite's chest. They found nothing and departed, but they left behind them a tradition that yet abides.

In time a ranchman named Hill acquired the land down the Lavaca River and stocked it with horses. The custom on the open range was to put a stallion and about twenty-five mares into a *manada* and loose-herd them until they were "broke in" to stay together. The *manada* was penned every night. Now, Hill had one negro herder who was particularly sleepy-headed. Every day this negro would take his mares to grass, turn them loose, stake his saddle horse, go to sleep, and wake up only in time to reach the pens by sundown.

One day he took his mares down to a flat along the river. He looked around for something to stake his horse to, but could see nothing but salt grass. He was kicking through it, hoping to find a stick that water or wood-rats had left, when he barked his shin against something hard and solid. It was a brass rod, fast in the earth, with a kind of knob or socket on the end of it—the very thing for a stake-pin.

The horse was not well broken to being staked, however, and in the course of the afternoon he got tangled up in the rope and "set back." When the negro, aroused from his nap, unwound him, he found the brass rod pulled far out of the ground. He pulled it on up and as a curiosity took it to the ranch, arriving considerably ahead of his usual time.

The minute Hill saw the rod he knew that it was a Jacob's staff, and he knew what a Jacob's staff stuck down in a salt grass flat near the Lavaca River meant. He at once ordered the negro to lead him back to the place where the rod had been found. Perhaps the negro was lazy and did not want to go so far; perhaps he was so ignorant of woodcraft that he could not find the place. At any rate, he did not lead Hill to it. He did, however, give an accurate description of the location with reference to the two famous mottes. Hill took the best trailer he had and spent all the next day and the next searching for the spot where the brass rod had been found. But the whole country was covered with coarse, thick grass tracked over everywhere by horses. Finally he quit the search.

Other searchers came and went. Then J. C. Wise began his search. This was only two or three years ago. Wise lives in San Antonio— that rendezvous for centuries of lost fortune seekers and filibustering adventurers. He had spent years in gathering evidence, then more years in perfecting a machine to locate minerals under the ground. In the very beginning he and his two associates made the mistake of hunting for a week on the Colorado River instead of the Lavaca. When they got near the Lavaca site, a ranchman refused to let him through his pasture. They went around the bay, procured a motor boat, and came up the river.

"The first thing we had to do," says Wise, "was to locate Laffite's old ship. Of course it had long since rotted, but we thought that by diving we might find some of the bulwarks. I think all the fish in the bay had a playground right where we wanted to work—and they weren't all red fish or mackerel either. Finally we located what was left of the ship and then took our measurements. With the wreck and the two mottes as marks, we felt reasonably sure of getting close enough to the treasure chest for our mineral machine to operate.

"It had rained and the salt grass flat was knee deep in mud. We

288

slushed about for five days, and that machine of ours never did indicate a thing. I know that the chest is there, though, and some day when I have more time I'm going back after it."

Not all authorities agree that *all* of Laffite's treasure on the Lavaca River is in a chest. Here is a letter from an old Texas ranger who lives five hundred miles upland.

"I was living in Lavaca County in 1870," the letter reads, "and while I was there my brother hired to a farmer named Bundick. One rainy day Bundick went turkey hunting, and just as he was crawling up on a flock of turkeys near the river, he struck his knee against something very hard. The pain almost sickened him, and when he looked down he saw what he took to be a pile of bricks, most of them half covered in the dirt. They were peculiar-looking bricks, and he wondered how they came to be out there. He picked up one, put it in his shot pouch, and when he got home showed it to my brother. Brother knew at once what it was. It was silver bullion hid there by some of Laffite's men. If Bundick had not been in such pain when he picked the thing up, he certainly would have noticed that it was silver or lead.

"Well, he and my brother went right back to get the whole pile of bricks. They found a moulted turkey feather that Bundick had noticed near the place, but they simply could not locate the bricks. There Bundick's tracks were too. Since that time, fifty-odd years ago, that pile of brick-looking silver has been stumbled on by two different persons ignorant of their worth, and in each instance the person when put wise has been unable to go back to the location. I myself have spent many days looking for the bullion, and while I am sure that I was often within a hundred steps of it, I never had the good fortune to stump my toe against it."

The mouth of the Colorado River is—or was—a better place than the Lavaca to look for pirate treasure. Along in the twenties William Selkirk, a prosperous citizen of New York, befriended a very sick sailor named Robinson. The sailor was exceedingly grateful. He was about to die and could, therefore, well afford to give away all he had to his benefactor. What he had, amounted to the story of his life—and a map.

The sailor had been a pirate under one of Laffite's captains, he said. Once while cruising for a prize in the Gulf of Mexico, the brig he was in awoke one morning to find herself under the guns of a towering

Spaniard. She ran for shore and about sundown slipped over a bar into the mouth of the Colorado River. However, she could not proceed upstream; she fully expected that her deep-draughted pursuer would be standing outside the bar at daylight ready to shell.

"There's a bare chance of getting away," said the captain. "If we don't, then we'll just fight back the best we can."

He was a desperate devil. Darkness came on. Three sailors, one of them Robinson, were sent ashore with the ship's treasure chest. It was very heavy. They buried it on a promontory, and then, returning, delivered to the captain a true and detailed description of the place—henceforth to be called Gold Point.

On the morrow, sure enough, the Spaniard beat up within range and opened fire. The captain was killed; so were the two sailors who had accompanied Robinson ashore with the chest. Thus he alone was left with exact knowledge of the treasure. He escaped the Spaniard, but he had no opportunity to take a sou with him. The winds of fortune, strong and in cross-currents, blew him for the next several years here and there over the sailing world. Now, at last, the treasure chest still unrecovered, he was dying, an object of charity, in New York.

William Selkirk had so much faith in the sailor's recital that he soon pulled up stakes, came to Texas, and purchased from the Mexican government 6000 acres of land at the mouth of the Colorado River—including Gold Point. Of his attempts to locate the pirate chest there is nothing unusual to tell.

The Selkirks have kept that land and paid taxes on it all these years. For the last forty years or so they have had a negro by the name of George Ellis watching certain marshy tracts of the land to keep off squatters—and treasure hunters. Not long ago some men came to Gold Point and, instead of asking George Ellis for permission to dig after a chest of gold, hired him to help them. George figured that by working with the intruders he could watch them and thus protect the Selkirk interests. He knew that if he scared them off, they would come back secretly and dig anyhow.

After they had dug a while, George felt his spade scrape against metal that he knew was the lid of a box.

"Boss," he said, "I jes' don' know what's come ovah me. There's a pow'ful mis'ry in my back; my hands is gettin' whicherly-like and my haid's all globble-globble. 'Deed, boss, I'se jes' bound to quit. You-all ain't goin' find nuthin' 'round 'mongst this sand nohow. You jes' as well quit too."

While he was making this speech the faithful George got right down over the box lid that his spade had scraped, so as to protect it against the discovery of another spade. He was mightily surprised when his employers declared that they were tired and disgusted and ready to quit also. They quit on the spot, and set out toward Bay City.

If it had not been for ha'nts, George the faithful would most certainly have returned under cover of dusk to finish unearthing what he had discovered, but "ha'nts is turrible, jes' turrible, about these yere old treasures." It was really after sunup before George got back to Gold Point. A rectangular hole in the earth showed where a chest had been lifted out during the night. One of the hunters, presumably, had struck it with his spade and recognized the *plumb* about the same time that George made his discovery. The negro's getting out of the way was just what the white men wanted.

Probably the earth was never visited by a more extravagant or a more uneasy ghost than the ghost of Laffite. Sometimes this ghost strains with all the agony of a purgatoried soul to get its treasure removed and put to uses of virtue. Again, the ghost—or perhaps it is the ghost of some man slain and buried over the treasure—repulses the most daring and godless prospectors as they come near the object of their search. Back in the days of Reconstruction one of the most hard-headed and upright lawyers in Texas used to get messages from Laffite's spirit trying to explain to him where a whole shipload of precious plunder was secreted on Galveston Island. The lack of coherence in the messages revealed plainly enough what torture the spirit was suffering.

Over on the Louisiana-Texas line a man by the name of Marion Meredith has, or used to have, a remarkable chart.[2] He got it from a neighboring widow whose husband had secured it from a Mexican woman. This chart was a kind of widow-maker.

It called for a tree with a chain about it, somewhere near the mouth of the Neches River. According to the history that went with the chart, some of Laffite's men had their ship cabled to the tree and had just finished planting a fine "wad" of loot near by when they were jumped by a Spanish galleon. They cut their hawser and got away only to be bombarded to the bottom of the ocean. One man alone survived, the man that handed down the chart.

Marion Meredith's neighbor, who finally came into possession of this chart, felt so sure of finding the treasure that he would trust no one to go with him in search of it. Without trouble he found the tree and the chain. Then he stepped directly to the spot at which he was to dig. After he had shoveled down a few feet, some unseen power seized him. At least his subsequent gesticulations were interpreted to indicate as much. When he reached home his organs of speech were paralyzed and in less than a week he was dead.

As soon as Meredith got hold of the chart—from the widow of the late searcher—he took in as partner a rough old character by the name of Clawson. The two men found the tree with the chain about it—a rather rusty chain. At the spot where the chart called for the treasure to be, they found a hole already started. Near at hand were some decayed tools.

They had not dug down very far before they came to a skeleton. They carefully removed it and laid it out on the bank. As the hole got deeper, only one man at a time could work in it. It was Clawson's turn to dig, and Meredith was peering down from above, expecting every minute to see a shovelful of doubloons pitched up, when all at once Clawson gave a wild leap for the surface. His face was haggard; his eyes had the look of the haunted; when he spoke his voice was terror itself.

"Come! For God's sake, let's get away from this place," he half whispered, half shrieked, clutching Meredith's arm in a viselike grip.

"What's the matter? What have you seen?" demanded Meredith, who had seen nothing.

"I have seen hell and its horrors. Come away from here, I tell you."

And Clawson pulled so powerfully and his terror was so contagious that they left without even taking their tools. Clawson would never make explanation. He only begged Meredith, as he valued his life, never to dig at that place again. In time Meredith returned to get his tools. He found the skeleton back inside the hole out of which he and Clawson had so carefully taken it. He covered it up, shoveling in sand and shell until the sink was level. Then he came away, never to go back. He had absolute confidence in Clawson's judgment. Long afterwards he met Clawson in Beaumont and again asked him for an explanation.

"For God's sake," Clawson replied, "never ask me about that matter again. It has haunted me all these years."

At La Porte, on the Gulf, not far from Houston, stands an abandoned house beneath which the spirit of Laffite, harried and desperate, keeps guard over his blood-marked booty. It leads any occasional sleeper in the house to a great mound of yellow coins, jeweled watches, bracelets, diamond rings, and strings of pearls. Then in an attempt to win absolution for sins committed on earth, sometimes in distress and sometimes in anger, it begs the visitant to take those things and dispose of them *without spending one penny evilly or selfishly*. No one has ever taken the treasure. Coast dwellers used to gather around firesides on northery winter nights, and while the rich juice of sweet potatoes roasting in the ashes oozed through the jackets, tell tales of the old house and its ghostly tenant. One such tale, written by Julia Beazley [3] under the title of *The Uneasy Ghost of Lafitte*, follows.

One time Lafitte and his buccaneering crew sailed up to what is now Bay Ridge (which is opposite the haunted house of La Porte). He anchored his schooner off shore, and rowed to the beach with two trusted lieutenants and the heavy chest which none dared touch except at his orders. When the skiff grounded, the watchers on the schooner saw their chief blindfold his helpers; then they saw the three disappear with the chest behind a screen of grapevine-laden trees. Two hours later Lafitte returned alone. He was in a black mood and no one had the temerity to question him. It was supposed that he had caught one of his helpers trying to mark the location of his cache, and had killed them both. Some say that he led them back to the pit they had dug and filled up, made them reopen and enlarge it, and while they were bent down digging, shot them dead. Soon afterwards Lafitte and his followers went down together in a West Indian hurricane, and his crime-stained treasure still lies buried in its secret hiding place.

Yet to many, as I have intimated, that place has not been secret. It is under the old house. As faithfully as I can follow the tale, I shall relate an experience connected with that old house as it was told me by a Confederate veteran who has now passed on. I shall call him Major Walcart, though that was not his real name.

"It was on a February night back in the eighties," the Major used to say. "The early darkness of a murky day had overtaken me, and I was dead tired. I do not think mud ever lay deeper along the shore of Galveston Bay or that an east wind ever blew more bleakly. When I came to a small stream, I rode out into the open water, as the custom then was, to find shallow passage. A full moon was rising out of the bay. Heavy clouds stretched just above it, and I remember the unearthly aspect of the blustering breakers in its cheerless light. The immensity and unfriendliness of the scene made me feel lonesome, and I think the horse shared my mood. By common consent we turned across before we had gone far enough from shore, and fell into the trench cut by the stream in the bottom of the bay.

"We were wretchedly wet as we scrambled up a clayey slope and gained the top of the bluff. A thin cry which I had not been sure was real when I first heard it now became insistent. It was like the wail of a child in mortal pain, and I confess that it reminded me of tales I had heard of the werewolf, which lures unwary travelers to their doom by imitating the cry of a human infant. By the uncertain light of the moon, which the next moment was cut off entirely, I saw that I had reached a kind of stable that crowned the bluff, and from this structure the uncanny summons seemed to come.

"The sounds were growing fainter, and I hesitated but a moment. Dismounting, I led my horse through the doorless entrance, and now the mystery was explained. Huddled together for warmth lay a flock of sleeping goats. A kid had rashly squeezed itself into the middle of the heap, and the insensate brutes were crushing its life out. I found the perishing little creature, and its flattened body came back to the full tide of life in my arms. Its warmth was grateful to my cold fingers, and I fondled it a moment before setting it down on the dry dirt floor.

"I tied my horse to a post that upheld the roof of the stable, and with saddle and blanket on my arm started toward the house, which I could make out in its quadrangle of oaks, not many yards distant. The horse whinnied protestingly as I left him, and when the moaning of the wind in the eaves smote my ears I was half in mind to turn back and bunk with the goats. It was a more forbidding sound than the hostile roar of the breakers had been in the bay.

"I called, but only the muddy waves incessantly tearing at the bluff made answer. I had scarcely hoped to hear the sound of a human voice. The great double doors leading in from the front porch were barred, but the first window I tried yielded entrance. Striking a match, I found myself in a room that gave promise of comfort. Fat pine kindling lay beside the big fireplace, and dry chunks of solid oak were waiting to glow for me the whole night through.

"I was vaguely conscious that the brave fire I soon had going did not drive the chill from the air so promptly as it should, but my head was too heavy with sleep to be bothered. I spread my horse blanket quite close to the cheerful blaze, and with saddle for pillow and slicker for cover I abandoned myself to the luxury of rest.

"I do not know how long I had slept when I became aware of a steady gaze fixed on my face. A man was looking down on me, and no living creature ever stood so still. There was imperious command in the unblinking eyes, and yet I saw a sort of profound entreaty also.

"It was plain that the visitant had business with me. I arose, and together we left the room, passed its neighbor, and entered a third, a barren little apartment through the cracks of which the wind came mercilessly. I think it was I who had opened the doors. My companion did not seem to move. He was merely present all the time.

" 'It is here,' he said, as I halted in the middle of the bare floor, 'that more gold lies buried than is good for any man. You have but to dig, and it is yours. You can use it; I cannot. However, it must be applied only to purposes of highest beneficence. Not one penny may be evilly or selfishly spent. On this point you must keep faith and beware of any failing. Do you accept?'

"I answered, 'Yes,' and the visitant was gone, and I was shivering with cold. I groped my way back to my fire, bumping into obstructions I had not found in my journey away from it. I piled on wood with a generous hand, and the flames leaped high. I watched the unaccountable shadows dance on the whitewashed walls, and marked how firebeams flickered across the warpings of the boards in the floor. Then I dozed off.

"I do not know how long I had been asleep when I felt the presence of the visitant again. The still reproach of his fixed eyes was worse than wrath. 'I need your help more than you can know,' he said, 'and you would fail me. The treasure is mine to give. I paid for it with the substance of my soul. I want you to have it. With it you can balance somewhat the burden of guilt I carry for its sake.'

"Again we made the journey to the spot where the treasure was buried, and this time he showed it to me. There were yellow coins, jeweled watches, women's bracelets, diamond rings, and strings of pearls. It was just such a trove as I had dreamed of when as a boy I had planned to dig for Lafitte's treasure, except that the quantity of it was greater. With the admonition, 'Do not force me to come again,' my companion was gone, and once more I made my way back to the fire.

"This time I took up my saddle and blanket and went out to the company of my horse. The wind and the waves were wailing together, but I thought I saw a promise of light across the chilly bay, and never was the prospect of dawn more welcome. As I saddled up and rode

off, the doleful boom of the muddy water at the foot of the bluff came to me like an echoed anguish."

But Laffite does not appear to every one who spends a night in the house, and any person seeking the treasure from purely selfish motives is likely to rue his pains. A story is told of an acquisitive and enterprising man who came hundreds of miles with the purpose of helping himself to the chance of finding pirate gold, but who abruptly changed his mind after spending a night in the house. As Laffite steadily pursues his object of finding a fit recipient for his dangerous gift, never succeeding, his disappointment is sometimes terrible, so they say, and some simple folk believe that when there is a particularly dolorous moan in the wash of the waves, it is the despair of the pirate finding voice.

Like the man Laffite, his treasures are uncertain, elusive, mysterious. Doubtless, too, most of the legends concerning them are, like many of those concerning Laffite, without foundation. Yet there are few monuments so potent to make a name remembered as its association with a great lost treasure. As long as Grand Terre and Galveston Island are above water, "Laffite's Treasure" is likely to keep the name of Jean Laffite green.

More than one writer has drawn a parallel between Laffite and Byron's Corsair. At least Byron's closing couplet seems proper to the Patriot and Pirate of the Mexican Gulf:

> *He left a Corsair's name to other times,*
> *Linked with one virtue and a thousand crimes.*

CHAPTER XIX

Shadows and Symbols

And after he went to the ship's board,
and wrote there other letters which said:
Thou man that wilt enter within me, beware
that thou be full within the faith, for
I ne am but Faith and Belief.
MALORY, Le Mort d'Arthur

Not long ago an Irishman from Indiana came to me and asked, "Did you ever hear of the Montezuma treasure buried in Sugar Loaf Mound at Del Rio?"

"Yes," I replied.

"Well," the Irishman responded, "that Montezuma treasure is buried all right, but not in Sugar Loaf Mound. I'm going to tell you something.

"When I was a boy, my father was foreman of a section gang working on the Southern Pacific Railroad. We lived for a time in a camp several miles east of Del Rio. Along about five o'clock one summer afternoon my brother and I were wandering around in the hills between the railroad and the Rio Grande. Looking up towards a rocky ridge, I saw a giant arrow pointing southward. We were traveling in that direction and before long I saw another enormous arrow, pointing down hill. We went on, and before long we saw a roughly formed ring of rocks, maybe fifteen steps in diameter. It was down in a swag.

"When we got back to camp, I told an old-timer about what we had seen. He said that the arrows pointed towards treasure and that the treasure was undoubtedly buried in the ring of rocks. The next morning my brother and I and this old fellow went back to examine the signs more closely. Well, we couldn't find those arrows at all and somehow missed the circle of rocks. I made a dozen other attempts to sight the arrows—all unsuccessful.

"We left the country. Years afterwards I learned that in giving secret directions the Spaniards sometimes made use of indirect lighting. They arranged rocks or timbers so that the shadows cast at a certain

298

time of day would point to the treasure they had concealed. Any man looking for the signs would have to be on the ground at a particular hour. Now, neither I nor my brother after the first and only glimpse of the arrows again looked for them at the exact hour in which we saw them—between two and three hours by sun on a summer afternoon. I have just returned from a trip to Del Rio, but the man I was with had little faith in my theory and our time was limited. I want to go back with some one really interested."

I could not go. I thought of how Jim Bridger once told a prospector that there was a diamond on top of a mountain in the Yellowstone country which could be sighted fifty miles away "if a man got the right range on it when the sun was right." The prospector offered the old scout a fine horse and a new rifle if he would show it to him.

Notwithstanding the advantages of shadows, buriers of treasure have from time immemorial generally marked their deposits with signs that are directly visible, though usually quite enigmatical. The Spaniards, since they buried most of the treasure in this country, developed, of course, the most elaborate code of symbols. A register of these signs, collected and deciphered for the most part by a lawyer who refuses to allow the disclosure of his name, is now—for the first time, I believe—printed.

X *On line to the treasure. X is also a common designation on landmarks.*

+ *Cross and other rich objects pertaining to the Church are buried here.*

> *The cross might mean many things. So potent was its symbolism that the very sign of it might protect a man's possessions as well as himself. It often said: "I have been here"; "A Christian has passed this way." When Coronado went east in search of the Gran Quivira, he gave instructions that he was to be trailed by means of wooden crosses which he would erect from time to time along his route. Again when Fray Marcos de Nizza set out in 1539 to hunt the Seven Cities of Cíbola, he had instructions, should he find himself on the coast of El Mar de Sur (the Pacific Ocean), "to bury written reports at the foot of a tree distinguished by its size, and to cut a cross in the bark of the tree, so that in case a*

ship was sent along the coast, its crew might know how to identify it by that mark."

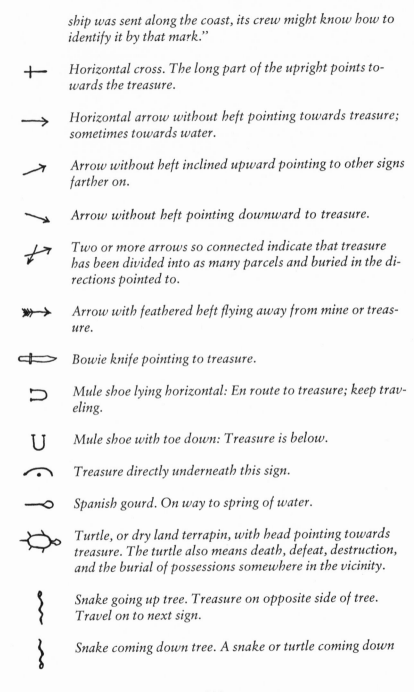

Horizontal cross. The long part of the upright points towards the treasure.

Horizontal arrow without heft pointing towards treasure; sometimes towards water.

Arrow without heft inclined upward pointing to other signs farther on.

Arrow without heft pointing downward to treasure.

Two or more arrows so connected indicate that treasure has been divided into as many parcels and buried in the directions pointed to.

Arrow with feathered heft flying away from mine or treasure.

Bowie knife pointing to treasure.

Mule shoe lying horizontal: En route to treasure; keep traveling.

Mule shoe with toe down: Treasure is below.

Treasure directly underneath this sign.

Spanish gourd. On way to spring of water.

Turtle, or dry land terrapin, with head pointing towards treasure. The turtle also means death, defeat, destruction, and the burial of possessions somewhere in the vicinity.

Snake going up tree. Treasure on opposite side of tree. Travel on to next sign.

Snake coming down tree. A snake or turtle coming down

a tree means that treasure is on that side of it. Measure distance from the tip of the reptile's tail to the ground. Step off ten times that distance straight out. At the termination of the distance stepped, one should find either the treasure or another sign.

Snake in striking position with head pointed toward treasure.

Snake coiled on tree or rock indicates presence of treasure directly beneath.

A straight line indicates a certain number of varas to be measured off, the vara being 33⅓ inches; the number of varas called for usually ranges between 50 and 100.

Two straight lines indicate double the distance of one line.

Flight of steps. This sign indicates that the treasure is down in a cave or shaft.

Treasure is to be found within a triangle formed by trees or rocks.

Over deposit, which is located within a triangle made by trees or rocks.

Triangle formed by trees or rocks enclosing treasure.

Triangle formed by trees or rocks with treasure in the middle.

This sign indicates that while the deposit is marked by a triangle of trees or rocks, it is to be found to one side of the triangle.

Deposit is around a bend or curve away from triangle formed by trees or rocks.

Treasure buried in box or chest.

⟋☐   *Peace pipe. Friendly Indians.*

⟋⌂   *Sombrero, or hat. The number of sombreros shown indicates how many people were in the party that buried the treasure. The sombreros may also indicate the number of men killed by an enemy.*

☼   *Mines close by. Any representation of the sun indicates proximity of mineral wealth.*

O R O   Oro *(gold) is short distance away.*

G   *Gold short distance away.*

[*A tunnel.*

⟩ OR ⟨   *Stop; change direction.*

⊕ OR ⊕   *Perhaps variant signs of the cross.*

🐕   *Greyhound. As to the meaning, there is some doubt.*

Whoever has read this book through will have found many other significations of treasure; as, fox fire, a white animal, ghosts, etc. Indeed, riches hoarded in the ground no more need a sign to signify their presence than good wine needs a bush. Like murder, they will out—but not out of the ground.

In addition to attracting divining rods, switches, and various other objects, buried treasure is supposed to have a particularly powerful attraction for mercury. I know of one man who put mercury in a bottle and went out to look for treasure. At a certain place the bottom fell out of his bottle. The treasure was so big and pulled so hard that it drew the mercury through the glass!

Treasure hunters often refer to the so-called "Sixth and Seventh Books of Moses." My own copy of this curious and absurd farrago of matter pertaining to black magic and other superstitions was printed in New York, 1880. The title page reads: *The Sixth and Seventh Books of Moses; or, Moses' Magical Spirit Art, Known as the Wonderful Arts of the Old Wise Hebrews, taken from the Mosaic Books of the Cabala and the Talmud, for the good of mankind. Translated from*

THE
Schemhamforas

Which will certainly bring to light the Treasures of Earth, if buried in the Treasure-Earth.

From the Arcan Bible of Moses.

FROM

P. Hoffman, Jesuit.

Composed ad Proxim.

L. MISCHINSKY, at RAOL, MDCCXLVI.

the German, word for word, according to old writings. Instead of tabulating signs that indicate the way to treasure, the work affords directions for recovering it. Thus, Mephistopheles is an effective agent to "bring treasure from the earth and from the deep very quickly." The best time to enlist the aid of angels in the business of recovering treasure is in the sign of the Scorpion, for then "they rule over legacies and riches." If devils and angels are lacking, certain cabalistic configurations will draw treasure upward.

I have in my possession an odd form of candle secured from a Mexican in San Antonio, who, with three companions, used it in an attempt to locate treasure. This candle is a lump of wax with four wicks protruding at right angles to each other. It is supposed to be taken on a windy night to a place near treasure, the *exact* whereabouts of which is unknown. Each of four men grasps a wick in his hand, against the mould of wax. Then the wicks, well greased, are lighted. The one that burns longest in the wind shows in which direction to proceed towards the treasure. By the method of trial and error the spot sought for may thus be arrived at—provided the wicks burn correctly.

But suppose a treasure hunter has no signs or shadows to go by, possesses no chart; suppose he does not believe in occultism and has no faith in any of the various instruments to be made or purchased. What resort is left to him? Why, dreams—for "dremes ben significaciouns."

This is a story related many years ago by a Confederate veteran.

"After the war I got back to Texas, broke like everybody else. But I bought a farm in Leon County—on credit—married, and began to make a home. I had the farm about paid off and was getting along very well when one summer I had a dream, or vision. At the time it appeared to me I was sleeping on a pallet on the gallery, my wife and two small children occupying the bed just inside the door.

"I saw a woman come into the yard through the gate, a strange-looking woman with strange headgear and queer dress, and I marveled that my fierce watch dogs did not attack her. She came to the side of the gallery and said in a clear voice: 'Dig in your little pasture and you will find treasure.'

"I sat up and watched her go out of the gate, just as she had come, and could hardly persuade myself that what I saw was a dream. The next morning I told my wife of the dream—and then forgot it. Now, the little pasture was a few fenced acres near the house where we kept

our milk calves. It was drouth stricken; the soil was hard and dry and had no growth except for a few brambles.

"Not many nights later, while I lay as before, the same woman came again. I saw her plainly in the moonlight. She spoke, very quietly but distinctly, the same words: 'Dig in your little pasture. Dig beneath the white rose.'

"I knew positively that there was no growth in the little pasture excepting the few brambles I have mentioned. But on my telling my wife of seeing the woman again in a dream, she said, 'Come on; let's look for roses.' And catching my hand, she laughingly dragged me to the pasture. There, as sure as I am a Reb, we found a rose bush with two white flowers on it. Then we got busy, but, after digging down about two feet, I struck a large rock and quit.

"The story got out and I became the butt of many jokes. A few months afterwards my brother-in-law offered me a fancy price for the place and I quit farming. Later on in the year I noticed that the little pasture had been plowed—the only improvement noticeable. About the same time I noticed my brother-in-law buying property, including a fine family carriage, sending his daughter to boarding-school, and getting himself elected to the state legislature. Maybe there was something under the roses."

And maybe there was. This is the dream that never dies.

Notes

I. The Lost San Saba Mine

1. Bolton, H. E., *Spanish Explorations of the Southwest*, pp. 283–284.
2. The account of this expedition is based on a Spanish transcript in the archives of the University of Texas entitled "Expedition to Los Almagres and Plans for Developing the Mines, 1755–1756." It is generally referred to as "The Miranda Report," and to it is attached a considerable amount of correspondence. It has never been published, and I am deeply indebted to Mrs. Margaret Kenney Kress, instructor of Spanish in the University of Texas, for the use of her careful translation.
3. In 1907 Doctor Herbert E. Bolton, "With Miranda's Report in hand, . . . beyond question identified the mine opened by Miranda with the Boyd Shaft, near Honey Creek Cove [in Llano County]. . . . On the basis of [this] identification the Los Almagres Mining Company was formed and [it] purchased about seventeen hundred acres of land round about Boyd Shaft."—Bolton, *Texas in the Middle Eighteenth Century*, p. 83. I have been unable to learn that the Los Almagres Mining Company has spent any money in developing mines.
4. One of the ubiquitous "authorities" relied on by various exploring parties has been a certain Don Ignacio Obregón, called Inspector Real de las Minas. According to John Warren Hunter, who printed at Mason, Texas, in 1905, an interesting but confusing pamphlet entitled *Rise and Fall of the Mission San Saba*, this Don Ignacio reported to the Mexican government, in 1812, that the Almagres ore tested out 1680 pesos to the ton. In a feature article, "The Lost Gold Mines of Texas May Be Found Again," by W. D. Hornaday, Dallas *News*, January 7, 1923, Don Ignacio bobs up again with even more sanguine news.

   Much credence has been placed in certain widely circulated letters purporting to have been transcribed from the archives at Monterrey, Mexico. See the *Texas Almanac* for 1868; also *History of San Antonio and the Early Days of Texas*, compiled by Robert Sturmberg, San Antonio, 1920, Chapter III.
5. The proposal to move the presidio south "to some rich veins of silver" is found in *Algunas Cartas á Don Pedro Romero de Terreros, . . . 1758–1759* (García Library, University of Texas).

   For a succinct history of the San Saba mission and presidio, see

William E. Dunn, "The Apache Mission of the San Saba River,"
Southwestern Historical Quarterly, Vol. XVII, pp. 379–414; also
H. E. Bolton, *Texas in the Middle Eighteenth Century*, pp. 79–93.

6. The story was printed in the Galveston *News*, date unknown, and was
contributed in abbreviated form, by E. G. Littlejohn to *Legends of
Texas*, pp. 22–23.

A word here concerning newspaper exploitation of the Lost Almagres Mine theme will not be out of place. In 1853, while the California gold strike was fresh in the minds of everybody, Texas newspapers gave it out that the "gold veins enclosed by the Colorado on
the east, the San Saba on the north, and the Llano on the south are
as rich as any in California." Men rushed into this region by the hundreds, two hundred gold hunters from New Orleans alone landing at
Lavaca Bay. The newspapers have never succeeded in bringing
about a Llano–San Saba gold rush, but the story never grows stale to
feature writers. Year after year, they reiterate it, generally in a very
diluted form.

For accounts of the gold rush, see the Galveston *Weekly Journal*,
May 13, June 6, and June 16, 1853.

7. "Several days previous to the fight [November 26, 1835] it was currently
reported in camp that there was a quantity of silver coming from
Mexico on pack mules to pay off the soldiers of General Cos. Our
scouts kept a close watch, to give the news as soon as the convoy
should be espied, so that we might intercept the treasure. On the
morning of the 26th, Colonel Bowie was out in the direction of the
Medina, with a company, and discovered some mules with packs approaching. Supposing this to be the expected train, he sent a messenger for reinforcements."—Baker, D. W. C., *Texas Scrap Book*, p. 92.

8. Mary Austin Holley, first historian of Texas, in *Texas*, Lexington, Ky.,
1836, pp. 161–173, quotes the Rezin P. Bowie account of the Indian
fight, said to have been printed first in a Philadelphia periodical. It
has been reprinted dozens of times. Less known, and differing little
in essential facts, is the account of the battle purporting to have been
written by James Bowie; it is to be found in J. C. F. Kyger's *Texas
Gems* (Denison, Texas, 1885, pp. 130–134) and also in John Henry
Brown's *History of Texas* (Vol. I, pp. 170–175).

9. Archives, University of Texas. For further account of Ham's experiences,
see James T. De Shields, *Border Wars of Texas*, Tioga, Texas, 1912,
pp. 74–76.

10. This is the theme of a Texan novel in which Bowie is the hero, William
O. Stoddard's *The Lost Gold of the Montezumas: A Story of the
Alamo*. Matt Bradley, editor and publisher of *Border Wars of Texas*,
said in a signed article printed in the Dallas *News*, January 28, 1923,
that only three months before the fall of the Alamo Bowie was trying

to reach the riches of which he alone among white men knew the secret.

Some notice of the recognition of the San Saba Mine in the literature of Europe as well as of America may here prove interesting. Henri Fournel, *Coup d'oeil . . . sur le Texas*, 1841, p. 23, speaks "*des richesses metalliques depuis longtemps signalées par les Espagnoles.*" I am unable now to verify the reference, but I am sure that Gustave Aimard introduces the subject in one of his romances, probably *The Freebooters*.

An English fabrication published in 1843 has this sentence: "The Comanches have a great profusion of gold, which they obtain from the neighborhood of the San Seba [*sic*] hills, and work it themselves into bracelets, armlets, diadems, as well as bits for their horses, and ornaments to their saddles."—Captain Marryat, *Monsieur Violet*, etc., p. 175.

Citation of all references to the San Saba mines in early Texasana would be both tedious and useless. Elias R. Wrightman, surveyor for Stephen F. Austin, in locating "the first three hundred" Texas colonists, made in 1828 a map of Texas that shows the general location of the San Saba Mine; in notes for a history of Texas written about the same time he describes the mineral riches in most extravagant phrases.—Mary S. Helm, *Scraps of Early Texas*, Austin, 1884, p. 136 ff.

So with most early histories of Texas, notably Kennedy's. In early fiction dealing with Texas use of the San Saba riches was freely made. "As soon as the Comanches, giving away, will permit the whites to work the mines north of San Antonio, the immense profits will prove an irresistible attraction," says Anthony Ganilk (pseudonym for A. T. Myrthe) in *Ambrosio de Letinez, or The First Texian Novel*, New York, 1842, Vol. II, p. 63.

The popular writer Charles W. Webber, who had been ranger with Captain Jack Hays, brought out in 1848 and 1849, respectively, two novels, *Old Hicks the Guide* and *The Gold Mines of the Gila*, that make effective use of tales about the San Saba Mine.

Later fictional uses of the same material are to be found in *The Three Adventurers*, a novel by J. S. (K. Lamity) Bonner, Austin, no date; and in "The Llano Treasure Cave," a short story by T. B. Baldwin (Dick Naylor), *The Texas Magazine*, Vol. III, pp. 195–204, reprinted in the *Dallas Semi-Weekly Farm News*, July 11 and July 14, 1922.

11. A son, Jeptha Billingsley, wrote two letters from Elgin, Texas, October and November, 1922, that afford the basis for this sketch. They are in the archives of the University of Texas. Walter Billingsley, of San Antonio, a nephew of "Captain Jess," knew many of the San Jacinto

veterans, and according to their story, the Billingsley men were so
relentless during the rout at San Jacinto that Houston, seeing the
Mexicans wanted to surrender, sent word to Captain Billingsley to
"slow down." "Present my compliments to General Houston," Billingsley is said to have replied to the commander-in-chief's messenger, "and tell him to go to hell."

12. Thus, three score years ago and more, B. F. Gholson, who was born on
the Texas frontier in 1842, who became one of the most noted Indian
fighters, cowmen, and all around frontiersmen of the Southwest, and
who gave his name to Gholson Gap, heard the story. Thus he told it
to me at a reunion of pioneer Texas rangers held at San Saba just
seventy-two years after Sinnet Musset's bullet halted Grumble and
the ransomed captive at that place.

13. See "W. A. McDaniel, Cowboy," etc., by Cora Melton Cross, the *Semi-
Weekly Farm News*, Dallas, Texas, June 22, 1928.

14. For this story and also for the one about the icicles of silver I am indebted to Clyde Smith, a lath plasterer of Beaumont.

15. The story that follows was clipped many years ago by E. G. Littlejohn,
of Galveston, from the Galveston *News* and contributed by him to
Legends of Texas.

16. See "A Legend of the Blanco Mine," by Julia Estill, *Legends of Texas*,
pp. 24–26.

17. Dr. S. E. Chandler, president of Daniel Baker College, at Brownwood,
Texas, frequently visited the home of Moses Kirkpatrick. He saw the
copper plates and other objects. I have interviewed various other people who saw them also. But nobody else can tell the whole story so
well as Dr. Chandler tells it. I thank him most emphatically.

18. The story of this exceptional man comes through Miss Julia Estill, of
Fredericksburg, who wrote it for *Legends of Texas*.

19. W. M. Longworth thinks, justly, that his street address should be given
so that people who know of hidden treasures may write to him and
secure his assistance with the "radio sleuth" in finding such wealth.
His address is 1110 Denver Boulevard, San Antonio, Texas.

II. Down the Nueces

1. For history of the establishments consult Bolton's *Texas in the Middle
Eighteenth Century*, using index.

2. See A. J. Sowell, *Early Settlers and Indian Fighters of Southwest Texas*,
Austin, 1900, pp. 405–408.

3. It is a pity that we have no unvarnished biography of Lieutenant-Colonel
Baylor. ("General" seems to have been a title of courtesy.) For the
account of his search for Spanish gold in the Nueces I am indebted

to his son, Henry Baylor, and to Henry Yelvington, both of San Antonio. *The War of the Rebellion: A Compilation of the Official Records of the Union and Confederate Armies* has scattered through its many and well-indexed volumes numerous facts concerning John R. Baylor.

4. An appalling amount of literature has been printed on the subject. Water Supply Paper 416, U.S. Geological Survey, Department of the Interior, 1917, entitled *The Divining Rod: A History of Water Witching*, by Arthur J. Ellis, contains a bibliography of nearly thirty pages listing books and pamphlets from 1532 to 1917. Men have claimed to be able to locate not only water and minerals but also criminals with the divining rod. The Orient and the Occident have both been familiar with it for centuries. Learned doctors and societies have repeatedly investigated it—and pronounced it a sham. Persons claiming to be expert with it have at times drawn to themselves the attention of whole nations. The wideness of the subject can not here be even suggested.

George Ray located, just outside the front gate of the Olmos ranch house, a vein of water that he said was between 25 and 29 feet underground. His manner of computing the depth was thus: After locating one vein, he stepped forward and 9 paces beyond located a second vein; 8 paces still farther on he located a third vein—8 and 9 make 17; a pace is 3 feet; 3 times 17 equals 51. There were 2 interstices between the three veins; 51 divided by 2 gives 25½, say 26 feet—the approximate depth necessary to go for water. Fortunately a lake affords a never-failing supply of water for Olmos headquarters; so no test of the vein that Mr. Ray located was made.

5. "Old Rip" Ford's men had a strange engagement at Fort Merrill. (See A. J. Sowell's *Early Settlers and Indian Fighters of Southwest Texas*, Austin, 1900, pp. 819–820.) It was located on land patented to the ambitious John McMullen. The McGloins came into a share of it, and before Live Oak County was organized, in 1856, the McGloin heirs agreed "that the houses and other improvements" situated upon the land should "be sold at public outcry." Barlow's Ferry, later replaced by the bridge near what is now Dinero, several miles down the river, diverted the public road on which the Fort Merrill crossing was once famous.

6. Corpus Christi *Star*, December 23, 1848.

IV. The Circumstance of War

1. Cannon were in early days not infrequently buried, thus giving a certain basis of fact for legend.

In 1759 Parrilla marched from San Antonio with a force of six hundred men and attacked the Taovayas villages on the Red River. He found the Indians "intrenched behind a strong stockade of breastworks, flying a French flag, and skilfully using French weapons and tactics." After a sanguinary battle resulting in heavy losses to both sides, the Spanish withdrew, leaving "two cannon and extra baggage" concealed behind. Seventeen years later the cannon were recovered; inhabitants of Cooke and Montague counties, Texas, are still looking for something buried about "Old Spanish Fort."

Traders journeying over the Santa Fe Trail used to cache cannon on the Big Arkansas River, for on returning east they left the "dangerous country" at that line and would not need the cannon until they got back with another west-bound cargo.

During the Civil War Confederate forces buried two cannon near Santa Fe, which were exhumed a generation later—thus giving courage to a host of treasure hunters.

2. For the story that follows, see "The Treasure Cannon on the Neches," by Roscoe Martin, *Legends of Texas*, pp. 84–89.

3. Noah Smithwick, *The Evolution of a State, or Recollections of Old Texas Days*, Austin, 1900, p. 83.

4. Five years after these stories of battlefield treasures appeared in *Legends of Texas*, Mr. Bob Nutt, of Beeville, who is responsible for Ramón's tale of Resaca de la Palma, received a letter from one Harley Johnson, written at Kerrville, as follows:

"My father Jim Johnson of Goliad, now dead went up the Kansas trail with cattle for Dillard Fant for four year hand running 1872–1875 and on last trip befriended the remuda Mexican who was very sick. Said Mexican told him how he and his troop buried this seven cart loads on Palo Alto Battle field (but the stuff was hurried thrown on 50 pack jacks and taken to hole). The Mexican took my father and some other men down to Palo Alto and they dug and uncovered it but it sank into quick sand of unknown depth when ten men jumped into the hole to roll one of the *maletas* out. I know the spot; have made 4 trips down there but could never get to it for quick sand. The original hole was 9 ft sq. x 6 ft deep. The stuff is some where at bottom. If you will pay all expenses to get it out I'll give you one tenth $25,000 of the $250,000. I taught Berclair school on Indian creek and knew your father also brothers. Have sick wife and need money."

5. Robert Hall. See *Life of Robert Hall*, etc., by Brazos (pseudonym), Austin, 1898, p. 85.

6. This account of Steinheimer came to me from L. D. Bertillion and was printed in *Legends of Texas*, pp. 91–95.

V. *Tales of the Cow Camp*

1. The original version of this tale was supplied by a ranch boy of Frio County named Charles A. Beever, through Leon Denny Moses, School of Mines, El Paso.
2. Peyote, "dry whiskey."
3. For allowing me to make use of this tale I am indebted to Mrs. G. B. Smedley, of Wichita Falls and Fort Worth. It will be found incorporated in her paper, "Legends of Wichita County," *Publications* No. VIII of the Texas Folk-Lore Society.
4. A "rep" is a cowboy who represents his brand on an "outside" range in order to bring in cattle that have strayed away.

VI. *Post Hole Banks*

1. Luther A. Lawhon, in *Trail Drivers of Texas*, San Antonio, 1920, pp. 176–177.

VIII. *The Lost Nigger Mine*

1. See El Paso *Herald*, "Week-end Edition," January 22, 1927.
2. Nothing is commoner in traditions of buried treasure than death cell maps. In his vivid autobiography, *Beating Back* (New York, 1914, pp. 44–45), Al Jennings tells of a hunt he once made in Oklahoma after treasure that a man about to be hanged gave directions to. Ben Hughes was an outlaw in the federal jail at Fort Smith, Arkansas. He had a cell mate named Jim Cash, who was charged with murder. "The case against him was so strong that he never stood a chance, and he went to the gallows. [Before he went, however, he] told Ben Hughes where he had buried seven thousand dollars in stolen money —gave him a map and full directions. The next spring a party of us— —all wanted by the law—went hunting for this buried treasure. We camped, leaving a negro to guard our horses. The map was perfectly plain; we found the place according to directions, and began to dig under a flat rock. Before we had gone a foot we heard a shot. We grabbed our guns, crawled to the bushes, and surveyed the camp. It looked peaceable, and we rushed in for our horses. We found the negro rolling and moaning with pain. He had got to monkeying with a loaded revolver, and, not understanding guns, had shot himself in the foot. We were patching him up when we spied a body of marshals

looking for gentlemen answering to our description. When the subsequent episode was finished we found ourselves miles from the treasure and afraid to go back. If that seven thousand dollars ever existed, it may be there yet. And there it will stay, for all of me."

"I understand," Jennings continues, "that people are digging all over Creek Nation for the buried treasure of the Jennings gang. I buried my treasure all right, but not that way. It used to run through my fingers like water."

Later he repented of his rash disbelief in outlaw treasure and, according to an article in *The Texas Monthly*, Dallas, June, 1929, went, in 1925, in search of a vast fortune purported to be buried at Nevas, Durango, by one of Pancho Villa's henchmen.

3. Following the appearance of an account of the Lost Nigger Mine which I wrote for *Holland's Magazine* (March and April, 1930), people from a dozen states wrote me seeking further guidance to the mine!

IX. On West

1. At a time when the principal town, Paso del Norte, was on the Mexican side of the river and what is now the city of El Paso was the village of Franklin, the Galveston *Daily News* (June 22, 1873) printed this dispatch:

"Franklin, June 4, 1873.

"A short time ago two old shafts were discovered in a mountain about a mile from town, and a company formed to clear them out and prospect them. This they have done, and have found a well-defined silver lead several feet in thickness, variously estimated at from $30 to $75 per ton. One of the shafts is 90 feet deep and the other over 100. There is an old Mexican tradition of a very rich mine about two and a half miles from the cathedral tower of El Paso [Juárez], and this mine, the locators at least seem to think, fills the bill."

2. See "The Legend of Cheetwah," by Edith C. Lane, *Legends of Texas*, pp. 130–132.

X. Los Muertos No Hablan

1. As a matter of fact, the army records show that only two negroes were killed and buried in the vicinity of Lobo—but history has no more business interfering with legend than legend has interfering with history.

2. Should anyone wish to know more about Jim Hughes, Red Curly (Sandy King), Zwing Hunt, and Russian Bill, he can do no better than read three books that have recently been published around the outlaws of the Southwest: *Helldorado*, by William M. Breakenridge; *Tombstone's Yesterday*, by Lorenzo D. Walters; and *Tombstone*, by Walter Noble Burns. Mr. Burns devotes a whole chapter to the Skeleton Canyon treasure, as Bill Cole's phantom is called in Arizona.

XI. *The Challenge of the Desert*

1. The extract is reprinted by permission of the publishers, The Arthur H. Clark Company, from Granville Stuart's *Forty Years on the Frontier*, Cleveland, Ohio, 1925, Vol. I, pp. 60–62.
2. Accounts—all poor—of the Gunsight, Pegleg, Breyfogle, and other lost mines of the Death Valley area have been printed in many places. I have dozens of newspaper stories on the subject. In 1924–1925 the *Western Story Magazine* ran a series of brief tales on lost mines of the West, written by Roderick O'Hargan. A flippant account of the Breyfogle Mine is to be found in Chapter LI of *Adventures in the Apache Country*, by J. Ross Browne, New York, 1869. In 1926 P. C. Kullman and Co., a brokerage firm of New York, issued an odd pamphlet entitled *Lost Mines in the Western Mountains* that contains brief legendary tales about several desert mines. A recent book, *Death Valley*, by Bourke Lee (1930), has an interesting chapter on "Mines and Miners" in which Breyfogle is slightly touched on.

   I list these sources merely to show the persistence of the traditions; I owe them nothing. For the stories of both the Breyfogle and the Yuma mines I owe everything to Donald F. MacCarthy, of Montrose, California, who has looked for them and who knows what makes a good story. For the story of the Mexican shepherd girl who found nuggets in the desert, I am indebted to my friend W. W. Burton, of Austin, now (1930) eighty-six years old.

XII. *In the Sunshine of the Pecos*

1. Bandelier began the study in 1880. Since 1915 it has been continued by Dr. A. V. Kidder, whose hospitable camp beside the Pecos ruins, which he has been years studying, has been my abode on more than one occasion and whose "History of Pecos" (in *An Introduction to the Study of Southwestern Archæology*, Yale University Press, 1924) has afforded the basis for this outline of the Pecos background.

2. A man like José Vaca does not require documentary proofs of *antigua* mines. Why should he? Other lost mine hunters do, however. For generations they have haunted the archives of Santa Fe. Some of the contradictions that they may there find to inspire their hopes follow.

"In like manner we discovered in said land [New Mexico] eleven silver mines of very rich veins, the ore of three of which was brought to this city [Mexico] and given to his excellency. . . . The assayer found one sample to run 50% silver . . ."—Report on Chamuscado's expedition to New Mexico, 1581–1582, in *Leading Facts of New Mexico History*, by R. E. Twitchell, Vol. I, p. 258.

"In New Mexico there were no mines [worked by the Spanish] until after 1725, and compulsory labor on the part of the Indians even after that date was limited to service in the missions."—A. F. Bandelier, *Investigations in the Southwest*, Final Report, Part I, p. 194.

Don Pedro Pino, from New Mexico, in reporting to a Spanish congress at Cádiz, 1812, said: "In this province mines have been found closed, some of them with work tools inside; but it is not known at what time they were discovered and worked. There are many mineral veins in the mountains of gold and silver."—Benjamin M. Read, *Illustrated History of New Mexico*, Santa Fe, 1912, p. 516.

"In 1803, in his report, Governor Chacón says that copper is abundant, but no mines are worked. . . . Pike in 1807 refers to a copper mine west of the Rio Grande . . . yielding 20,000 mule loads of metal annually. . . . This must have been the Santa Rita. . . . The metal was transported to the City of Mexico by pack mules and wagons, 100 mules, carrying 300 pounds each, being constantly employed. There is very little of record which shows any mining done in New Mexico during Spanish rule."—R. E. Twitchell, *Leading Facts of New Mexico History*, Vol. I, p. 475.

3. For description of these remarkable sites in Arizona see *Mesa, Cañon, and Pueblo*, by Charles F. Lummis, New York, 1925, pp. 294–306.

4. The Pecos Indians kept the sacred fire for Montezuma burning until 1840, when the remnants of the village moved to Jémez.—A. F. Bandelier, "A Visit to the Aboriginal Ruins in the Valley of the Pecos," *Papers of the Archæological Institute of America*, Boston, 1881, p. 112. In Willa Cather's recent *Death Comes for the Archbishop*, a noble and beautiful novel, use is made of the secret fire-chamber.

For an account of the Pima Indian belief in Montezuma as their ancestor, see Major William H. Emory's *Report on the United States and Mexican Boundary Survey*, Washington, 1857, Vol. I, p. 117. The Papago Indians applied the name of Montezuma to a character, "Elder Brother," that had existed in their myths probably centuries before they heard the name of Montezuma. See "The Papago Migration Myth," by J. Alden Mason, *Journal of American Folk-Lore*, Vol. 34, pp. 254–268. Compare also with "The Pima Indians," by Frank Russell, *26th Annual Report of the Bureau of American Ethnology*, p. 225.

The rise of the Montezuma cult in the Southwest has been brilliantly traced by Adolph F. Bandelier in *The American Anthropologist*, Vol. V, October, 1892, pp. 319–326. As Bandelier shows, neither the war chieftain Montezuma nor his ancestors had anything more to do with the Southwest than had Julius Cæsar. The name of Montezuma was hardly known among the aborigines of the Southwest prior to the Mexican War of 1846. At that time, however, officials of the Mexican government had manuscripts circulated in New Mexico representing that Cortés had married "the Malinche," a character familiar to Indians through the "Matachines" dance. As a matter of history, Marina—in the Aztec tongue, Malinche—was mistress to Cortés. The common people hated her. This Malinche, so the government document circulated in New Mexico asserted, was the daughter of a great Indian from the north named Montezuma, and thus she brought to the conqueror of New Spain, as a part of her dowry, the territory of New Mexico. Such a tale was fabricated to inspire loyalty to the Mexican republic among New Mexicans, most of whom detested the *gachupines* and therefore had a sympathy for the symbolic object of *gachupín* tyranny—Montezuma. What such propaganda really inspired was legend.

5. This, of course, is but a variation of the ordinary "mineral rod," "switch," described elsewhere in this book. The Mexicans call it *vara de virtud*, or *vara de San Ignacio*.

XIII. The Pecos Barricade

1. For Beale's Report (35th Congress, 1st Session, House of Representatives, Ex. Doc., No. 124) and the whole story of the camels, which is also the story of the Texas-California route, see *Uncle Sam's Camels*, edited by Lewis Burt Lesley, Harvard University Press, 1929. Quotation is from pp. 154–155.
2. Santleben was king of the freighters. His book, *A Texas Pioneer*, New York, 1910, is a mine of information. For record of his transportation of money see pp. 104, 153, 182, 195, 200.
3. This legend has been supplied by J. A. Rickard, of O'Donnell, Texas, who heard it from a frontiersman named T. J. Kellis.

XIV. The Secret of the Guadalupes

1. To D. F. MacCarthy, generous gentleman, of Montrose, California, who has looked for the Lost Breyfogle Mine in Death Valley and the Yuma Mine of Arizona as well as for Guadalupe gold; to J. Evetts Haley, whose rich store of information relating to West Texas is partly revealed in his excellent history *The X I T Ranch*; to Ralph H. Shuffler, newspaper man and good fellow of Odessa, who interviewed various old-timers in my behalf; to my good friend Clabe Robinson, of Live Oak County; to Green Ussery, New Mexico ranchman; to J. E. Ellison, Marietta, Ohio, once a hunter of the Guadalupe gold; to J. J. Walker, a lawyer of Barstow, Texas; to a newspaper article of unknown origin reprinted in *Hunter's Frontier Magazine*, Melvin, Texas, October, 1916, and then again reprinted in *Legends of Texas*; to a newspaper interview that appeared in the El Paso *Times* in 1912 and was reprinted in *Frontier Times*, March, 1924; and to a summary account under the general title of "Legends of Lost Mines," by Frederick O'Hargan, in *Far West* magazine, July, 1928—to all of these I express my indebtedness for traditional material relating to the lost gold of the Guadalupes—and I wish I were out again with Asa Jones on his Culberson County ranch breathing the air from the Guadalupe Mountains themselves.

2. I have not seen the article written by Lew Wallace, nor have I been able to determine the magazine in which it appeared, but I have a copy of part of it as Donald F. MacCarthy transcribed it in Helena, Montana, in 1889. General Wallace was much interested in mines, as witness his article "The Mines of Santa Eulalia, Chihuahua," *Harper's New Monthly Magazine*, November, 1867, pp. 681–702, and also as witness one of his sanguine mining ventures related by Henry F. Hoyt, *The Frontier Doctor*, Boston, 1929, pp. 160–177. General Wallace likewise was a historical romancer.

3. Although the Rustler Hills rise 3700 feet above sea level, they are hardly more than 250 feet higher than the adjacent plains. They are capped by massive grey limestone and are not nearly so rough as the Guadalupes proper. An excellent description of the topography and geology of the whole region, with especial attention to mineral resources, is to be found in George Burr Richardson's *Report of a Reconnaissance in Trans-Pecos Texas*, University of Texas Mineral Survey Bulletin No. 9, Austin, 1904.

XV. Not Only Gold and Silver

1. When the great Washoe boom of Nevada was on in 1860 and everybody in Virginia City as well as in San Francisco was a potential millionaire

and stocks in the "Wake-up-Jake," the "Root Hog or Die," the "Let Her Rip," the "Gouge-Eye," and hundreds of other "mines" were doubling in value over night, ledges of iridium, platinum, and plumbago were claimed by prospectors. Men tunneled into the granite of Mount Davidson, which towers above Virginia City, in order to tap a lake—an ocean—of coal oil that "spirits," through mediums, had directed them to.—See Charles Howard Shinn, *The Story of the Mine*, New York, 1896, p. 141; also Dan De Quille, *History of the Big Bonanza*, Hartford, Conn., 1877, pp. 100–102.

2. George A. Bruffey, *Eighty-one Years in the West*, Butte, Mont., 1925, pp. 131–132.

3. The story of the "Minnie Moore" is taken from a privately printed but exceedingly interesting and valuable book entitled *Reminiscences of Alexander Topence*, Ogden, Utah, 1923, pp. 214–217.

4. This legend of the rangers' quicksilver was contributed by Edgar B. Kincaid, who ranches near Sabinal, to *Legends of Texas*, p. 62.

5. My informant is G. T. Bludworth, State Department of Education, Austin.

6. J. W. Wilbarger, *Indian Depredations in Texas*, Austin, 1889, pp. 15–19; James T. De Shields, *Border Wars of Texas*, Tioga, Texas, 1912, pp. 212–215. The legend of Goacher's mine appeared under the title of "The Legend of a Lost Lead Mine," by John Knox, in the Houston *Post-Dispatch*, Sunday, August 29, 1926.

7. It is said that during the Civil War settlers worked a vein of lead to the north of Smithville, which is in the same formation that Rabb's Creek is in. That mine has been lost also. In a letter published in the Brenham, Texas, *Banner-Press*, February 26, 1927, "Prof." Rundus exhorts the farmers to look out for lead, copper, quicksilver, and other minerals likely to occur in the country.

8. Grateful acknowledgment is here made to Bennett Lay, of Hallettsville, Texas, for furnishing this story of the lost lead of Lavaca County.

9. This account of Hoffman's mine was written for *Legends of Texas* by Edgar B. Kincaid.

10. See *Legends of Texas*, pp. 77–78.

11. In 1774 De Mézières reported Spaniards gone in search of mines that Indians said were "in the direction of the Brazos de Dios." In 1823 Daniel Shipman and two other men went from Austin's settlement on the coast in search of "an inexhaustible silver mine" reported to exist up the Brazos River. In 1836 the Reverend David B. Edward was strong in his belief in "a mountain of iron" on the headwaters of the Brazos. In the remarkable *Narrative* (1839) of her capture by the Indians and subsequent experiences Mrs. Rachel Plummer described "a large lump of platina" near the Brazos in the Cross Timbers. In 1844 the Houston *Telegraph and Texas Register* urged prospectors to go

up the Brazos River a hundred miles above the mouth of the Bosque and there locate copper deposits "laid down on all old Spanish maps." In 1867 and 1868 at least three expeditions left Parker County to prospect for copper on the Brazos; some of them pushed on to the Wichita and there found "favorable sign."—H. E. Bolton, *Athanase de Mézières*, Vol. I, p. 104, and Vol. II, pp. 33, 34, 47; Daniel Shipman, *Frontier Life*, 1879, pp. 23–26; David B. Edward, *History of Texas*, Cincinnati, 1836, pp. 44–45; Mrs. Rachel Plummer, *Narrative of the Capture and Subsequent Sufferings*, 1839, reprinted at Palestine, Texas, 1926, p. 111; *Telegraph and Texas Register*, Houston, May 1, 1844; *Pioneer Days in the Southwest*, compiled by Emanuel Dubbs, Guthrie, Okla., 1909, pp. 180–187.

12. See *Five Years a Cavalryman*, by H. H. McConnell, Jacksboro, Texas, 1899, pp. 294–296—a delightful book.

13. "The existence of copper ores in the Permian measures of Texas has long been known, and these ores have been, from time to time, the object of geological researches and mining developments. . . . The ore appears principally in two zones of Permian rocks, namely, the Red River zone in the counties of Archer, Wichita, Montague, Hardeman, and Wilbarger, and the Brazos River zone in the counties of Haskell, Baylor, Stonewall, and Knox."—E. J. Schmitz, *Transactions* of the American Institute of Mining Engineers, Vol. 26, p. 97 ff., 1897, quoted in *The Minerals and Mineral Localities of Texas*, by Frederic W. Simonds, University of Texas Mineral Survey Bulletin No. 5, Austin, 1902, p. 23.

14. *Legends of Texas*, pp. 72–77.

XVI. Sartin for Sure

1. It is reproduced from *Legends of Texas*. The account, traditional in her family, of the Moros of Tamaulipas comes from Jovita González.

2. The legend follows closely the telling by E. O. McNew, "Palo Duro May Be Treasure's Hiding Place," in the Fort Worth *Star Telegram*, Sunday, November 25, 1928.

XVII. The Treasure of the Wichitas

1. Dr. John Sibley, U.S. Indian Agent (Thoburn's *A Standard History of Oklahoma*, Vol. I, pp. 20–21), after making a reconnaissance of the Wichita country in 1805, reported a traveler thus: "Amongst these mountains of mines we often heard a noise like the explosion of can-

non or distant thunder. The Indians said it was the spirits of the white people [Spaniards] working in their treasure."

In *Astoria*, Chap. XXVI, Washington Irving notes that Lewis and Clarke heard the same kind of mysterious explosions in the Rocky Mountains, attributed by Indians "to the bursting of rich mines of silver." Irving cites similar phenomena over Spanish America.

XVIII. Laffite and Pirate Booty

1. In the Autumn number of *The Yale Review*, 1928, appeared an article of mine entitled "The Mystery of Lafitte's Treasure." Anyone comparing the chapter on "Laffite and Pirate Booty" with that article would observe that various remarks dealing with the man Laffite have been changed. The changes are due to the work of Mr. Stanley Faye, of Aurora, Illinois, with whom *The Yale Review* article brought me in contact and who with extraordinary generosity placed the manuscript of his rarely scholarly work *Privateers of the Gulf* at my disposal. I cannot express sufficiently my obligation to Mr. Faye. It is to be hoped that his ripe and revealing work will soon be in book form.

Of articles on Laffite there has been no dearth, but hardly one of them shows any critical sifting. The best biographical sketch heretofore obtainable is that entitled "Life of Jean Lafitte," by "W. B." (William Bollaert), in *Littell's Living Age*, Vol. XXXII, March 6, 1852, pp. 433–446.

"The Cruise of the Enterprise–A Day with La Fitte," by "T.," in *The United States Democratic Review*, Washington, D.C., Vol. VI, July, 1839, pp. 33–42, affords an interesting picture of the privateer boss's headquarters at Galveston at the time the United States government ordered him to leave.

De Bow's Review, New Orleans, 1851–1853, ran several articles dealing with Laffite. See Vol. XI, pp. 372–387, "Life and Times of Lafitte"; Vol. XIII, pp. 378–383, "Early Life in the Southwest—The Bowies"; and Vol. XV, pp. 572–584, "Early Life in the Southwest."

The Pirates' Own Book, Boston, 1837 (reprinted at Salem, 1924), contains an anonymously written sketch twenty-five pages long entitled "Life of Lafitte, the Pirate of the Gulf."

The *Papers* of Mirabeau Buonaparte Lamar, one time president of the Republic of Texas, edited by Charles A. Gulick, Jr., and Winnie Allen, Austin, 1925, contain some excellent material on Laffite. See *Papers* Nos. 19, 24, and 2492 (old Jim Campbell's story).

Fortier, Phelps, Gayarre, Cable, Grace King, and other Louisiana writers have all treated of Laffite; among them Miss King is best. The

Texas historians have copied each other without saying much of anything. However, Moses Austin's deposition in the *Austin Papers*, edited by Barker, is interesting, if erroneous.

The articles in the *American Mercury*, February, 1926, and the *Atlantic Monthly*, June, 1903, add nothing, though the latter entertains.

As for newspaper articles, they have been printed by the score, one feature writer rehashing another until the hash has generally become very thin indeed. An exception is an article compiled by Harry Benge Crozier for the Galveston *Daily News*, April 11, 1917. Another article signed by W. L. Bradley in the same newspaper, April 28, 1895, has some good stories in it.

Among fantastic things on Campbell and other characters associated with Laffite are to be mentioned the account, pp. 125–131, in Charles Hooten's *St. Louis Isle, or Texiana*, London, 1847; also articles in the Galveston *News* for February 8, 1878; April 21, 1878; and May 25, 1879.

The bibliography of hearsay dilution might be extended indefinitely. Some legendary material on Laffite that appears in *Legends of Texas* has not been used in this chapter. A very large number of weak novels and short stories have been built around Laffite. I want to thank the staff of the Rosenberg Library of Galveston for having placed at my disposal their voluminous Laffite material.

2. The story of Meredith's chart is appropriated from "Life and Legends of Lafitte the Pirate," by E. G. Littlejohn, *Legends of Texas*, pp. 179–185.

3. Taken from *Legends of Texas*, pp. 185–189.

Glossary of Mexican
and Other Localisms
of the Southwest

It would be possible to write of the folk of the Southwest in language free from colloquialism—but not to write them down. Their language, seasoned as it is with Mexicanisms and metaphor peculiar to the range, is as much a part of the folk's lore as are the legendary tales themselves.

acequia: irrigation ditch.
adios: good-bye.
allá: yonder; *más allá*: farther on.
almagre: red hematite.
amigo: friend; *por amigo*: for the sake of friendship.
amo: master.
antigua: ancient; an old-timer.
Arroyo Colorado: Red Creek.
artillery: pistols, personal weapons.

bad man: outlaw.
bandera: flag.
bandido: bandit.
bayo coyote: dun horse with a black stripe down his back.
black ivory: negro slaves.
borrowed: euphemism for stolen.
bozal: nose-hitch.
bravo: fierce, brave.
Brazos de Dios: Arms of God.
bronco: wild; *los indios broncos*: unchristianized Indians.
brujo: wizard.
brush popper: brush hand; cowboy expert at running in the brush.
Buena Vista: Fine Prospect.
bulto: bulk, object.

caballada: band of horses.
caballero: horseman, gentleman.
cabestro: hair rope.
caboodle: lot, aggregation, amount.
cafecito: cup of coffee.

323

camino real: public highway.
candelilla: a plant from which wax is extracted.
caporal: boss.
carabina: carbine, rifle.
carajoing: shouting "*Carajo!*"—an exclamation much used by mule drivers, vaqueros, and other outdoor workers.
carbón: charcoal.
carga: load.
carreta: old-fashioned wooden-wheeled Mexican cart.
cartucho: cartridge shell.
Casa Blanca: White House.
cerro: hill.
chaparro: brush.
chapote: Mexican persimmon.
Chihuahua: name of a state and city in Mexico—used as a harmless expletive.
Chihuahua cart: a heavy wooden cart. See *carreta*.
"chimney": mining term for a "blow out" or "shoot" of ore.
chisos: phantoms.
chivarras: leggins, chaps.
chouse: to chase.
cienaga: marsh.
cocinero: cook.
coma: an evergreen, thorny tree; also small berry borne by the tree.
comancheros: traders with Comanches.
compadre: (1) co-godfather; (2) close companion. See *compañero*.
compañero: partner, companion.
concha: shell-shaped ornament of silver.
conducta: a guard or convoy.
conquistador: conqueror.
corrida: cow crowd, outfit of cow hands.
cow chips: dried cow dung.
cowpen Spanish: illiterate Spanish.
cristianos: civilized people, Christians; tantamount to "white people."
crow-bait: a poor, decrepit animal (usually a horse).
curandero: one who cures; a kind of quack doctor who uses both home remedies and something of the Indian medicine man's magic.
cut for sign: to examine the ground for tracks and droppings (the two "signs").

dally: to wrap a rope around the horn of a saddle. (From *dar la vuelta*, to give a turn.)
derrotero: a set of directions, a chart; also a diary.
difficulty: a quarrel, often resulting in a "killing."

dinero: money.
Dios: God.
dueño: owner.
duffer: codger.
duffle: personal effects; clothes, etc.

embrujada: bewitched.
empleado: officer; name often applied by Mexicans to Texas rangers.
enchilada: a highly seasoned Mexican dish.
escondida: hidden.
espantosa: haunted, horrible.
excavad: dig (imperative form).

fandango: a dance; more freely, any gay party.
fire-water: whiskey.
frijoles: dried Mexican beans—a staple diet in the ranch country.

gachupín: upper-class Spaniard.
gallery: porch.
gente: people.
granjeno: one of various thorned bushes of the Southwest.
grubstake: (as verb) to furnish provisions; (as noun) provisions.
gully-washer and fence-lifter: a very hard rain.

hablar español: to speak Spanish.
hacienda: a plantation or ranch; a landed estate.
hard money: coin.
hear the owl hoot: to have many and varied experiences.
high lonesome: a big drunk.
historia: a tale; historical account.
hombre: man.
horn in: to intrude.
horqueta: a fork.
huajilla: a bush, valuable for browsing, belonging to the catclaw family.

iguana: lizard; name of an ore formation.

jacal: hut, cabin.
jarro: earthen pot. See *olla*.
jato: wallet.
javelina (from Spanish *jabalina*): peccary.

ladrón: robber.
lagarto: alligator.

lay for: lie in wait for.
lechuza: owl, screech owl.
like the devil beating tan bark: fast and furious.
llano: prairie; a flat, open plain.
lobo: "loafer" wolf.
loose-herd: to herd loosely so as to allow animal to graze.
loma: hill; Loma Alta: High Hill.

machete: cutlass.
macho: mule.
Madama: Madam.
maldiciones: bad words.
maleta: bag made out of rawhide; also, satchel.
manada: bunch of mares with stallion.
mano: (1) hand; (2) stone (used in the hand) for grinding corn against the
    metate.
mantilla: head shawl.
mañana: tomorrow; sometime.
maravillas: wonders.
marihuana: a narcotic.
mayordomo: overseer, major-domo.
mecapal: basket for carrying ore out of shaft.
mediano: half grown.
medicina: medicine.
mesa: flat-topped hill; mountain shaped like a table (mesa).
mescal: the agave, or century, plant; liquor made from the plant.
Mestizo: a Mexican of mixed blood.
metate: a stone on which corn is rubbed to meal.
mina: mine.
mocho: gotched; droop-horned.
montezuma: ruin; name of Aztec ruler.
Moro: Moor; Mexican vigilantes who dressed like Moors.
morral: fiber bag, usually carried on horn of saddle.
mota: clump of trees; motte.
mucha: much.
muerto: dead man. *Los muertos no hablan*: the dead do not talk.
mujer: woman, wife.
mulero: mule driver.
música: music.
mustang: (as verb) to catch mustangs; (as noun) wild horse.
muy malo: very ill.

nueces: pecan, nut.

ojalá: an exclamation of surprise or encouragement.
olla: pot, jar.
olmos: elms.

padre: (1) father; (2) priest.
paisano: road-runner, chaparral bird.
palo: tree; Palo Alto: High Tree.
palo blanco: hackberry.
palo duro: (literally, hard wood) a bush common on the upper Texas
    plains, from which Palo Duro Canyon takes its name.
párate: halt.
parientes: relatives.
parihuela: hod for carrying ore.
pasajero: traveler.
pasear: (1) a journey or trip; (2) to travel.
paso: (1) a pass, a ford; (2) a double-step, six feet.
pastor: shepherd.
pata: foot; Pata de Venado: Deer's Foot.
patrón: (1) owner, employer, patron; (2) ghostly warden.
Pecos: as verb, to throw into the Pecos River; hence, to kill by drowning.
pecoseños: inhabitants of Pecos.
pelado: low-class Mexican.
peón: laboring class of Mexicans.
perdida: lost.
peso: dollar.
picachos: peaks.
pido por Dios: I beg in God's name—a beggar's cry.
pinto: (1) spotted horse; (2) spotted bean.
piñon: dwarf pine.
pirooting: meandering, "fooling around," probably from pirouetting.
plata: (1) silver, (2) chart.
play out: cease to be.
plug: a broken down horse.
poor doe: lean, tough venison of any kind.
porción: an allotment, or portion, of land.
presidio: fort; Presidio del Norte; Fort of the North.
pronto: quickly, soon.
pueblo: town.
puente: bridge; Puente de Piedra: Stone Bridge—a rocky ford.
pull freight for the tules: take to the wilds, or "tall timber."
pull in your horns: stop.

quién sabe: who knows?

Glossary

Quill: a pure-blooded Indian of Mexico.

raíz diabólica: (literally, devil root), peyote or "mescal button," a drug.
ranchero: ranchman.
reach: to make a motion as if to draw a pistol.
reata: rope; more especially a rawhide rope.
remuda: bunch of saddle horses.
rep: (as noun) a cowboy who represents his brand at outside ranches; (as verb) to represent.
República Mejicana: Mexican Republic.
resaca: marsh; Resaca de la Palma: Palm Marsh.
rib up: persuade.
rico: rich, a rich man.
rural: Mexican peace officer corresponding to Texas ranger.
rustle: (1) to wrangle, or herd, horses; (2) to steal.

sacaguista: a kind of coarse, salt grass.
señor: sir.
serape: shawl, blanket.
set back: to pull back.
shank of the afternoon: late afternoon.
shuck: (1) cigarette made with corn shuck for wrapping; (2) slang name for Mexican.
siesta: afternoon nap.
sitio: grant of land.
sotol: a plant of the yucca family having long, stiff, saw-edged leaves.
sow bosom: salt pork.
Spanish dagger: yucca plant.
squat: a bit of land, a claim.
stake: (1) as verb, to furnish supplies or money for an enterprise; (2) "to pull up stakes," to leave; (3) "to make a stake," to make a beginner's fortune.
stake-pin: a pin or peg used for tying a stake-rope to.
stamping ground: home range.
stick-and-mud chimney: constructed of adobe (mud) and sticks.
stomp: stamp; stomp dance, war dance.
string up: hang.
stuff: buried treasure.
swag: (1) quantity, load; (2) a low place, coulee.
swallow fork: (1) an ear-mark; (2) used as a verb, to "sashay," to travel carelessly.
swing a wide loop: live a free life.

talache: grubbing-hoe.

tarantula juice: whiskey.
tequila: alcoholic drink made from the maguey plant.
Terlingua: a name meaning Three Tongues.
Tigers of the desert: Apaches.
tinaja: a rock water hole.
toboso: a coarse grass.
tomahawk: often used for hatchet.
tortuga: turtle, tortoise.
tracks: to make, to leave, travel.
trigueño: a brown horse.

vaciero: supply agent for several sheep (or goat) camps; also, a kind of boss over *pastores*.
vámonos: let us go.
vaquero: cowboy.
Vara de San Ignacio: mineral rod.
vara de virtud: mineral rod.
vereda: trail; Veredas Coloradas: Red Trails.
vega: a meadow; a stretch of low, flat country.
viznaga: a species of cactus.
voucher: Indian scalp.

war bag: a sack or bag for personal belongings.
wet stock: cattle or horses smuggled across the Rio Grande.
white man: (1) English-speaking Caucasian as distinguished from Mexican; (2) a decent human being.
wrangle: to herd horses; to drive them.

zurrón: a bag fastened to the head for carrying ore in.